Democracy and Coercive Diplomacy

Kenneth Schultz explores the effects of democratic politics on the use and success of coercive diplomacy. He argues that open political competition between the government and opposition parties influences the decision to use threats in international crises, how rival states interpret those threats, and whether or not crises can be settled short of war. The relative transparency of their political processes means that, while democratic governments cannot easily conceal domestic constraints against using force, they can credibly demonstrate resolve when their threats enjoy strong domestic support. As a result, compared to their nondemocratic counterparts, democracies are more selective about making threats, but those they do make are more likely to be successful – that is, to gain a favorable outcome without resort to war. Schultz develops his argument through a series of game–theoretic models and tests the resulting hypotheses using both statistical analyses and historical case studies.

KENNETH SCHULTZ is Assistant Professor of Politics and International Affairs at the Department of Politics and Woodrow Wilson School of Public and International Affairs, Princeton University. He has published articles in such journals as the *American Political Science Review*, *International Organization*, and the *British Journal of Political Science*.

CAMBRIDGE STUDIES IN INTERNATIONAL RELATIONS: 76

Democracy and Coercive Diplomacy

CAMBRIDGE STUDIES IN INTERNATIONAL RELATIONS

Series list continues after index

Democracy and Coercive Diplomacy

Kenneth A. Schultz

Princeton University

CAMBRIDGE
UNIVERSITY PRESS

CAMBRIDGE UNIVERSITY PRESS
Cambridge, New York, Melbourne, Madrid, Cape Town, Singapore, São Paulo, Delhi

Cambridge University Press
The Edinburgh Building, Cambridge CB2 8RU, UK

Published in the United States of America by Cambridge University Press, New York

www.cambridge.org
Information on this title: www.cambridge.org/9780521796699

First published 2001

A catalogue record for this publication is available from the British Library

Library of Congress Cataloguing in Publication data

Schultz, Kenneth A.
Democracy and coercive diplomacy / by Kenneth A. Schultz.
   p.   cm. – (Cambridge studies in international relations; 76)
Includes bibliographical references and index.
ISBN 0 521 79227 4 (hardback) – ISBN 0 521 79669 5 (pbk.)
1. Diplomatic negotiations in international disputes.   2. Threats.
3. International relations.   4. Democracy.   I. Title.   II. Series.
JZ6374.S38   2001
327–dc21   00–050258

ISBN 978-0-521-79227-1 hardback
ISBN 978-0-521-79669-9 paperback

Transferred to digital printing 2009

To Heather and Aaron

Contents

Figures

Tables

Preface

In March 1999, as the first draft of this manuscript was being completed, the United States and its allies launched an air war against Yugoslavia over its treatment of ethnic Albanians in Kosovo. While this conflict was fascinating for many reasons, one aspect that particularly struck me was President Clinton's decision to announce, both before and during the air campaign, that he had no intention of introducing ground troops into Kosovo. Why Clinton was reluctant to use ground forces is not very puzzling. Given the costs that were anticipated and the lack of strong public support, any such operation would have been politically and militarily quite risky. The decision to announce his intentions publicly, however, came under strong criticism, especially when the air campaign failed to produce immediate results. "How does it make sense," asked Republican Senator John McCain, "to tell your enemy before you go into a conflict that you will not exercise whatever options are necessary to achieve victory?" (US Senate 1999). Asked this very question in an April 19 *Newsweek* interview, Vice President Al Gore defended the president's strategy: "We have an obligation to candidly communicate with the American people about what we're doing and why, and what we're not doing and why. And if candor and clarity are costs of democracy, it's not the first time."

This book explores how the transparent political process within democracies influences the way these states use threats of force, how the targets of those threats respond, and whether or not crises are resolved short of war. While Gore's response reflects a common perception that the requirements of open deliberation and debate impose liabilities on democratic foreign policy, my findings suggest a more mixed and, on balance, more positive conclusion. The Kosovo episode reflects a class of cases in which the demands of domestic politics and the demands of international diplomacy clashed. President Clinton ruled out ground troops in large part to hold together fragile domestic support for the intervention, both in the United States and in Europe. He traded off some of his bargaining leverage against Yugoslavia in order to mute domestic oppositions that were leery of where the engagement would lead. I find that this is a common pattern, in which democratic governments are constrained in the threats they can make or find their threats rendered ineffective because of domestic opposition to the use of force.

This is not, however, the only pattern associated with democracy. In many other cases, democratic states have managed to use threats very effectively because open competition and debate reveal the *strength* of domestic support. In the strategic environment of an international crisis, convincing a rival state that one is willing and able to carry out a threat to use force is difficult. Thus, the ability to signal resolve in a credible manner bestows important advantages. I show that, when democratic states are strongly resolved to use force, they are better able to convince their opponents of that fact than are nondemocratic states. The support of domestic opposition parties, freely given, provides confirmation of the government's political incentives to carry out its threats. Nondemocratic governments, which routinely coerce support and suppress dissent, have no comparable mechanism for signaling unified resolve.

Thus, while democracies cannot readily conceal domestic constraints against waging war, the fact that they are consequently more selective about threatening force means that the threats they make tend to be particularly effective. Indeed, I show that democratic states are less likely to initiate crises by issuing threats, but, conditional on their doing so, those threats are less likely to be resisted. The danger of war is consequently lower.

Many friends and colleagues have contributed their time and insight to this project. I am particularly grateful to the following people who read and commented on the manuscript or its various components: Bruce Bueno de Mesquita, Michael Doyle, James Fearon, Kurt Taylor Gaubatz, Hein Goemans, Joanne Gowa, Stephen Krasner, Jack Levy, Jeffrey Lewis, Edward Mansfield, James Morrow, and Alastair Smith. I would also like to thank Paul Huth both for his comments on the manuscript and for providing the data that serve as the basis for the empirical tests in Chapter 6. The Eisenhower World Affairs Institute and the Woodrow Wilson School of Public and International Affairs provided financial support.

Parts of chapters 3, 4, and 5 are based on articles that were published in the *American Political Science Review* and *International Organization* (Schultz 1998, 1999).

This book is dedicated to my wife and son. Heather has been by my side through the entire process; indeed, the inspiration that would become the central thesis of this book came to me only a few weeks before our wedding. I am eternally grateful for her unconditional love and support. Aaron was born while the first draft of the manuscript was coming together. He is my proudest accomplishment and a source of immeasurable love and joy.

1   Introduction

This book explores the effects of democratic politics on the use of coercive diplomacy in international crises. It considers how the institutions and practices of democracy influence a government's decision to threaten force to resolve a dispute, the way the targets of such threats choose to respond, who wins and who loses in bargaining, and most important, whether the matter is settled through the threat of force or through its actual use – that is, war. I argue in these pages that democracy generates distinctive patterns and outcomes because of the public nature of political competition within democratic polities. Open deliberation and debate, essential for representation and accountability domestically, have profound effects on whether and when democratic governments can effectively use threats of force to prevail in international crises.

Contrary to the pessimism one often sees in scholarly and popular opinion, I find that these effects are not wholly negative. It has long been common to argue that the open nature of democratic polities is a liability in international politics. In his massive *Study of War*, for example, Quincy Wright argues that the demands of public deliberation and participation make democratic states "ill-adapted to the successful use of threats and violence as instruments of foreign policy" (Wright 1965, p. 842). For a threat to be successful, the target must be convinced that the issuer really means to carry it out. Democratic governments, however, are at every turn susceptible to criticism from domestic oppositions, which can raise doubts about their willingness and ability to act. Autocratic governments, on the other hand, can more easily conceal or suppress their internal divisions. "Consequently," Wright concludes, "in the game of power diplomacy, democracies pitted against autocracies are at a disadvantage" (1965, p. 842).

This pessimistic view is at best incomplete. The public nature of decision making and competition in democratic polities generates both benefits and liabilities. Indeed, I find that democratic states have in general been quite successful at using threats to get their way in international disputes and to do so without actually waging war. While domestic dissension can at times undermine their threats, democratic governments also enjoy unique advantages due to the public debate that surrounds a decision to threaten or use force. In particular, when there is strong domestic consensus behind the government's threats, the support of domestic opposition groups – freely given – can send a signal of resolve that is more effective than can be sent by a government that routinely coerces such support. Moreover, while it is true that democracies cannot readily conceal domestic constraints against waging war, the fact that they are consequently more selective about threatening force means that the threats they do make tend to be particularly credible. Indeed, I will show that democratic states are less likely to initiate crises by issuing threats, but, conditional on their doing so, those threats are less likely to be resisted. As a result, the probability that a democratic state initiates a crisis which then escalates to war is less than the corresponding probability for nondemocratic states.

Why examine this issue? From a scholarly perspective, this book fits into a large and growing body of research on the influence of domestic political institutions and behavior on international outcomes. While there has long been a vigorous debate about the relative importance of international and domestic factors in foreign policy, the last decade has witnessed an explosion of interest in moving away from the traditional unitary state model of international relations to consider the impact of domestic institutions and actors (esp., Putnam 1988; Pahre and Papayoanou 1997; Milner 1997). Scholars have moved beyond simply arguing that "domestic politics matter" to thinking systematically about how, why, and when they matter.[1] This book contributes to this research program by exploring the impact of democratic politics on how states use and respond to threats of military force.

From a practical perspective, the interest in this question stems from two observations about the current international system. First, there are

---

[1] Any list of citations to this literature is bound to be incomplete. Some recent works include Evans, Jacobson, and Putnam (1993), Downs and Rocke (1995), Bueno de Mesquita and Siverson (1995), Siverson (1998), Gaubatz (1999), Smith (1998a, b), Goemans (2000), Milner (1997), Bueno de Mesquita *et al.* (1999). A large subset of this literature is work on the democratic peace; see citations in fn. 3, below.

more democratic states in the world, both in absolute terms and as a percentage of all states, than ever before in history. According to Freedom House, an organization that tracks such developments, there were 120 democratic countries in 1999, an all-time high. Democracies represented 63 percent of all countries, up from 40 percent only ten years before (Karatnycky 2000). The second observation is less heartening: the threat and use of military force remain persistent features of international politics. While there has been considerable interest in the well-known claim that democratic states do not wage war against one another – a point to which I will return below – the issue of how democracies wield the threat of force remains a pressing one. Despite the hopes that accompanied the end of the Cold War, the decade since then has witnessed numerous episodes in which democratic states have contemplated, threatened, and/or used military force: the Persian Gulf War, various efforts (and non-efforts) to intervene in the break-up of Yugoslavia, the 1996 Taiwan Straits crisis, the 1999 air campaign over Kosovo – just to name some of the most prominent. In most of these cases, the decision to threaten or use force was publicly debated within the democratic nations involved (Jakobsen 1998). The relative consensus that prevailed during the Cold War has been replaced by more frequent contention over both the ends and means of foreign policy. Hence, a careful examination of how domestic competition influences the use of threats in crises is clearly warranted.

The argument

The argument in this book builds on a recent literature that focuses on uncertainty as the driving force behind crises and wars (e.g., Fearon 1992, 1994a, 1994b, 1995, 1997; Kilgour and Zagare 1991; Morrow 1989; Powell 1990, 1999; Bueno de Mesquita, Morrow, and Zorick 1997).[2] This literature starts with a simple insight: because wars are costly for all sides, states generally have incentives to find peaceful settlements of their disputes that allow them to avoid these costs. After all, even the eventual winner of a war would do at least as well by getting the spoils of victory up front without incurring the associated costs. To explain why some disagreements escalate into crises and some crises escalate into wars, writers in this tradition have pointed to the role of

---

[2] These works build on earlier arguments about the role of uncertainty as a cause of war, such as Schelling (1960), Blainey (1988), and Stoessinger (1974).

uncertainty and, particularly, a specific kind of uncertainty known as *asymmetric information*.

Asymmetric information arises when states have information about their willingness and ability to wage war that other states cannot observe. When states bargain in a crisis, their expectations about the outcome and costs of war determine the range of negotiated settlements that are acceptable *ex ante*. If these expectations are based on information that is commonly available – a condition known as *complete information* – then it is relatively easy to identify a settlement that both sides prefer to war. A condition of incomplete and asymmetric information arises whenever at least one state has information that others cannot observe regarding the factors which determine its evaluation of war. For example, a government's expectations about war depend in part on the willingness of its domestic constituents to bear the costs (Mueller 1973; Bueno de Mesquita and Lalman 1990, 1992; Goemans 2000). A government that faces a hawkish electorate faces fewer political risks in waging war than one that faces dovish constituents. If the government has more or better information about the preferences of its constituents than do those in other states, then information is distributed asymmetrically. Information which one actor possesses and which another cannot directly observe is *private information*.

The main danger associated with this condition is that actors uncertain about their rivals' preferences may take actions that bring about escalation and war. A state may be unsure, for example, how its opponent would respond to a demand to change the status quo: will it acquiesce to such a demand, or will it resist? Faced with a choice between accepting the status quo or making a threat that could lead to war but might also generate profitable concessions, a state might gamble on the latter. Similarly, a state confronted by such a threat may be unsure how the challenger would react in the face of resistance: will it back down from its challenge, or will it wage war? Again, faced with a choice between giving in to a threat or gambling that that threat is a bluff, the target might choose the latter. Under conditions of uncertainty, states face hard choices which sometimes favor actions entailing a risk of war. Although the costs of fighting make war sub-optimal *ex post*, strategies that might lead to war can be optimal *ex ante*.

In this view, crises are primarily driven by efforts to communicate resolve, as states try to convince one another that they are willing to wage war if their demands are not met. Threats and displays of force are the primary means of communication. Whether or not such threats succeed depends crucially on the credibility with which they are sent – that is, the belief they generate in the target that the threatened actions will be carried out. A state will make concessions in the face of a threat only if it believes that failure to do so will lead to a worse outcome with sufficiently high probability. To be sure, a threat must also be backed by material capabilities, the military forces necessary to inflict damage, seize territory, defeat opposing armies, etc. A completely credible threat backed by negligible capabilities will rarely coerce an opponent into making concessions or otherwise changing its behavior. Nevertheless, the reverse is also true: overwhelming military capabilities can be rendered impotent if the threat to wield them is incredible.

Credibility is at a premium precisely because states' willingness to carry out their threats is inherently suspect. There are two related reasons why this is so. The first is that carrying out a threat to wage war is costly. Once called upon to do so, the threatening state might very well decide that the potential benefits of getting its way in the dispute do not, in the end, warrant the costs and risks associated with war. Unless the stakes are great and the costs of fighting small, it is often cheaper to make a threat and back down than it is to wage war. If, however, the stakes and costs are such that it does make sense to fight in the face of resistance, it may still be difficult to convince the target of this fact. This gets to the second reason that credibility is problematic: states have incentives to lie (Fearon 1995). The conflict of interests inherent in crisis situations means that states have incentives to exaggerate their resolve in the hopes of getting the other side to back down. Hence, they may engage in bluffs or limited probes: threats intended to scare the target into making concessions, even if the issuer has no intention of carrying them out. Because of these incentives, not all threats can be believed – even those that, after the fact, turn out to have been genuine. Overcoming asymmetric information requires that actors find ways to reveal their resolve in a credible manner, given a strategic environment which encourages deception.

It is here that we can find leverage for thinking about the effects of domestic institutions in general and democracy in particular. A central difference between democratic and nondemocratic systems is that the former permits what Robert Dahl (1971) refers to as "public contestation" – the ability of parties or groups openly to compete for political office. In a democratic system, the government does not monopolize the country's political discourse. Rather it must share the stage with opposition parties that are free to make public appeals for political support, if necessary by publicizing the government's actions and shortcomings. As a result, much of what democratic governments do and why is exposed to public debate and scrutiny.

From the perspective of democratic theory, this process is desirable because it helps create an informed electorate and ensure genuine choice over representation. At the same time, the open nature of politics in democratic systems has unintended effects on the availability of information internationally. Because of the demands of publicity, mechanisms that exist to inform voters also provide information to decision makers in foreign states. Hence, the domestic and international levels are inextricably linked: institutions and practices which generate information *within* states also affect the informational problem *between* states. To the extent that international crises are driven by states' efforts to communicate and/or exploit private information, there is good reason to believe that the outcomes of such interactions are influenced by domestic political institutions in general, and democracy in particular.

Open political competition creates conditions that are highly favorable for revealing information to both domestic and foreign audiences. A general finding in the literature on information and signaling is that two information sources are better than one, especially when they have conflicting interests (Milgrom and Roberts 1986; Krehbiel 1991, p. 84; Lipman and Seppi 1995; Shin 1998). When private information is shared by agents with conflicting interests, two effects occur, both of which facilitate credible revelation. The first is that each actor can constrain the other's ability to conceal or misrepresent what it knows. If there is information that one agent would like to keep secret, it is generally the case that an agent with opposite interests would like that piece of information to be revealed. At the same time, when actors with conflicting interests agree on the content of their private information, the resultant signal has greater credibility than if it were sent by one actor with known incentives to misrepresent. With competing information sources, then, neither agent can exploit its informational advantage *vis-à-vis* some third party to the same degree as it could if it monopolized the information in question. Moreover, the possibility of confirmation means that some signals that emerge are highly reliable.

This logic has important implications for the behavior of democracies in international crises. The government's ability to conceal or misrepresent information about its preferences for war and peace is highly constrained in democratic systems. Institutions and practices of democracy not only force the government to compete in public with its political rivals, but they also create favorable conditions for that competition to be both informed and informative. Opposition parties are free to engage in open debate over the desirability of different policies, such as the wisdom of using force to change the status quo. Turnover in office and access to legislative institutions and other resources ensures that these parties, while out of executive power, have access to information that is relevant to such debates. The policy process in a democratic polity, therefore, resembles an ongoing and very public debate in which the government may be the loudest voice, but not the only voice. The situation is very different in nondemocratic polities in which the government is better able to monopolize information and/or suppress alternative information sources. Although the policy process in such systems may entail substantial debate in private, within the regime, its public aspect more closely resembles a monologue.

In addition to publicizing a good deal of "raw" information about a state's capabilities and intentions, the interaction of political parties aggregates information about the government's political incentives into readily observable signals: the public strategies that parties adopt during international crises. The main argument on this point is developed through a formal model in Chapter 4. The model permits us to perform the following comparative-static exercise: how do behaviors and outcomes change when we move from an interaction between unitary states to an interaction in which one state is composed of two strategic actors, a government and an opposition party. It combines a standard crisis bargaining game with a simple model of two-party electoral choice. These parties vie for the support of the electorate through their public actions in the international crisis – in particular, the government's decision whether or not to threaten force and the opposition's decision to support or oppose the threat. Because these actions are observable, they reveal to the rival state information about the government's underlying political incentives and, hence, its willingness to wage war.

The model shows that the probability of war is lower when informative signals can be sent by both parties than when the government is the lone voice of the state, as it is in polities in which competition is poorly developed or actively suppressed. This result is driven by two reinforcing effects that decrease the danger of war due to informational asymmetries: what I call the restraining and confirmatory effects of domestic competition.

The restraining effect

Relative to their nondemocratic counterparts, democratic governments have fewer opportunities to exploit their private information by engaging in deception and bluff. When military and political conditions are such that the resort to force would be politically undesirable, democratic governments cannot easily conceal this fact because domestic opposition parties have incentives to publicly oppose the use of force. From the standpoint of domestic politics, this strategy positions the opposition party to capitalize on the electorate's unease about the use of force and to exploit what is expected to be an unpopular foreign policy outcome. From the standpoint of international politics, this strategy effectively reveals the government's constraints, casting doubt on whether it will actually want to carry out its threats. Although the prospect of domestic dissent does not always prevent the government from bluffing, it does make the practice riskier and hence less attractive. Democratic governments have to be more selective about the threats they make. Nondemocratic governments, on the other hand, are better able to conceal evidence of military or political weakness; as a result, they are better able, and more willing, to engage in bluffing behavior.

At the aggregate level, this means that democratic governments should be less likely than nondemocratic governments to initiate crises by threatening to settle disputes by force. In Chapter 5, I present evidence consistent with this claim using data sets that cover more than 170 countries from 1816 to 1984 and include information on roughly 1800 crises. I estimate that if a state switches from a nondemocracy to a democracy, holding everything else constant, the probability that it will initiate a crisis decreases by a third to a half. Moreover, there is evidence from historical cases that actual or anticipated dissent by opposition parties induces caution in democratic decision makers, making them hesitant to threaten force. In Chapter 7, I examine four such cases, taken from the experience of Great Britain: the 1899 crisis with South Africa which led up to the Boer War, the 1936 crisis over German remilitarization of the Rhineland, the 1956 crisis over Egypt's nationalization of the Suez Canal, and the 1965 dispute over Rhodesian independence. Although these cases are different in their particulars, in all four the British government took into account the expected reaction of domestic opposition parties and believed that their public opposition to the use of force would make it difficult to send a credible threat. There is also evidence that the governments in the rival states observed the domestic political situation within Britain and interpreted the signals from the opposition party as evidence that a threat to use military force would be difficult to carry out or sustain.

The confirmatory effect

The flip side of this argument is that the threats that democratic governments do choose to make are more effective than those made by their nondemocratic counterparts – in the sense that they are more likely to get their targets to back down without a fight. In part, this follows directly from the previous observation: if a state is constrained from bluffing, the threats that it does make are more likely to be genuine. The model of political competition, however, provides a more explicit causal mechanism for this effect. When the costs of war are anticipated to be low relative to the stakes of the dispute, the opposition party has electoral incentives to publicly support the government's threats. Domestically, this strategy permits the opposition party to "match" the government, blunting the electoral salience of what is expected to be a foreign policy success. Internationally, this strategy signals to the rival state that the government has political incentives to carry out its threat.

It makes intuitive sense that a threat that receives support from other parties is more credible than a threat that is greeted by domestic dissent. The logic of multiple signalers goes even further: a threat made by a democratic government and supported by its domestic political adversaries is more credible than a threat made by a nondemocratic government that serves as the lone voice of the state. The political conflict between the government and the opposition, along with the fact that the latter's support is freely given rather than coerced, gives their show of unity particular meaning. The competing interests of the government and opposition mean that, although the government has incentives to bluff, the opposition generally has little incentive to collude in a bluff. As a result, the threats that the opposition chooses to support are very likely to be genuine. The target of such a threat is thus more likely to make concessions or otherwise avoid escalation of the crisis.

Again, this logic suggests patterns both at the aggregate level and in individual crises. The probability that a target state resists, conditional on its having been challenged, should be lower when the initiator of the challenge is democratic than when it is nondemocratic. In Chapter 5, I present evidence consistent with this prediction. In crises initiated by democracies, the probability that the target reciprocates with militarized action is roughly 30 percent lower than in crises initiated by nondemocracies. In

Chapter 6, I delve deeper into this effect by looking at fifty-six cases in which states attempted to deter attacks on valued protégés (Huth 1988). The evidence suggests that democratic defenders were generally more successful in such attempts, but especially when their deterrent threat was supported by all major opposition parties.

Together, the restraining and confirmatory effects suggest that democracy should lower the probability that a state enters a crisis which then escalates to war. Because democracies choose their threats selectively, and because of the additional credibility some of their threats enjoy, democratic states are less likely to issue a threat that leads to war due to the target state's uncertainty. The evidence in Chapter 5 supports this prediction. In particular, I estimate that a shift to democracy decreases by 40–60 percent the probability that a state will initiate a crisis that escalates to the point of war, or at least to the use of force by both sides. Hence, democracy mitigates the problems associated with asymmetric information, reducing the attendant danger of military conflict.

Alternative approaches: democratic peace theories and neorealism

Inevitably in the background of any analysis of democracy and war lies the "democratic peace," the now well-known claim that democratic states do not fight wars against one another.[3] It would not be an exaggeration to say that the academic study of international conflict has been preoccupied with this matter for much of the last decade. At the core of this literature are two findings, both of which have attracted some controversy. The main observation is that there are few, if any, clear cases of war between democratic states. The highly qualified wording here – "few, if any, clear cases" – reflects the fact that, depending upon how one treats some ambiguous cases of democracy and/or war, the number of wars between democratic states can be zero or some number greater than zero but still smaller than otherwise would be expected.[4] The

---

[3] The literature on this subject is too large to cite in a single footnote. The main works which have sought to establish the democratic peace claim are Small and Singer (1976), Doyle (1983), Maoz and Abdolali (1989), Bremer (1992), Russett (1993), and Ray (1993). Citations of the main theoretical contributions to this literature, and further empirical work, can be found throughout the text of this chapter. For a recent review of the literature, see Chan (1997).

[4] See Russett (1993) and Ray (1993) for a discussion of some of the ambiguous cases.

second claim is that democratic states are not less war-prone in general than nondemocratic states.[5] In other words, although democracies do not fight one another, they fight other kinds of states sufficiently often that their overall rate of war participation is not appreciably smaller. Neither of these claims is universally accepted, however, and researchers tend to fall in one of three camps: those who believe both findings, suggesting that democracies enjoy a special relationship that does not extend to other states; those who believe the first but not the second, suggesting that peace among democracies is an outgrowth of a general disinclination to wage war; and those who believe the second but not the first, suggesting that democracies are no different from other kinds of states, either singly or in their relations with one another.

This book is *not* primarily about the democratic peace. Although motivated by a similar set of theoretical and practical concerns, it does not directly address whether or why democratic states have not fought wars against one another. In large part, this departure is motivated by concerns that the democratic peace observation is inconclusive and overdetermined, as a number of critics have pointed out (esp., Gowa 1999; Farber and Gowa 1995, 1997; Gartzke 1998). One need not accept the theoretical conclusions of these writers to agree with their central contention that the empirical basis of the democratic peace claim has serious weaknesses. War is a rare event and, until relatively recently, democracy has been a rare form of government. As a result, it is difficult to accept any relationship between the two with great statistical confidence, especially prior to World War II. After 1945, when the empirical finding is more robust, we have reason to believe that other factors – most prominently, the Cold War – influenced the tendency of democratic states to fight one another. It is difficult to disentangle the common strategic interests uniting democratic states from other factors that might arise from their common political norms and structures.

None of this means that there is no meaningful relationship here, but it does suggest that there are limits to what we can conclude on the basis of the available data and that there is little to be gained from additional tests of the democratic peace. These results also suggest that the research program on domestic institutions and war has to show that it can uncover new empirical propositions. After all, there is legitimate

---

[5] For the main works establishing this claim, see Chan (1984), Weede (1984), Maoz and Abdolali (1989), Maoz (1996). Main dissenters include Rummel (1983, 1995) and Benoit (1996). Gleditsch and Hegre (1997) present evidence on both sides.

work to be done on this topic *even if there is no democratic peace.* Those interested in the larger research program need to show that it does not stand or fall with this single observation. A primary purpose of this book is to develop a theory that is consistent with the democratic peace but also generates new hypotheses for empirical testing.

The literature on the democratic peace, however, does provide some alternative perspectives on the relationship between democracy and war. While the purpose of this book is not to falsify these theories, it is important to show that they cannot account for the empirical regularities we uncover here. Hence, we will at times contrast the predictions of the informational theory of democracy developed here with those of three alternative approaches that have dominated the debate on the democratic peace: the normative school, the institutional constraints school, and neorealism.

Normative theory

Normative approaches to the study of democracy and war take several different forms, but all share a common assumption that state leaders are motivated by normative ideas or ideologies that dictate how political relations should be structured. In some such accounts, decision makers are thought to internalize the norms and values that prevail within their own domestic political environment (Russett 1993; Dixon 1994). In this view, actors are socialized to a certain way of seeing the world and resolving conflicts, and they attempt to carry out these practices in their foreign policy. Alternatively, state leaders might find themselves constrained to act according to these norms due to institutions of accountability which permit liberal publics to exert influence on elites (Doyle 1983, 1986; Owen 1997).

Two broad sets of norms are thought to be prevalent in democratic, and particularly liberal democratic, polities. One is a preference for nonviolent dispute resolution. In democratic societies, the use of violence or threats of violence is considered illegitimate as a means of resolving conflicts (Russett 1993, pp. 31–35). Democratic institutions and norms seek to replace force with peaceful alternatives such as voting mechanisms or courts. Thus, to the extent that state leaders implement internationally the practices that they consider legitimate domestically, they should be motivated to resolve international disputes through negotiation, compromise, third-party mediation, and arbitration (Dixon 1993, 1994; Raymond 1994; Mousseau 1998). The second norm emphasized by writers in this tradition is a norm of respect for legitimate, liberal governments (Kant 1983 [1795]; Doyle 1983, 1986; Owen 1997). Liberal ideology holds that a government is legitimate if it is based on the consent and representation of the governed. Regimes so constituted are true reflections of their citizens' preferences, and, consequently, their international demands deserve the respect of other liberal states. Regimes based on force and oppression, by contrast, merit no such deference, because their goals are assumed to run contrary to their citizens' interests.

Theorists in the normative school claim that the absence of war between democracies follows logically from these assumptions. Democratic leaders prefer to settle disputes in a nonviolent manner and in a way that respects the rights of all parties. Moreover, they expect leaders in rival democratic states to share those preferences. Knowing that their desire for peace will be reciprocated, democratic states readily engage in negotiations without fear of attack. War is thus avoided because both sides want a settlement that recognizes the rights and needs of the other. At the same time, this theory leaves open the possibility of war between democratic and nondemocratic states. Such wars can arise either because autocratic leaders may try to exploit the natural pacifism of democratic states (Russet 1993) or because a commitment to their ideals may impel liberal states to convert others by force (Owen 1997; Doyle 1986).

Institutional constraints

The institutional constraints perspective is rooted in the observation that war is less likely when the people who would bear its costs get to decide. This school traces its lineage to Immanuel Kant's observation that a republican political system makes it difficult for state leaders to wage war because doing so would require the mobilization of societal support (Kant 1983 [1795]). This explanation focuses on the constraining effects of democratic institutions, which ensure that decision makers are responsive to the public's wishes. In this framework, the People are generally assumed to be pacific, largely because it is they who would personally suffer in the event of war (Gaubatz 1999, p. 10). Though state leaders may face no personal costs in war – such as the loss of family or property – institutions of accountability can expose them to political costs – in particular, the costs of being removed from office for waging a war opposed by the voters. For an autocratic leader, on the other hand, waging war is "the easiest thing in the world to do" because none of the costs of war are borne by the leader or those close to him (Kant 1983

[1795], p. 113). Thus, democratic leaders face costs of war to which their nondemocratic counterparts are less vulnerable.

Though Kant's argument about the democratic peace mixes normative, ideational, and institutional factors (Doyle 1983), his observation about the effect of electoral accountability has spawned a set of arguments focusing primarily on this factor. Bueno de Mesquita and Lalman (1992) argue that democratic institutions facilitate the mobilization of opposition, making it easier for challengers to unseat a government that undertakes costly or failed policies. War is thus an especially risky prospect for democratic leaders, who may find themselves in early retirement if things go badly; nondemocratic leaders, by contrast, are better insulated from such risks. Morgan and Campbell (1991) add that constraints on executive decision making, political competition, and the diffusion of decision-making authority make it easier for those with dovish preferences to veto a resort to force. These arguments suggest that those who control the sword in democratic polities tend to have lower expected value from going to war, and a greater incentive to avoid violent conflict, than their nondemocratic counterparts (see also, Rummel 1979; Lake 1992; Siverson 1995).

While this argument has intuitive appeal, there are legitimate concerns about the basic assumption that war is systematically less attractive to democratic leaders. Contrary to the stylized view of autocracy that often appears in international relations, studies of politics within such systems tend to emphasize the pervasive insecurity that haunts the dictator. Tullock (1987, p. 212) concludes his study of autocracy with the proposition that "Dictators and other autocrats are fundamentally insecure." Wintrobe (1998, p. 25) notes that the absence of a legal procedure for removing dictators from office generates advantages as well as disadvantages: "dictators typically enjoy income, privileges, and perquisites of office unknown to any democratic leader. But they also experience the other end of the spectrum of consumption possibilities: One common method for removing a dictator is assassination." Put another way, democratic political institutions make it easier to sanction failed leaders, but they also tend to limit the magnitude of the punishment that is imposed. Removal from office may be unpleasant for a democratic politician, but ex-office holders can generally retire with a public pension, find a lucrative job in the private sector, or even run for office again. Life is not always so pleasant for nondemocratic rulers who run afoul of their domestic constituents. While the lack of institutionalized mechanisms for removing undesired leaders means that removal is relatively rare, it also means that the associated punishment can be quite severe. Indeed, Goemans (2000) presents evidence showing that, while democratic leaders face a higher probability of removal in the aftermath of a war, nondemocratic leaders are much more likely to face exile, imprisonment, or death in the event that they are removed. Thus, institutions of accountability generate two countervailing effects, and it is not clear which dominates.

Neorealism

The third theoretical tradition to engage this debate is neorealism, which has entered this literature primarily to refute the claims of a democratic peace (esp., Layne 1994; Gowa 1999). Neorealism starts from the assumption that all states are like units whose domestic political characteristics do not fundamentally alter their international behavior. Instead, state behavior derives first and foremost from the anarchic nature of the international system (Waltz 1959, 1979). Because anarchy implies the absence of supranational constraints on the use of force, states must pursue power as a means to security. This imperative leads them to acquire military capabilities and to seek out allies among states with similar strategic interests. It also generates conflict because of the relative nature of power: the gains of one state must come at the expense of others (Gilpin 1975; Grieco 1988). Many interactions are inevitably zero-sum, and war is a natural outgrowth of this conflict. In such a world, variations in domestic political structures are overwhelmed by the constraints of international competition. The key determinants of international outcomes are power and interests, where the latter derive primarily from external factors such as the relative power of other states, geography, and technology.

This emphasis on power and interests is clearly evident in the realist response to the democratic peace literature. Gowa (1999), Farber and Gowa (1995, 1997), and Gartzke (1998) have argued that what appears to be a democratic peace in the Cold War period is actually a product of shared strategic interests: most democracies faced a common threat in the Soviet Union and hence had incentives to mitigate conflict among themselves. Layne (1994) presents case studies showing that conflicts between democratic states have been resolved peacefully not because of democratic norms but because of clear differentials in state power. Thus, neorealism makes both positive and negative claims, both of which need to be addressed. The positive claim is that, in trying to explain crisis behavior and outcomes, we must adequately account for power and strategic interests. The negative claim is that domestic political institutions have no systematic impact on international outcomes; neorealism thus provides the null hypothesis that we seek to reject.

Information *versus* preferences

In a sense, the approach presented in this book sits in between neorealism and democratic peace theory. Neorealist theory sees war as an inevitable outgrowth of conflicting interests. Democratic peace theories consider the absence of war between democratic states a result of a mutual desire for peace that is driven by shared norms and/or institutional constraints. I start with the observation that war need not always stem from incompatible interests, nor is peace the inevitable result of shared interests. What neorealism fails to address is the fact that war entails costs for all sides and is thus an inefficient way for rational states to settle their conflicts (Fearon 1995). Fighting wars leads to destruction of human, financial, and material resources. Because of these costs, states generally share a common interest in finding some negotiated settlement that avoids war. Thus, while anarchy and the quest for relative power might generate conflict among states, it does not explain why states sometimes fail to settle those conflicts efficiently – that is, without incurring the costs of war.

What democratic peace theory fails to address is the fact that a mutual desire for harmony and cooperation does not always guarantee success. Indeed, we observe many cases in which actors with shared interests cannot achieve outcomes that make them collectively better off. The Prisoner's Dilemma and related issues of collective action are perhaps the most widely treated examples of this in international relations theory (e.g., Keohane 1984; Oye 1986). In the context of crisis bargaining, informational asymmetries can cause bargaining to fail even when a mutually beneficial deal is known to exist, a point I will develop more fully in Chapter 2.

Put another way, most existing theories about democracy and war are primarily arguments about interests or preferences. Normative theorists see democratic leaders as motivated by a shared desire for peace – a desire which presumably does not motivate nondemocratic leaders. The institutional constraints argument suggests that democratic leaders face a different cost-benefit analysis when thinking about war and peace; in particular, elected officials in a democracy are thought to face higher average costs for using force. Realist criticisms of the democratic peace also base their arguments on interests. Farber and Gowa (1997) argue that the absence of war between democracies is an artifact of the Cold War, caused by "common interests" rather than "common polities."

This book departs from these other theories by focusing primarily on information rather than on interests. It does so, not because interests are unimportant, but because they do not tell the full story. The availability of information, and the nature of strategic interaction under conditions of uncertainty, intervene in the causal chain between interests and outcomes. By focusing purely on whether and how democracy affects preferences for war and peace, the other perspectives overlook the fact that a central obstacle to peace lies not in states' preferences but in their information and expectations. Whether crises develop and how they evolve depends not simply on what states want but also on whether or not they can communicate their demands credibly.

Thus, domestic political institutions can have a substantial impact on crisis behavior and outcomes even if, as I assume here, they have no systematic influence on preferences over war and peace. What is different about democratic systems is that their preferences are more transparent. Hence, whether or not institutional and/or normative constraints bite in any given case is something that rival states can learn by observing the signals that emerge. On the other hand, the constraints that operate on nondemocratic leaders can be harder to perceive. Because open political opposition is suppressed or marginalized, it is more difficult for outside observers to learn the factors that influence the decision-making calculus of the autocratic leader.

In taking this approach, the theory developed here shares some features with that of Fearon (1994a), who has argued that democratic governments have an advantage when it comes to signaling their resolve in international crises. According to his argument, state leaders incur "audience costs" if they make threats which they later fail to carry out. The magnitude of these costs helps determine how credible a threat to use force is. When a threat generates large audience costs, there is a strong possibility that the government intends to – indeed, has to – carry through on that threat. When a threat generates small audience costs, the government has more leeway to engage in bluffing behavior – that is, to make empty threats from which it can readily back away if necessary. This argument suggests a role for political institutions, because the magnitude of these costs should depend on how effectively domestic audiences can sanction their leaders. Since electoral institutions provide a low-cost mechanism for this purpose, Fearon hypothesized that democratic governments could generate higher audience costs and hence send more credible signals of resolve.

The argument developed here builds on this line of reasoning to some degree, but it also departs from it in important ways. The main similarity lies in the fact that both theories shift the focus on domestic political institutions away from the question of how they influence a government's preferences for war and toward the question of how they influence the government's ability to reveal its preferences. I also rely on Fearon's (1992, 1994a) work by adopting his assumption that leaders expose themselves to audience costs when they make public threats in international crises. I do not, however, follow Fearon in assuming that threats by democratic governments generate systematically higher audience costs than threats by nondemocratic governments. The difficulty with this assumption is that, like the institutional constraints approach, it relies on the premise that democratic leaders are politically more insecure than their nondemocratic counterparts and subject to greater penalties for failure. As I argued above, although democratic institutions increase the likelihood that leaders will be sanctioned for failure, they also cap the magnitude of the punishment that can be imposed. Nondemocratic leaders, by contrast, are less likely to be sanctioned but more likely to incur severe punishments when they are. Accounts of the Gulf and Falklands Wars, for example, suggest that both Saddam Hussein of Iraq and the military junta in Argentina would have put their regimes at risk had they chosen to back down after initiating those crises (Karsh and Rautsi 1991, p. 221; Gamba 1987, p. 163). One can well imagine that being forcibly removed from power in such systems, though not inevitable, could be exceedingly unpleasant. Hence, while the probability of incurring audience costs may be lower in a nondemocratic system, the severity of those costs may be considerably higher. It is unclear which effect dominates.

Ultimately what matters is not whether the audience costs generated by a threat are large but whether the rival state understands when the government has political incentives to carry through on the threats it has made. The problem faced by nondemocratic leaders is not that their threats generate no political risks but rather that the political risks generated by their threats are not obvious to outsiders. When Iraq invaded Kuwait, Hussein may have exposed himself to audience costs that made it difficult for him to back down, but could we know for sure one way or another? In the absence of additional information, it was difficult to know what his political incentives were. The public nature of political competition in democratic systems provides precisely this kind of information.

The plan of the book

This book is divided into two main parts. Part I, which comprises Chapters 2, 3, and 4, develops the theoretical argument. Part II, comprising Chapters 5, 6, and 7, presents a series of empirical tests. The underlying framework of crisis bargaining under incomplete information is laid out in Chapter 2. This chapter uses a simple game-theoretic model to show why informational asymmetries can cause bargaining to fail and why it is inherently difficult for states to overcome such asymmetries in the context of an international dispute. Chapters 3 and 4 then present the argument that domestic political institutions in general, and democracy in particular, affect crisis behavior and outcomes by determining a government's ability to reveal and conceal private information about its preferences. Chapter 3 argues that the institutions and practices of democracy foster meaningful debate among competing parties – debate that is meaningful both for its domestic political effects and for the information it can reveal to outside observers. Chapter 4 links this insight with the crisis bargaining game from Chapter 2. It presents a model in which one state experiences public competition between the government and an opposition party. This model permits us to explore how behavior and outcomes change when we move from a game in which states are treated as unitary actors to one in which the state is composed of two strategic parties which compete for political office.

The empirical tests in Part II combine statistical analyses and historical case studies. Chapter 5 uses statistical tests to explore a series of hypotheses relating regime type to three dependent variables: whether or not a state initiates a crisis, whether or not the target of a threat resists militarily once challenged, and the probability of war. Chapters 6 and 7 then explore hypotheses about the way government and opposition parties in democratic states behave in international crises and how these behaviors influence the expectations of foreign states. Using both quantitative and qualitative analysis, these chapters look at how the support and dissent of opposition parties influence the government's decision to issue threats and how the targets of those threats respond.

The concluding chapter summarizes the theory and evaluates its strengths and weaknesses in light of the empirical evidence. It also considers the implications of this theory for international politics. In light of the arguments developed here, what does the spread of democracy mean for the future of war and threats to wage war? I then turn to the question of national welfare. From the perspective of individual liberty, institutions that expose state policies to public scrutiny and permit unfettered competition for political office are unquestionably desirable. But when it comes to national security and the need to defend the national interest in a dangerous world, the answer is less obvious. Are transparency and informative competition in the national interest?

Part I

Theory

2 Information and signaling in international crises

The natural starting point for an inquiry into the effects of democracy on war is some consideration of the factors that cause international disputes to become crises and crises to escalate into wars. A fully specified theory of war is, of course, well beyond the reach of a single book, much less a single chapter. The aim here is to lay out, in a general manner, some of the core strategic issues that arise when states bargain in international crises. In particular, this chapter motivates the book's emphasis on the informational properties of domestic political institutions by demonstrating the role that information plays in accounting for crisis behavior and outcomes. It considers the difficulties of bargaining under conditions of incomplete and asymmetric information, the role of threats and other signals, and the counterintuitive relationship between preferences and outcomes that can arise under uncertainty. Using these insights, it builds a baseline model of crises into which we can later embed a model of democracy.

The focus on uncertainty arises from a simple observation: War is an extremely risky and costly way for a state to pursue its interests. The human losses are the most obvious of these costs. There are also financial and economic costs in terms of forgone consumption, investment, and economic growth. For the governments that choose to bring their countries into war, there are serious political risks as well. A number of recent studies have emphasized the link between government survival and war outcomes, and all of them suggest that political leaders expose themselves to the prospect of removal – or worse – when they chose to wage war (esp., Bueno de Mesquita, Siverson, and Woller 1992; Bueno de Mesquita and Siverson 1995; Goemans 2000). A sample of results from these studies suggests the magnitude of the risk and the fact that it is not confined to democratically elected leaders. Bueno de Mesquita,

Siverson, and Woller (1992) study the incidence of domestically instigated, violent regime change as a result of war participation. Although the probability of such a change depends significantly on the outcome of the war and on whether or not the country in question initiated the conflict, their most startling result is that the very act of participating in war *doubles* the chances that a regime will be violently overthrown. Goemans (2000) has compiled evidence on the fate of individual leaders who take their countries into war. He finds that 65 percent of democratic leaders and 41 percent of nondemocratic leaders were removed from office within two years after the war, regardless of whether or not they won or lost. Even more dramatic, 77 percent of the nondemocratic rulers who were removed ended up in prison, exiled, or dead. Clearly, the costs associated with war are considerable, however one chooses to measure them. Seen in this light, it is worth asking why war has nevertheless been a persistent feature of international politics.

The framework employed here sees war as the result of a bargaining failure. Because war is costly, states would generally be better off if they could solve their disputes through negotiation, rather than through war. The question then becomes: under what conditions will states succeed in achieving peaceful bargains, and under what conditions will bargaining fail? Borrowing from a substantial literature in economics and a growing literature in international relations, I argue that bargaining can fail due to asymmetric information combined with conflicting preferences over the allocation of disputed goods.[1] Incomplete information about states' military and political attributes creates uncertainty over precisely which negotiated settlements are mutually acceptable. Overcoming this uncertainty is problematic because states generally have incentives to engage in strategic misrepresentation. Hence, much of state behavior in international crises revolves around efforts to communicate – and exploit – private information, and the outcomes of crises depend crucially on the success or failure of these efforts.

The literature on information and signaling in international crises is quite large, and much of it relies on models of greater sophistication than those developed here (e.g., Morrow 1989; Fearon 1992, 1994a, 1995, 1997; Powell 1990, 1999). The purpose of this chapter is not to provide an exhaustive review of this literature but rather to set out some of the basic intuitions that are crucial for the argument in this book. There are three

---

[1] For a summary of the economics literature on bargaining under incomplete information, see Fudenberg and Tirole (1991, ch. 10).

main insights in particular that provide a necessary starting point for an inquiry into the effects of domestic institutions on international crises:

(1) A shared preference for a peaceful bargain does not ensure that such a bargain will be found. Under conditions of asymmetric information, peaceful outcomes that both sides prefer to war may not be realized.

(2) Overcoming information asymmetries is complicated by the fact that actors have conflicting interests in a crisis and so have incentives to misrepresent their preferences in order to get the best possible deal. A crucial determinant of crisis behavior and outcomes is the ability of states to signal information credibly, given a strategic environment which encourages deception, concealment, and bluff.

(3) While states' power and interests influence the outcomes of crises, their effect is mediated by information and beliefs. The nature of strategic interaction under uncertainty means states' preferences over war and peace need not influence the likelihood of war and peace in a predictable or straightforward manner.

Together, these insights suggest that arguments about democracy and war that focus purely on how institutions or norms shape leaders' preferences for war and peace are at best incomplete and at worst indeterminate. They are incomplete to the extent that they assume a shared preference for peace is sufficient to explain a peaceful outcome. In fact, such preferences are necessary but not sufficient to explain the absence of war. Such arguments may also be indeterminate to the extent that the relationship between preferences and outcomes is itself indeterminate when states interact with incomplete information. An increase in the costs of war for one or both states in a crisis can lead to an increase, decrease, or no change in the probability of war. At the same time, the logic developed here suggests that there is analytical leverage in exploring how domestic political institutions influence the availability of information internationally, and particularly how they affect a state's ability to reveal or conceal its preferences for war and peace.

The structure of an international crisis

The basis for this analysis is a simple formal model of crisis bargaining, different versions of which will appear throughout this book. In basing the analysis on a stylized model, I do not deny that every crisis, or potential crisis, has unique considerations that influence the choices states make and the outcomes we observe. The modeling enterprise is built on the assumption that there are some common trade-offs and strategic decision problems inherent in any such interaction. It is these commonalties that the models try to capture. Thus, the games presented here do not reflect international crises in all their complexity, nor do they attempt to. Rather, the goal is to use simple, stylized models to cut away complexity and focus on the underlying strategic logic. Though descriptive accuracy is sacrificed, these models help to uncover general insights and propositions.[2] This section considers the basic assumptions of the model and the underlying view of international crises.

An international dispute begins with a conflict of interests over some issue. From the perspective of this analysis, the exact issue that drives the dispute is unimportant. We can think of it as being anything that states value, such as territory, wealth, a policy, etc. The crucial thing is that the states must have conflicting preferences over how the good in question is allocated or how the issue is resolved. In principle, this is not an overly restrictive assumption: as long as the two states' preferences are not identical, there is always the potential for such disputes to arise. In practice, of course, many such differences may be so small that the use of military force to resolve the dispute is unrealistic (e.g., Keohane and Nye 1977). A crisis occurs when one state makes at least a threat to use military force to change the status quo. The models in this book address how states choose to turn disputes into crises, how crises evolve, and how domestic political institutions affect both of these processes.[3]

The generic crisis game on which this analysis is based has the following structure, depicted in Figure 2.1. There are two states, a challenger and a target. The interaction begins with the challenger's decision either to accept the status quo allocation of the good or to issue a challenge – that is, to threaten the target with force unless it concedes to a change in the status quo. If the challenger chooses to maintain the status quo, the game ends. If the challenger issues a threat, the target faces a choice between conceding to the challenger's demand or resisting. In the event the target concedes, the game ends peacefully with some or all of the

---

[2] For some excellent recent discussions of the role of formal models in theory building in international relations, see Powell (1999) and Milner (1997).

[3] Obviously, coercion can take any number of forms, not all of them involving military force. Given our substantive interest in interstate war, however, a focus on the use and threat of military force is appropriate.

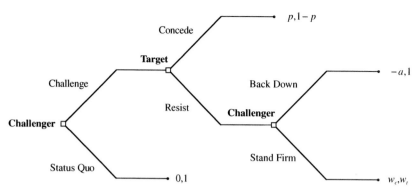

Fig. 2.1 Crisis bargaining model

good being reallocated to the challenger. If the target resists, the challenger must then decide either to stand firm and follow through on its threat or to back down. If the challenger backs down, the status quo allocation of the good is preserved. If the challenger stands firm, we assume that it carries out its threat and attempts to take the good by force. We will call this outcome war, although the use of force entailed in carrying out the threat need not always meet the standards of full-scale war.

Given this structure, the interaction can have four different outcomes: the status quo (*SQ*), the target makes concessions (*CD*), the challenger backs down in the face of resistance (*BD*), and war (*WAR*). To understand how the game will be played, we have to make assumptions about how the states assess these outcomes – in particular, how they order them from least to most preferred. For the most part, these assumptions are quite straightforward. Because the challenger is demanding a greater share of the good than it initially possesses, it prefers concession by the target to the status quo. If the challenger backs down from its threat, this action preserves the status quo allocation. There may, however, be some cost to the challenger for making the threat and then backing down in the face of resistance – a cost that comes from a loss of face in the eyes of international and/or domestic audiences (Fearon 1994a; Sartori 1998). I will return to this issue later in the chapter. For now, it is sufficient to assume that the challenger's payoff from backing down is equal to or less than its payoff from the status quo. From the target's perspective, any concessions reduce its share of the good. Hence, the target prefers both the status quo and the outcome in which the challenger backs down to making concessions.

27

The states' preference orderings over the peaceful outcomes are thus quite clear: For the challenger, $CD > SQ \geq BD$, and for the target $SQ = BD > CD$. Notice that, from the perspective of how the good is allocated, the two states have diametrically opposed preferences: the best outcome for the challenger is the worst outcome for the target.

To reduce notation, it will be useful to attach some concrete values to these outcomes. There is no loss of generality in doing so, because any set of assumptions that preserves the basic orderings will generate similar results. In particular, assume that the good in dispute has a value of one, and that the target possesses the good in the status quo. In the event that the target makes concessions, let x denote the proportion of the good that is transferred. Finally, we let a denote the cost, if any, that the challenger incurs for backing down from a threat, with $a \geq 0$. Given these assumptions, the payoff to the challenger is zero in the event that it selects the status quo, x if the target makes concessions, and $-a$ if it makes a challenge and backs down. The payoff to the target is 1 if the challenger selects the status quo or backs down and $1 - x$ if the target is forced to make concessions. For now, we leave the level of concessions made by the target unspecified.

How do the states evaluate the war outcome? At its most general level, the value a state places on going to war is a function of five factors: the value it places on winning, the value it places on losing, the probability with which it expects to win, the costs it expects to incur, and its attitude toward risk (Bueno de Mesquita 1981, 1985; Morrow 1985, 1989). Assume that war is a winner-take-all event: the state that wins gets to determine the post-war division of the good and will, by assumption, take it all. In reality, of course, the winner of a war is rarely in a position to dictate terms without constraint. This assumption, however, has little substantive impact on the results and is made largely to keep the notation simple. We further assume that the actors are risk-neutral: each actor values getting half of the good the same as it values a lottery in which it has a 50 percent chance of receiving the whole good and a 50 percent chance of receiving nothing. The assumption of risk neutrality is common in this literature. All of the results would also hold if the actors were assumed to be risk-averse, in which case they would prefer the certain half to the even lottery. Some aspects of the analysis might change if the actors were highly risk-acceptant, a point to which I will return below.

In this stylized setting, each state's expected value for war reduces to a simple function of two variables: the probability that it will win and the costs that it will incur by fighting. Let p denote the probability with which the challenger will win the war, and let c_c and c_t represent the costs that the challenger and target, respectively, expect to incur in the event of war. It is important to note that, because the value of the good in dispute has been normalized to one, these terms reflect the costs of war *relative* to the value of the good. They increase if either the costs of war go up or the value of the good goes down; they decrease if either the costs of war go down or the value of the good goes up. Given these assumptions, the states' expected values for war, w_c and w_t, are:

$$w_c = p - c_c, \text{ and} \tag{1a}$$

$$w_t = 1 - p - c_t. \tag{1b}$$

No state can be forced to accept less from a peaceful outcome than it expects to get from fighting. This is a fundamental consequence of international anarchy: states can wage war whenever it is in their interests to do so (Waltz 1979). Moreover, the absence of a central authority capable of enforcing contracts means that all settlements must be self-enforcing – that is, they must give each state at least as much as it can expect to get from breaking the contract (e.g., Oye 1986). As a result, when states bargain in a crisis, their expected values for war determine the range of settlements that are mutually acceptable and self-enforcing. Hence, for any settlement of the dispute to be mutually acceptable, it must be the case that the challenger gets a share of the good which is at least as great as w_c and the target gets a share of the good which is at least as great as w_t. In terms of the game described above, this means that the level of concessions offered by the target, x, must meet two requirements: To be acceptable to the challenger, $x \geq w_c$, and to be acceptable to the target, $1 - x \geq w_t$.

An important implication of this set-up is that a division of the good that meets both of these requirement always exists. The existence of such a settlement is ensured by the fact that war imposes costs on both sides (Fearon 1995). We can see this from expressions (1a) and (1b): Whereas the total value of the disputed good is 1, the total value of war to the two states is $1 - c_c - c_t$. As a result, allocating the good peacefully, rather than through war, generates a surplus of $c_c + c_t$. For example, a division of the good such that the challenger gets a share of p while the target gets a share of $1 - p$ would give each at least as much as it expects to get from war no matter what the costs of war are – indeed, even if those costs are effectively zero. Though a division of $(p, 1-p)$ is only one of the possible deals that might satisfy this condition, we will focus on this level of concessions for two reasons. First, it is a division of the good that is guaranteed to be mutually acceptable under all conditions (i.e., even when the costs of war are zero). Second, this allocation has some intuitive appeal because it roughly corresponds to the distribution of military power between the two states.[4]

It is important to emphasize that w_c and w_t reflect *expectations* about the outcome of war. While we assume that states try very hard to generate accurate expectations based upon the information available to them, *ex post* outcomes can vary markedly from *ex ante* expectations. Evidence that a state had high expected value for a war that it went on to lose disastrously does not contradict this assumption. Moreover, in claiming that concessions of magnitude p are always acceptable to the challenger, we do not rule out the possibility that the challenger could generate a better outcome by fighting a war. If it won the war at little or no cost, its actual payoff could be greater than p. All we are assuming is that the challenger's payoff cannot exceed this value *in expectation*. That is, while the challenger might assign positive probability to war outcomes that exceed p, it also assigns positive probability to outcomes that are less than p. The assumptions that war has positive expected costs and that actors are risk-neutral ensure that the probability-weighted average of all possible outcome has value less than p. The same logic ensures that the expected payoff from war to the target cannot be greater than $1 - p$.

Once the prospect of war is introduced, a purely conflictual interaction is transformed into a game of "mixed motives." Although the two states still have conflicting interests over the distribution of the good, they have a common interest in avoiding war. From the perspective of the target, war is the worst possible outcome. While the status quo allocation is clearly better than making concessions of magnitude p, the latter is still preferable to fighting a war. The challenger also prefers concessions to war – and all other outcomes, for that matter. How the challenger evaluates war relative to the remaining outcome depends upon the actual values of p and c_c. Of particular importance in what follows is whether or not the challenger prefers war to backing down – that is whether w_c is greater than or less than $-a$. The direction of this relationship determines what the challenger will do in the event that its threat is

---

[4] For further discussion of a similar assumption, see Bueno de Mesquita and Lalman (1992, pp. 42–43).

resisted. Clearly, the challenger would rather wage war than back down if and only if

$$w_c > -a. \tag{2}$$

If this condition holds, we say that the initial challenge is "genuine": the challenger will implement its threat to use force if the target resists its demand. If this condition does not hold, then the challenge is a "bluff" or "limited probe": the challenger will back down rather than carry out its threat. As we will see below, the target's beliefs about whether or not condition (2) holds play an important role in determining the success or failure of the challenger's threat and the prospects for a peaceful settlement.

We have now specified most of the key elements of the basic crisis game: the actors, the sequence of moves, the possible outcomes, and the preference orderings over these outcomes. What remains is to discuss the central variable in this analysis: the distribution of information, and particularly the actors' beliefs about each other's preferences. Before moving on to this point, however, a comment is in order about the game structure. Obviously, this basic model rests on a number of simplifications. The demand made by the challenger and the level of concessions made by the target are fixed exogenously. There is only one round of "bargaining" because the target's refusal to make concessions is irreversible; it cannot change its mind once the challenger has shown itself willing to stand firm. The target cannot make demands of its own. The good is infinitely divisible, so that any level of concessions is possible. The actors are assumed to be risk-neutral. In assessing the impact of these simplifications, the key question is not whether the model fully captures real-world crises – it does not and, like all formal models, is not intended to. A more appropriate question is whether the simplifications distort the insights we get from the model. In other words, would a more complex model yield fundamentally different results? For most of the results discussed below, the answer to this question is 'no'; the basic insights have been confirmed using models which relax some of the restrictive assumptions made here. The assumptions of divisibility and risk-neutrality, on the other hand, do have some substantive impact, so I will return to them in my concluding remarks.

The distribution of information

The crucial element of the game that remains to be specified is the distribution of information: what do the actors know about each other's preferences and particularly their willingness to wage war? In any strategic interaction, actors must form some expectations about what the other side is likely to do. In this context, the target's actions depend upon its information and beliefs about how the challenger will respond to resistance: Is its threat genuine or a bluff? Similarly, the challenger's decision whether or not to make a threat depends upon its assessment of the target's likely response: How willing is the target to resist? To answer these questions, states form beliefs about each other's preferences. Of particular importance in the crisis game are each side's beliefs about the other's value for war. The target's beliefs about w_c determine its expectations about whether the threat is genuine; the challenger's beliefs about w_t determine its expectations about whether the target will resist. These beliefs are based on the information that states have about one another and particularly about the political and military factors that determine their value for war. When the relevant information is observable to both sides, information is said to be complete: each side knows the other's preferences, and this fact is common knowledge. When states have information about their own attributes that others cannot directly observe, a condition of asymmetric information arises: each state has more or better information about its own preferences than it does about the preferences of the other side.

To start the analysis of how the distribution of information influences behavior and outcomes in this game, consider what happens when the states have complete information about each other's expected values for war. To be clear, a condition of complete information does not require that the states know *every* fact that is relevant to their assessment of war; what it requires is that the states make these assessments using the same information. Thus, it leaves open the possibility that the states are uncertain about some factors that affect the outcome of war – as long as this uncertainty is shared. When this is the case, the two states arrive at the same assessment of w_c and w_t.

Under complete information, the target state knows whether or not $w_c > -a$ and, thus, whether or not the threat it faces is genuine. If the threat is genuine, then the target knows that resistance will lead to war. Facing a clear choice between concessions and war, it will always choose the former: as long as it has positive costs for war, the target always prefers making concessions, for a payoff of $1-p$, to war, which delivers a payoff of $1-p-c_t$, in expectation. On the other hand, if the threat is known to be a bluff, then the target will always resist; after all, there is no reason to make concessions if the challenger will certainly back away from its threat. Given the target's responses, the challenger's strategy is clear. If $w_c > -a$, then the challenger knows that the target will make concessions. Since these are preferred to the status quo, it always makes sense to issue the challenge in this case. On the other hand, if $w_c \leq -a$, then any threat would be a bluff, and the target, knowing this, will certainly resist. Since the challenger can anticipate that it would have to back down, it is better off refraining from threats altogether.

Thus, under complete information, the game has two equilibrium outcomes, both of them peaceful: either the challenger makes a genuine threat, and the target makes concessions, or the challenger accepts the status quo, anticipating that a bluff would be resisted. Peace is assured not only because the costs of war ensure that some peaceful outcome is mutually acceptable, but also because each state can perfectly anticipate what the other will do. The target knows whether or not the threat is genuine, and the challenger knows whether or not the target will resist. As we will see, a condition of asymmetric information creates uncertainty about the other state's intentions and leads to the possibility of conflict.

A condition of asymmetric information can arise from several sources. One possible source is in the evaluation of material outcomes: that is, the relative probabilities of victory and defeat on the battlefield, the number of casualties that will be incurred, the financial and material costs. All of these outcomes depend upon a number of factors which it is reasonable to assume are not always common knowledge. Consider, for example, the probability of victory. A number of studies have considered what determines who wins and who loses a war (Organski and Kugler 1980; Stam 1996; Reiter and Stam 1998). A partial list includes such factors as relative military resources, each state's ability to mobilize those resources for war, the choice of strategy and tactics, the effectiveness of military technologies, the quality and morale of the troops, and the reliability of third party allies. Whenever one state has information about these military and political attributes that the other cannot observe, a condition of asymmetric information arises. So, for example, if the challenger has private information about the effectiveness of a new technology or the strategy it would employ, then its estimate of p will be based on more and better information than will the target's estimate (Bueno de Mesquita, Morrow, and Zorick 1997). Similarly, if the challenger's estimate of casualties were based on private information, then it would know more about its costs of war than would the target.

A second, and more vexing, source of uncertainty deals with the way in which material outcomes translate into the payoffs upon which actions are based. Winning is always better than losing, and fewer casualties are always better than more. But the crucial question is how the state evaluates the prospect of war relative to the alternatives, such as the status quo or some negotiated bargain. This evaluation involves comparing outcomes that are not directly comparable. If, for example, a state has 50 percent chance of winning a piece of territory and expects to incur 10,000 battle deaths and spend 5 percent of its gross national product in the process, is this preferable to a status quo in which it possesses none of the territory? The answer to this decision depends upon how each of these factors trade off and combine to determine the decision maker's ultimate payoff; even if all of these terms were common knowledge to both sides, a condition of asymmetric information would arise if the one side had private information about this process of aggregation.

Consider the effect of casualties on the decision maker's expectations about war. The relationship between the absolute number of casualties incurred and the political ramifications of war is not fixed across political systems or across events in a given political system. Larson (1996), for example, surveys US public opinion during four wars – World War II, the Korean War, the Vietnam War, and the Gulf War – and two recent military interventions – in Panama and Somalia. He finds that there is no constant trade-off between casualties and public support; instead, tolerance for casualties varies from case to case depending upon the perceived stakes of the conflict. Where core values and interests are thought be in jeopardy – such as in World War II – the public has been willing to tolerate very large numbers of casualties; where peripheral interests are seen as being at stake – such as in Somalia – support for the conflict can dissolve after only a small number of casualties. Thus, even if the costs of war were only measured in human lives lost, and even if both sides in a dispute could come to the same conclusion about the likely number of casualties, there is still room for uncertainty surrounding the translation of these numbers into the payoffs that are relevant for decision making. If the state wins the war and incurs the expected number of casualties, will that outcome be viewed by the relevant domestic audience as a success or failure? What division of the good would be preferable to taking that gamble? How does a given level of benefits and costs influence the welfare of those who control the state's foreign policy? Asymmetric information would arise if the leader of one state had more or better information than his rival with which to answer these questions.

The very act of listing these factors, even in general terms, suggests how likely it is that such a condition will arise. It should be unproblematic to assume that elites within a state have better access to information about their own political and military attributes than do decision makers in other states. The former generally sit on top of bureaucratic and political organizations that collect and analyze information about how the state can perform internationally and how politically important groups will react domestically. Decision makers in foreign countries, by contrast, have fewer resources to devote to this end. For the purposes of this analysis, it is necessary neither to make claims about nor to empirically verify the frequency of informational asymmetries at the international level. Nor does this analysis dispute that, under certain conditions, actors may operate with information that is close to being complete. We will assume, however, that complete information is problematic, in the sense that it is not the natural state of affairs. Instead, complete information is a special case that arises when actors find ways to overcome uncertainties that are inherent in the political environment.[5]

Any or all of the factors that determine a state's expected value for war might be sources of asymmetric information. In order to make the analysis tractable, we need to introduce this kind of uncertainty in a simple, and at the same time general, manner. Following standard practice (e.g., Fearon 1992, 1995; Powell 1999), assume that actors hold private information about how costly war is relative to the value of the disputed good – a factor which is often referred to as "resolve." Whereas the p term in expression (1) depends heavily on the balance of military capabilities, resolve, as we noted above, rests on a more complicated, and less obviously material, set of factors: how much is the good in question worth? What costs are we willing to pay? What risks are we willing to take? From the perspective of foreign states, the answers to such questions are harder to observe than, say, the number of tanks and

---

[5] Given this discussion, one might legitimately wonder whether state leaders are really all that well informed about their *own* attributes. The questions of whether state leaders have accurate information on which to base their decisions and how political institutions influence the flow of information to key decision makers are important and interesting ones. But they are not questions that we must consider here. Nothing in the discussion that follows requires that leaders be fully and accurately informed about the factors that determine their own expected values for war. For a condition of asymmetric information to arise, it is only necessary for a leader to have *more* information about his own attributes than does the leader of a rival state.

airplanes each side possesses. Thus, it makes sense to focus on this kind of uncertainty. Moreover, none of the fundamental results we consider here depend upon this particular formulation.

We generate asymmetric information about these values for war by assuming that each state knows its own costs for war but is uncertain about those of its rival. The basic idea is that there are multiple "types" of challenger and target, and each type has a different value for war. Each state knows what type it is but has only inexact beliefs about the type of the other (Harsanyi 1967–68). Formally, we assume that a non-strategic actor – generally known as "nature" – randomly draws the challenger's costs for war, c_c, from the range $[0, \bar{c}_c]$. The challenger then observes the value of c_c, but the target knows only the probabilities associated with each possible draw. This probability distribution describes the target's prior beliefs about the challenger's costs of war. Similarly, assume that nature draws c_t from the range $[0, \bar{c}_t]$. Again, the target observes the exact draw of c_t, but the challenger knows only the shape and range of the probability distribution. The result is that each side knows exactly what its own expected value for war is but is incompletely informed about that of its rival. The situation is identical to that of two poker players, each of whom sees his own cards but can only form inexact expectations about his opponent's. This set-up implies that w_c can be anywhere in the range $[p - \bar{c}_c, p]$ and w_t can be anywhere in the range $[1 - p - \bar{c}_t, 1 - p]$.[6]

What is the impact of asymmetric information in this game? We answer this problem in two stages: first by considering the problem the target faces in deciding whether or not to resist and then by looking at the challenger's problem in trying to make its threat credible. In this way, we will move backward through the game tree, starting with the target's decision given that it has been challenged and then looking at the challenger's decision about whether to threaten force in the first place.

Responding to threats under asymmetric information

How does the target respond to a demand for concessions? The general insight from the bargaining literature is that, under conditions

---

[6] To keep the analysis general, we need not specify the exact probability distributions that represent the states' prior beliefs. As shown in Appendix A, the results highlighted here hold for any distribution.

of asymmetric information, states face a trade-off between lowering the risks of war and increasing the returns to peace (Fearon 1995; Powell 1999). The more generous is the offer they make, the greater is the likelihood that the offer will be accepted, thus preventing war or further escalation. Of course, if they are accepted, generous concessions also deliver a lower payoff to the side making them. Put another way, it is easy to ensure peace, but only if one is willing to pay any price. The alternative is to make a stingy offer which, if accepted, will lead to a more favorable allocation of the good. Such offers entail a higher risk of war, however, because they are more likely to be rejected by the other side. Thus, as the concessions offered decrease, the payoff from peace increases, but so too does the likelihood of war.

The existence of this trade-off helps to explain why states might take actions that entail a risk of war. While others have explored this trade-off formally using models with continuous offers (Fearon 1995; Powell 1999), the basic point can be seen even with the simpler framework considered here, in which the target must choose between making concessions of magnitude p, which the challenger is sure to accept, and resisting, which is equivalent to offering nothing. The former is a "safe" strategy which entails no risk of war. By conceding part of the good, the target ensures a payoff of $1-p$, which is at least as great as its expected payoff from war. Even though the target always prefers concession to war, however, it does not always make sense to concede. After all, it does not face a stark choice between these two options. If there is some chance that the challenger will back down at it final node – that is, if there is some chance that the challenge is a bluff – then resistance entails a gamble: the challenger might back down, giving the target its best possible payoff, or the challenger might stand firm, leading to a war. Thus, the target faces a choice between getting its second-best outcome for certain (*CD*) and taking a gamble between its first- (*BD*) and third-best outcomes (*WAR*). Here we see the trade-off: making concessions eliminates the danger of war but also reduces the payoff to peace; by resisting the target might be able to retain the entire good, but it can only do so by embracing some risk of war.

Given this trade-off, the key question facing the target is: What is the likelihood that the challenger will stand firm if I resist? In other words, how credible is the threat? In terms of the model, what is the probability that $w_c > -a$ given that a challenge has been made? Let q denote that probability. For now, we take this belief to be exogenous; in the next section, we will see how it arises endogenously from the challenger's strategy at its initial decision node. In the event it resists, the target expects war with probability q, and it expects the challenger to back down with probability $1-q$. Thus, the target's expected utility from resisting is given by

$$EU_t \text{ (Resist)} = qw_t + (1-q). \tag{3}$$

The target prefers to resist if and only if this expression is greater than or equal to $1-p$, the certain payoff from conceding, which occurs when

$$c_t < p \cdot \frac{1-q}{q}. \tag{4}$$

In equilibrium, then, the target resists only if its costs from war, c_t, are sufficiently low to make the gamble worthwhile. Let c^* denote the value on the right-hand side.

It is worth looking at this expression more closely. If the target is certain that the challenger will stand firm in the face of resistance, then $q = 1$, and $c^* = 0$. Because c_t can be no smaller than zero, there is no possible type of target for which expression (4) holds, so the target never resists. Similarly, if the target is certain the threat is a bluff, or $q = 0$, then c^* goes to infinity, meaning that all possible types of target will resist. These two extremes reflect the two possibilities that hold under complete information, as we saw above. Under incomplete information, however, the target may face uncertainty about the nature of the threat it faces – uncertainty that is captured by values of q between zero and one. In this case, $c^* > 0$, and some types of target – i.e., those for which $c_t < c^*$ – prefer to resist, gambling that the challenge is a bluff. Hence, the probability that the target resists increases the more it doubts the genuineness of the threat. As q goes up – meaning that the target is increasingly sure that the challenger will stand firm – the range of types which are willing to resist the challenge shrinks. Conversely, as q goes down – meaning that the target is increasingly sure that the challenger is bluffing – the range of types which are willing to resist grows. The target's decision is thus a function both of its beliefs – captured by q – and of its preferences – captured by c_t. Those with the lowest costs of war are the most motivated to resist, but how low those costs must be depends upon the target's beliefs about the genuineness of the threat.

Even though all targets prefer making concessions to fighting a war, some will nevertheless choose to resist as long as there is some uncertainty about the challenger's intentions. When the challenge is a bluff, this gamble pays off; when the challenge is genuine, the result is war.

The general insight here is crucial: *Although war is suboptimal* ex post, *strategies that entail a positive risk of war may be optimal* ex ante. Under incomplete information, the target state faces a choice between making generous concessions, thereby ensuring peace, and trying to get the best possible settlement – and risking war in the process. Actors who always make a settlement whenever one is possible generally benefit less from those settlements than they could (Roth 1985, p. 3). On the other hand, maximization of expected utility reduces the probability that a deal will be struck – and increases the chances of war.

Strategic misrepresentation and the search for credibility

In the preceding analysis, the target's beliefs about the genuineness of the challenger's threat was taken to be exogenous. Here we take the next step back in the game tree to consider the challenger's initial decision on whether to issue a threat and how this decision shapes the target's expectations. We have seen that uncertainty about the challenger's preferences can lead the target to gamble on strategies that might lead to war. How can the statements and actions of the challenger influence the degree of uncertainty the target faces? Thinking about this question raises a more general puzzle. If asymmetric information can cause bargaining to fail, it would seem to follow that states can ensure peaceful outcomes by disclosing their private information. Why can a state not simply reveal its type and thereby eliminate the danger of war?

The answer to this question lies in two additional problems, one arising from the nature of the actors, the other arising from the nature of their strategic environment. The first problem is that political actors are prone to opportunism, or "self-interest seeking with guile" (Williamson 1985, p. 47). In a world of honest people, informational asymmetries would present little problem since all actors would faithfully reveal what they know. In reality, though, governments and state leaders are opportunistic actors who will engage in "calculated efforts to mislead, distort, disguise, obfuscate, or otherwise confuse" (*ibid.*, p. 47). A diplomat is, after all, "an honest man, sent abroad to lie for the good of his country." Furthermore, the strategic interaction implied by an international dispute promotes such behavior (Morrow 1986, 1994a; Fearon 1995). A crisis arises when states have conflicting preferences over the division of some international good. Although both states prefer a peaceful outcome to war, their interests collide when it comes to deciding which one to implement. The challenger naturally prefers concessions to the status quo, while the target's ordering is exactly opposite. As a result, each state has incentives to exploit its private information strategically in order to get the best possible settlement for itself. Since this incentive is well known to all players, states are necessarily skeptical about the signals sent by their rivals.

Consider the model presented above. The challenger would like the target to believe that its costs from war are sufficiently low so that it would stand firm in the event of resistance. If we were to add a stage to the game in which the challenger publicly announces its costs of war, then it would always have an incentive to understate its costs. To see this, consider what would happen if the target took such announcements at face value – that is, when challenger announces "My costs are m," the target believes this to be true. The target would then make concessions whenever m was such that the challenger's value for war exceeded the payoff for backing down – that is, as long as $m < p + a$. Thus, regardless of its actual type, the challenger is always better off announcing that its costs satisfy this condition. As long as the target understands these incentives, of course, it should not believe any such statements. Once all types of challenger announce that their costs are low, it no longer makes sense for the target to take these statements at face value. Thus, an equilibrium in which the challenger reveals its costs honestly and the target takes the announcement seriously does not exist. Simple communication is ruled out as a reliable means of information revelation.[7]

Asymmetric information is thus compounded by that fact that states have known incentives to conceal and misrepresent their type. Such behavior does not always foreclose information revelation, but it does make the task of overcoming informational asymmetries problematic. States can, and do, attempt to convey information about their preferences and intentions, often through the use of threats, mobilizations, or shows of force (Schelling 1960; Fearon 1992). When states issue threats

---

[7] The same would be true if we added another bargaining stage to the game. Assume that if the challenger stands firm, then rather than going to war, the target gets another opportunity to make concessions. It might seem reasonable that if the challenger stands firm the first time it faces resistance, then the target should make concessions when given a second chance. However, this is not the case. Unless there is some cost or risk to doing so (something which will be addressed below), all types have an incentive to stand firm the first time, in hopes of getting concessions later. As a result, nothing can be learned of the challenger's true type. The target enters the second stage with exactly the same belief as it had going into the first. This point explains why the one-stage bargaining model, though simplistic, captures much of the essential strategic logic.

to use force, they are generally trying to convince their rivals that they are willing to go to war unless their demands are met. Of course, such a threat might also be a bluff issued by those with high costs in hopes of getting a better deal. Whether or not the threat is believed depends on whether it was sent in a credible manner.

How can states send credible signals of their type given that they are opportunistic actors in a strategic environment that encourages dishonesty? A fundamental result in the literature on information is that actors can reveal their type credibly if the signals they send are costly in such a way that some types are more likely to send those signals than others (Spence 1974). This logic suggests a distinction between "cheap" signals, which can be sent by anyone and thus convey no information, and "costly" signals, which can reveal information if certain types are more likely to bear the costs than others.

To see why a threat must entail some cost in order to convey information, consider what would happen in the crisis model if the payoff the challenger received from backing down from its challenge was the same as its payoff from the status quo – that is, if $a = 0$. In this case, the worst payoff the challenger can get from making a challenge is exactly zero; even if its value for war is less than zero, it can always avoid this outcome by backing down. Because of this, there is no reason for the challenger not to make a threat: it can do no worse than the status quo, and it might do better. Since all challengers, regardless of their costs of war, face the same incentive, the act of making a threat reveals nothing about the challenger's true type. The equilibrium in this case is "pooling": all types behave exactly the same way, so the target cannot update its prior beliefs.

History provides numerous examples of how such cheap signals were ineffective in conveying resolve. One comes from China's efforts to deter the United States from attacking North Korea during the Korean War. On October 3, 1950, Chinese diplomats conveyed a message through the Indian ambassador that a US move across the 38th parallel would trigger Chinese intervention. Although the threat turned out to be sincere, it was dismissed at the time by Secretary of State Dean Acheson as "a Chinese Communist bluff." An October 4 memorandum describes Acheson's reasoning:

> The Secretary pointed out that the Chinese Communists were themselves taking no risk in as much as their private talks to the Indian Ambassador could be disavowed . . . [I]f they wanted to take part in the "poker game" they would have to put more on the table than they had up to the present. (US, Dept. of State 1976, pp. 868–69)

Acheson dismissed the Chinese threat because it was conveyed in a costless manner. Under these conditions, a true threat could not be distinguished from a bluff. Acheson chose to ignore the signal and act on his prior belief that China would not in fact get involved (Jian 1994, pp. 169–71).

A second example comes from Iraq's invasion of Kuwait prior to the 1991 Gulf War. In mid-July, 1990, US intelligence observed a build-up of Iraqi troops on the border with Kuwait. The number, type, and arrangement of forces clearly gave Iraq the ability to overrun its neighbor in a quick assault, and some in the intelligence services concluded that this was precisely what Iraqi leader Saddam Hussein intended to do (Woodward 1991, pp. 184–97). Nevertheless, US decision makers dismissed the move as an effort to intimidate Kuwait and gain some concessions in their border dispute. Again, we know from hindsight that the signal was not a bluff, but the manner in which it was sent meant that it could easily be regarded as such. As Woodward (1991, p. 200) reports, "[Defense Secretary Richard] Cheney agreed that everything Saddam had to do to prepare for an invasion was exactly what he also had to do if his intention was simply to scare the Kuwaitis. There was no way to distinguish between the two." US decision makers understood Iraq's incentives to overstate its willingness to fight, and the relatively costless manner in which the threat was made meant that they could easily dismiss the build-up as a bluff. The nature of the signal was such that Cheney could not distinguish a type that was actually willing to invade from a type that was not.

Separation of types occurs if the signal entails some cost or risk that certain types are more willing to bear than others. When this is the case, the decision to send the costly signal reveals some information about the sender's type, prompting the receiver to update its prior belief. Schelling's (1960) classic argument about the role of threats and brinkmanship in nuclear crises suggests one possible mechanism for sending costly signals. Schelling argued that states could signal their resolve by using threats, mobilizations, or limited uses of force to escalate a crisis. With each such action, states approach the "brink" of war, which Schelling saw, not as a "sharp edge of a cliff where one can stand firmly, look down, and decide whether or not to plunge," but rather as "a curved slope that one can stand on with some risk of slipping, the slope gets steeper and the risk of slipping greater as one moves toward the chasm" (1960, p. 199). As Powell (1990) has observed, if states are differentiated according to their value for war, then so too is their willingness to step on to the slope and risk slipping into the chasm. The higher a state's expected value from war is, the less it has to lose by increasing the likelihood of war, and hence the more willing it will be to take actions which do precisely that. By contrast, a state that has low expected value from war will generally shy away from actions that make war more likely. High and low types can thus be separated according to their willingness to take actions that increase the probability of war.

This is an important theoretical result, because it suggests that, when states have asymmetric information and conflicting interests, the cure can often be as dangerous as the disease. For states to reveal information about their type credibly, they may have to take actions that increase the probability of war. The act of signaling thus entails a risk of bringing about the very outcome that the signals were intended to prevent. At the same time, this result is somewhat unsatisfying on substantive grounds. It treats the onset of war as a purely stochastic event, with state leaders manipulating the probability of war but having no say over the actual decision to start one. This view perhaps reflects Schelling's (1960) and Powell's (1990) substantive interest in nuclear brinkmanship crises and the sense that nuclear war would not be a consciously chosen event, but rather an accident caused by heightened tensions. I agree with Fearon (1994a, p. 579) that this feature limits the general applicability of models based on "slippery slope" signaling.

In part reacting to this concern, Fearon (1992, 1994a) suggests an alternative mechanism for costly signaling which leaves the decision to wage war in the hands of decision makers. In this view, states use threats, mobilizations, and the like to generate an expectation that they are willing to use force in the event that their demands are not met. In doing so, they expose themselves to "audience costs" – which are costs that the leader incurs if he fails to carry through on his commitment. So, for example, when President Bush stood before Congress in January 1991 and declared that the Iraqi invasion of Kuwait "will not stand," he exposed himself to such costs. By publicly committing himself to the liberation of Kuwait, Bush put his credibility – and that of the United States – on the line. Had he failed to carry through on that commitment, Bush would, in this view, have suffered costs for making the empty threat. Most of Fearon's (1994a) treatment of audience costs focuses on costs imposed by domestic audiences, such as voters who might punish leaders for tarnishing the "national honor." In this view, making a public threat and then backing down would be seen by the domestic audience, and exploited by challengers, as a foreign policy failure. Smith (1998a,

1998b) builds on this logic by arguing that rational voters would interpret the failure to carry through on a commitment as an indicator that the leader is incompetent when it comes to foreign policy. The general formulation, however, does not rule out costs imposed by international audiences. Sartori (1998), for example, generates an effect akin to international audience costs by assuming that states that are caught bluffing in one crisis will have a harder time conducting diplomacy in the future.

Actions that generate audience costs serve to tie the leader's hands and to signal the state's willingness to wage war. Once a threat has been made, the leader no longer faces a simple choice between waging war or settling for the status quo; instead, he faces a choice between waging war and incurring audience costs. Because of these costs, a leader who would not want to wage war in the absence of the commitment may be "locked into" fighting once the commitment has been made; in that sense, he has tied his own hands. At the same time, the act of doing so serves as a signal, since states that intend to carry out a threat are more likely to expose themselves to the audience costs than those with very low expected values for war, which are better off avoiding costly commitments.

The models that follow will assume that public threats expose state leaders to audience costs. In the present context, it is not necessary to be explicit about whether these costs arise primarily from domestic or international audiences, since the basic strategic logic does not depend upon this distinction. The model in Chapter 4, however, will incorporate Fearon's (1994a) and Smith's (1998a, 1998b) claim that audience costs derive from domestic audiences' negative assessment of leaders who make threats and then back away from them. We also leave aside, for the present, Fearon's (1994a) hypothesis that democratic and non-democratic governments are systematically different when it comes to their ability to generate audience costs and, in particular, that democratic leaders are in a better position to send signals in this manner.

Making costly threats under asymmetric information

How does the ability to generate audience costs affect the challenger's decision to make threats and the target's interpretation of those threats? Because an exact derivation of the challenger's strategy is somewhat complicated, the formal details are provided in Appendix A. Here, I present the main results and the intuition behind them. The challenger's strategy at its initial decision node takes the following general

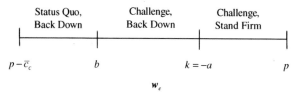

Fig. 2.2 The challenger's equilibrium strategies as a function of its value for war

form. The possible types of challenger form a continuum from the lowest possible value, $p - \bar{c}_c$, to the highest possible value, p, as shown in Figure 2.2. The challenger's strategy choice is described by two cutpoints along that continuum. The first, which we denote k, separates types that make genuine threats from those that do not. In particular, if $w_c > k$, the challenger makes the challenge and stands firm at its final node. Recall that since only types for which $w_c > -a$ stand firm, it must be the case that $k \geq -a$; it turns out that, in equilibrium, $k = -a$, meaning that all types that can make genuine threats do so. The second cutpoint, which we denote b, separates types that bluff from those that choose the status quo. Thus, if $-a \geq w_c > b$, the challenger makes the challenge but backs down in the face of resistance. Finally, if $w_c \leq b$, the challenger selects the status quo. This strategy effectively divides the continuum of possible types into three ranges, as shown in the figure.[8]

Given this strategy, what should the target conclude about the credibility of the threats it faces? Formally, what is the target's "updated" or "posterior" belief that $w_c > -a$ given that it has been challenged, the probability that we labeled q above? This conditional probability can be readily derived using Bayes' rule, as follows:

$$\Pr(w_c > -a \mid \text{Challenge}) = \frac{\Pr(w_c > -a)}{\Pr(w_c > b)}. \tag{5}$$

This means that the posterior probability that the threat is genuine given a challenge is equal to the prior probability that $w_c > -a$ divided by the prior probability of seeing a challenge (which happens whenever $w_c > b$). The main implication of this expression is straightforward: as long as some types of challenger forego making threats, the act of making a threat reveals information about the challenger's type. That is, as long as the

---

[8] As shown in the appendix, all three ranges need not exist for all possible values of the parameters, $p, a, \bar{c}_c$, and $\bar{c}_t$. The formal solution includes a full treatment of all cases.

probability of a challenge is less than one, the posterior probability that $w_c > -a$ given a challenge is greater than the prior probability that this relationship holds. Thus, the fact that challengers with very high costs for war are unwilling to make a threat means that the target can learn something from the threat and update – as well as upgrade – its assessment of the challenger's intention to stand firm. Hence, some separation of types occurs due to the costliness of the signal.

It is also true, however, that the threat does not completely resolve the target's uncertainty. Even once we have added costly signaling in the form of audience costs, the decision to make a challenge only imperfectly separates types that are willing to wage war from those that are not. The reason is that, in general, some types of challenger bluff in equilibrium. Those types whose expected value of war falls between k and b make a threat at the initial node but back down in the event that the target resists. As a result, not all threats are genuine. This is a natural consequence of asymmetric information: actors have an incentive to exploit their private information for strategic gain. In this case, states with low expected value for war have incentives to make threats in the hope that the other side will concede rather than call the bluff. This incentive is not wholly eliminated by the introduction of costly signaling. Those states that bluff do so knowing that they will have to incur audience costs in the event that the target resists; they bluff nevertheless because the prospect of getting away with it balances out the risks of getting caught.[9]

This insight leads to another key insight: because there is bluffing in equilibrium, there is a lingering danger of war. As we saw, even though the target always prefers conceding to fighting, the fact that some threats are not genuine generates incentives for it to resist some challenges. Again, war is suboptimal *ex post*, but an action that entails a risk of war – in this case, resisting the challenge – may be optimal *ex ante*. The expected probability of war in this model is the probability that the challenger will make a genuine threat times the probability that the target will resist if challenged, or

$$\Pr(\text{War}) = \Pr(w_c > -a) \cdot \Pr(c_t < c^*). \tag{6}$$

As long as there is some probability that the target will resist, and as long as some types of challenger can make genuine threats, there is a nonzero probability of war.

---

[9] Only in extreme cases in which the audience costs are high relative to the maximum possible costs of war (so that $a > \bar{c}_c - p$) does no bluffing take place in equilibrium (Fearon 1997).

The continuing danger of war in this model reveals a fundamental insight into the dilemma of signaling when actors have conflicting interests. Although costly threats do reduce the probability of war and help separate types, for them to work in this manner *there must be some chance that they will fail* (Fearon 1992, p. 40). To see why, consider what would happen if all threats that exposed the challenger to audience costs were interpreted as genuine. In this case, the target would never resist, opting for concession over certain war. Once the target adopts this strategy, however, all types of challenger, regardless of their value for war, prefer to make the challenge. After all, the audience costs are incurred not for bluffing but for being caught in a bluff; if the target never resists, then bluffing is riskless and, indeed, highly profitable. Thus, the target must resist some challenges for there to be separation of types. The positive probability of resistance induces restraint on those challengers that have low expected value for war, causing them to challenge with lower probability than types with high value for war. At the same time, this need to resist some challenges leaves open the possibility of war, which occurs whenever the target resists a threat that was actually genuine.

Moreover, the introduction of audience costs changes the bargaining dynamics in an important way. Once states have exposed themselves to these costs, outcomes that might have been acceptable at the outset of the crisis are foreclosed. Before making a costly threat, challengers for whom $w_c < 0$ are content to accept the status quo rather than fight a war; after the challenge is made, however, those types for which $0 > w_c > -a$ can no longer accept the status quo, since doing so entails costs. Thus, bargaining positions become more intransigent as states take actions to increase the costs of backing down. Concerns about credibility and reputation that are captured by audience costs can start to overshadow the actual object of the dispute. This dynamic is evident in a famous 1965 memo by Assistant Secretary of Defense John McNaughton who quantified US goals in the Vietnam War as follows (Sheehan 1971, p. 263):

> 70 percent – To avoid a humiliating US defeat (to our reputation as a guarantor).
>
> 20 percent – To keep SVN (and the adjacent) territory from Chinese hands.
>
> 10 percent – To permit the people of SVN to enjoy a better, freer way of life.

Clearly, as the US effort in Vietnam grew, the desire to avoid the reputational costs of backing down began to overshadow the original objective of intervention – and justified further escalation. Although costly signals help reveal information by separating some types of challengers, they are not wholly benign in their effects.

Indeed, the introduction of audience costs need not decrease the probability that this interaction will end in war. The reason is that, as audience costs increase from zero, there are two countervailing effects. On the one hand, the probability that a threat is genuine increases with the audience costs, and consequently, the probability that the target state resists a challenge decreases. Thus, by clearly committing the challenger to stand firm, threats that entail high costs are effective at encouraging the target to make concessions. On the other hand, an increase in the audience costs also increases the range of challengers that can no longer accept the status quo once the threat has been made – i.e., those challengers for which $0 > w_c > -a$. Hence, more types of challengers may be in a position to make challenges from which they can not back down. As we saw in (6), the probability of war equals the probability that the challenger makes a genuine challenge times the probability that the target resists conditional on being challenged. Because an increase in audience costs can increase the first term and decrease the second, the overall effect on the probability of war is ambiguous. It is true that extremely high audience costs can decrease the probability of war to zero; if $a > \bar{c}_c - p$, then all types of challenger must stand firm, and knowing this, the target never resists. We cannot rule out, however, that in some instances the danger of war is higher when costly signals are available than when they are not.

This last insight reinforces a crucial point about the dilemma of communication in crisis situations. When actors have incentives to misrepresent their preferences, efforts to reveal information credibly may require them to take actions that can increase the probability of war. Thus, while asymmetric information is necessary for war to occur in this model, a signal that reveals information does not necessarily reduce the danger of war. This finding is common to crisis bargaining models involving two unitary states (e.g., Fearon 1994a, 1995; Powell 1990). One of the main arguments of this book is that domestic political competition can, under some circumstances, reveal information in a way that helps bypass this dismal logic.

Information, preferences, and the probability of war

We have seen, then, that a mutual desire for peace does not always guarantee a peaceful outcome. The above model started with the assumption that there always exists some deal that both sides prefer to war. Moreover, both sides know that such a deal exists; after all, it is common knowledge that a division of the good in which the challenger receives p and the target receives $1-p$ is one such deal. And yet, the existence of such a deal – and the states' mutual interest in reaching it – does not eliminate the danger of war under incomplete information. Even if the states prefer some deal to war, as long as they prefer a good deal to a bad deal, bargaining may fail.

This insight motivates a more general point: behavior and outcomes in international crises depend not only on power and interests, but also on information and beliefs. Holding constant the states' interests – that is, the value they place on the good and the costs they expect to incur from fighting – and holding constant the probability of victory for each side, the strategies they select, the ultimate distribution of the good, and the likelihood of war can still vary with the distribution of information. Most dramatically, of course, a given configuration of power and preferences can lead to peace under complete information and war under asymmetric information. Other outcomes vary as well. Figure 2.3 shows the equilibrium outcome for each possible configuration of w_c and w_t and whether information is complete or asymmetric. Notice that, in three of the six cells (shaded) the ultimate resolution of the crisis varies as the informational environment changes. Hence, *the distribution of information mediates the relationship between preferences and outcomes.*

The distribution of information also complicates the relationship between preferences and outcomes. As noted in Chapter 1, democratic peace theories in both their institutional and normative versions are primarily arguments about preferences – in particular, the supposed disincentives which democratic leaders have to use force. It is generally assumed that such disincentives can account for differences in the propensity of democracies and nondemocracies to engage in war. I will show, however, that, under conditions of incomplete information, the relationship between preferences and the probability of war is not straightforward. In particular, as the average costs of war for a state increase, the probability of war can go either up or down. Hence, disincentives to wage war do not inevitably translate into a diminished probability of war.

To see this, assume that some states have constraints that systematically increase their average costs of war. If we assume that democracy is one such constraint, then this assumption captures the institutional constraints perspective, but the argument here can apply to any factor which is thought to have this effect. In particular, we assume that, if the

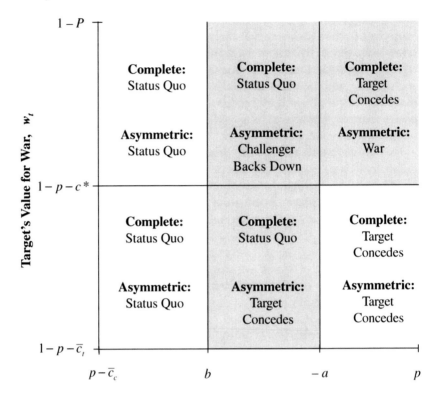

Challenger's Value for War, w_c

Fig. 2.3 Equilibrium outcomes under complete and asymmetric information

challenger state has this constraint, then its expected value for war is diminished by some amount, $d_c > 0$, or

$$w_c = p - c_c - d_c. \tag{6}$$

If the challenger does not have this constraint, then its expected value for war is as given in (1a), which is equivalent to assuming that $d_c = 0$. As before, we assume that c_c is drawn from a probability distributions over the range $[0, \bar{c}_c]$ and that this distribution is common knowledge. Thus, the target's prior beliefs going into the crisis are that w_c can take any value in the range $[p - \bar{c}_c - d_c, p - d_c]$. The constraint effectively shifts the distribution of w_c downward, meaning that, all other things being equal, a state with this constraint has a lower expected value from war, on average, than does a state that is not similarly constrained. We can similarly deduct d_t from the target's value for war, w_t, if the target state has the constraining feature.

We can explore the impact of these constraints by performing the following comparative-static exercise: what happens to the probability of war when d_c and/or d_t move from zero to some positive number, thus reflecting the constraints operating on the challenger and/or the target? A treatment of the modified game is presented in Appendix A. Two results emerge from this exercise. The first is that, as constraints increase on the target state, the probability of war generally moves in the expected direction – that is, it decreases. As the costs of war increase for the target state, the probability that it will choose to resist a challenge weakly decreases – which is to say, the probability of resistance decreases under some configurations of the parameters and is unchanged in others, but never increases. As a result, the same is true of the probability of war: More constrained targets are less likely to end up in war. The second result, however, is perhaps counterintuitive: as the constraints on the challenger increase, the probability of war may increase, decrease, or remain unchanged. In other words, the relationship between the challenger's constraints and the likelihood that it will end up in war is indeterminate.

What explains this indeterminacy? The relationship between the costs of war and the likelihood of war need not be straightforward because war is the outcome of an extended strategic interaction involving (at least) three discrete decisions: the decision to make a challenge, the decision to resist, and the decision to stand firm.[10] Only the last of these entails a direct choice between war and peace, and only at this node is the relationship between the costs of war and the decision to wage war straightforward: the challenger is less likely to choose war the higher are its expected costs from doing so. Each of the earlier decisions is made under some uncertainty about the ultimate outcome and is shaped not only by the state's own payoff from war but also by its beliefs about the other side. The result of this strategic interaction is that an increase in the average costs of war for one or both states generally has two countervailing effects: the state whose costs have increased becomes less likely to take actions which might lead to war, but the other state becomes more likely to take such actions. Thus, as the challenger's costs increase, it

[10] See Signorino (1999) for a good discussion of how strategic interaction can lead to nonmonotonic relationships.

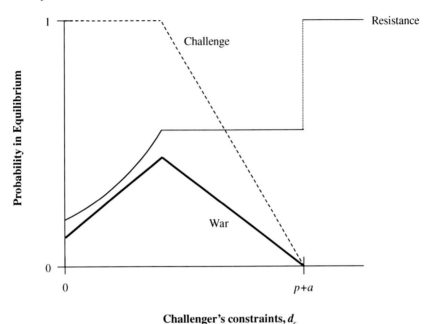

Fig. 2.4 Predicted outcomes as a function of the challenger's constraints

becomes less likely to initiate a challenge and less likely to stand firm in the face of resistance. At the same time, such an increase can encourage the target to resist the threat. After all, when d_c is subtracted from the challenger's expected value for war, the target's beliefs about w_c adjust as well. The challenger's added disincentive to wage war is factored into the target's calculations about whether or not to resist if challenged. As these disincentives increase, the target becomes more willing to resist. Because the probability of a genuine threat decreases with d_c and the probability of resistance increases with d_c, the probability of war – which is the product of these two terms – can move in either direction.

Figure 2.4 depicts this intuition graphically, by showing the probability of a challenge, the probability of resistance, and the probability of war as a function of d_c, holding d_t constant.[11] The main result is evident in the bold line corresponding to the equilibrium probability of war. As d_c

[11] Because we have kept the probability distributions of the cost terms general, the exact curvature of the lines need not always be as depicted. The lines were drawn roughly to reflect the relationships that hold when the costs are distributed uniformly. Moreover, the probability of war that holds when $d_c = 0$ need not be exactly as drawn.

increases, this probability first increases and then decreases, suggesting again the non-monotonicity of the relationship. The other two lines focus on the probabilities of two distinct steps on the road to war: the decision by the challenger to initiate a crisis and the decision by the target to resist when challenged. Notice that the probability of a challenge is weakly decreasing in d_c – that is, it either stays constant or falls as d_c goes up. This makes sense: The challenger only makes a threat when its expected value from war exceeds a certain threshold. As this expected value decreases, the likelihood that the challenger will be in a position to make a challenge decreases as well. The second, and more important, result is that the target's inclination to resist is weakly *increasing* in d_c. The reason, very simply, is credibility. As we saw, the target's willingness to resist depends entirely upon how likely it is that the threat is genuine. An increase in the costs of war for the challenger casts doubt on its ability to implement the threat in the face of resistance, thus emboldening the target to resist with greater probability. At the extreme, when the constraints are so great that no type of challenger can make a credible threat, the probability of resistance is exactly one. Non-monotonicity in the probability of war is the net effect of a weakly decreasing rate of challenges combined with this weakly increasing rate of resistance.

Though I have focused quite generally on the effect of constraints that increase the costs of war, the relevance of this analysis to the existing literature on democracy and war should be obvious. The specification considered here captures well the view of democracy that appears in the institutional constraints literature. Bueno de Mesquita and Lalman (1992, pp. 156–57), for example, treat democracy in a very similar way, by assuming that costs of using force are drawn from a distribution with a higher mean when the state is democratic. Moreover, the fact that these additional costs are reflected in the prior beliefs of the rival state mirrors their assumption that democratic institutions "signal" the state's higher than average costs of war. As we have seen, the effect of such constraints on the likelihood of war may be indeterminate.[12]

[12] One might make a similar argument about normative theories of the democratic peace, which similarly rely on assumptions about the undesirability of war. One could model this theory by assuming that the challenger and target face constraints only when both are democratic. The main result of this exercise is that a joint increase in the costs of war need not reduce the likelihood of war, for the same reasons discussed above. I am reluctant to capture normative arguments in this way, however, because writers in this tradition believe that shared democracy not only increases the costs of war but also delegitimizes the use of threats (e.g., Doyle 1983, 1997; Russett 1993). Capturing norm-driven behavior in a model of rational choice is bound to be *ad hoc*.

A real world example, again from events leading up to the Gulf War, will help show that this result is not simply an artifact of the model. As Iraq's military buildup against Kuwait grew throughout the last two weeks of July 1990, the Bush administration decided to warn Saddam Hussein about the possibility of American intervention. On July 24, the United States announced joint naval exercises with the United Arab Emirates. On the same day, the State Department spokesperson warned Iraq against using coercion and affirmed that the United States had a commitment to "the individual and collective-defense of our friends in the Gulf with whom we have deep and longstanding ties" (Freedman and Karsh 1993, pp. 51–52). Iraq's response, as we know, was contemptuous. Hussein called the US ambassador to his office the next day and told her that he was not scared by American threats. After all, he reportedly said, "Yours is a society which cannot accept 10,000 dead in one battle."[13] Thus, the Iraqi leader's view that the United States operated under constraints against the use of force made him more willing to ignore demands that he back off. Indeed, his strong prior belief that the United States could not stomach a long and costly war shaped much of his strategy in this crisis and the ensuing war. As the model suggests and this example illustrates, if democracy does systematically increase the costs of using force, and if other states adjust their expectations accordingly, then the effect of democracy on the probability of war need not be negative.

Conclusion

This chapter laid the groundwork for those that follow by exploring some of the dilemmas that arise when states interact under conditions of asymmetric information. The costs of war generally ensure that there exists some range of peaceful bargains that all sides prefer to war. Unfortunately, when information pertaining to the states' expected value for war is distributed asymmetrically, identifying and agreeing upon such a bargain can be problematic. When bargaining under such conditions, states face a risk–return trade-off and often find that the strategy with the highest expected return also entails some positive risk of war. This problem is compounded by the fact that states have conflicting interests over the distribution of gains. Because of this conflict, states

---

[13] A transcript of their meeting can be found in the *New York Times* of September 22, 1990, p. 19.

have incentives to misrepresent their private information in hopes of getting a more favorable settlement. Thus, informational asymmetries can persist due to a strategic environment which encourages concealment and bluff.

In this model, asymmetric information is a necessary condition for war. Without it, a peaceful outcome – either the challenger maintains the status quo or the target makes concessions – is guaranteed. Of course, this result rests on a number of assumptions that help ensure the existence of a deal that both sides prefer to war. It is not unreasonable to question whether these assumptions always hold in the real world. For example, what if the good in dispute is not divisible? Some issues that states contest in international politics are not easily divided into shares or otherwise split through compromise. If the target cannot make concessions short of handing over the entire good, then there may be no peaceful outcome that both sides prefer to war. If the costs of fighting are sufficiently small that both states have positive expected value from war, then the challenger prefers war to the status quo, and the target prefers war to making concessions. As a result, war must be the outcome, even under complete information. Similarly, while the assumption that actors are risk-neutral or risk-averse makes good sense in general, there may be leaders who are highly risk-acceptant, in which case they place value on the gamble associated with war. If both actors in a dispute were sufficiently risk-acceptant, it is possible that their combined values for war would exceed the value of the good, again precluding any mutually acceptable deal. This might also be the case if there are benefits to war that offset the costs. As the voluminous literature on diversionary conflict suggests, there might be benefits to war that can only be achieved through fighting – and hence cannot be bargained over (see, e.g., Levy 1989). Such factors would generate war under complete information in the event that these benefits exceed the costs of war to *both* states.

Does introducing these possibilities contradict the argument presented here? No. If conditions are such that there would be war under complete information, war would also take place under incomplete information; the reverse, however, is not true. If the good is indivisible and both states have positive expected value for war, war will occur regardless of the distribution of information because there is no deal that both sides prefer to war. As we saw, however, if a mutually acceptable deal does exist, then it will always be found under complete information but may not be when information is distributed asymmetrically.

Thus, even if we were to admit the possibility that some conditions may generate war under complete information, the basic insights of this chapter are not contradicted. Whether or not the probability of war is zero under complete information, that probability is always higher under incomplete information. Even if this kind of uncertainty is not a necessary condition for war, it is at least a contributory condition.

When information is asymmetric, the successful use of coercive diplomacy gives rise to a search for credibility. Threats escalate to war precisely because, when actors have incentives to overstate their resolve, not all threats can be believed. Sending signals in a reliable manner requires constraints on states' ability to engage in deception and/or mechanisms for bolstering the credibility of genuine threats. As we saw, if domestic institutions systematically increase the costliness of war, they may exacerbate the problem of credibility by raising doubts about a state's ability to carry out its threats. The question that arises, then, is whether domestic political institutions – and especially those that are associated with democracy – do provide reliable solutions to the dilemmas of bargaining under incomplete information. It is to this issue that we now turn.

3   Democratic politics in international crises

While the arguments in the previous chapter captured the core strategic dilemmas that arise in crisis bargaining, they were built on a stylized view of what states are and how they choose policies. In this view, common to models of international relations, states are unitary actors with a monopoly on some pertinent information about the political and military factors that determine their costs of war. While other states can learn about some of these factors, the primary mode of communication is through external actions: threats and displays of force directed by one state against another. States, in short, are "black boxes": their external behavior is observable, but their internal workings are largely hidden from view.

For some kinds of states, the black box model is entirely appropriate. Because of the closed nature of their political systems, countries like communist North Korea and Iraq under Saddam Hussein provide outsiders with few glimpses of the processes by which decisions are made. Even in less extreme cases, political structures that bestow influence and authority on a small number of actors can be quite opaque to foreign observers. On the other hand, the black box model is less appropriate when dealing with states whose political institutions generate greater openness and publicity. Democratic states, in particular, have a number of institutions and practices which ensure that decisions are made and debated in a public manner, that information can flow freely between government and governed, and that the government does not monopolize the nation's political discourse. As a result, the state is not a black box, but a transparent or open box into which outside actors can look for clues about the government's motivations and constraints. What foreign decision makers learn from observing the internal communication within such states supplements the information that is conveyed by the external communication of diplomacy and threats. There is thus good reason to believe that crisis behavior and outcomes differ systematically between democratic and nondemocratic political systems.

This chapter and the one that follows develop this argument. In Chapter 4, I revise the basic crisis bargaining model in order to capture some of the salient features of democracy. We can thereby derive specific hypotheses about how democratic institutions influence the initiation and resolution of crises. This chapter sets the stage for that exercise by elaborating and justifying the view of democracy and democratic politics underlying the analysis.

While democracy is many things, the theory developed here focuses on a particular feature that is central to democratic theory, what Dahl (1971) calls "public contestation": competition for political office between government and opposition that takes place through public appeals for support. The two components of this phrase – publicity and competition – are both central to the argument. The public nature of democratic politics ensures that the process of decision making is observable by foreign states and can thus influence international behavior. Competition between contending parties, as we will see, helps to ensure that the signals that emerge are credible. In particular, the quest for political office gives opposition parties incentives to take actions that reveal information about the government's opportunities and constraints. Through their public actions in crises, and particularly whether they support or oppose the government's policy, these parties generate additional signals about the political incentives to use force – signals that are harder to obtain from polities in which oppositional activity is suppressed or kept behind closed doors.

Underlying this view of democracy are two sets of assumptions that are elaborated in this chapter. The first deals with the nature of democratic institutions. I argue that the rules and norms of democracy make meaningful debate possible by ensuring: (1) that competition takes place in public; (2) that dissent against the government is legitimate; (3) that the rules governing political competition are institutionalized; and (4) that opposition parties have access to policy-relevant information. The second set of assumptions deals with the motivations of the key political actors: contending parties or candidates. A competitive dynamic arises between government and opposition when these parties are motivated by the desire to hold political office. I argue that office-seeking motivations lead to meaningful variation in the strategies that opposition parties take during international crises – meaningful both at the domestic and international levels. Here, I focus primarily on the domestic implications, showing how the opposition party's strategies influence and are influenced by the expected electoral impact of a crisis. These arguments set the stage for the next chapter, which explores the effect of democratic competition at the international level, through its effect on the information and beliefs of foreign actors.

The nature of democratic competition

Competition for political office is generally seen as a *sine qua non* of democracy. Joseph Schumpeter's classic work defines democracy as "that institutional arrangement for arriving at political decision in which individuals acquire power to decide by means of a competitive struggle for the people's vote" (1947, p. 269). Similar definitions appear in the seminal works of Lipset (1959) and Dahl (1971). In principle, there is nothing in this definition that requires competition to take place through organized political parties. In practice, however, modern democracies have invariably developed some kind of party system, though there is wide cross-national variation in the strength and stability of political parties. Hence, it is no great leap to move from a conception of democracy as competition to a conception of democracy as party competition (Strom 1992, pp. 377–78).

To be clear, the term competition refers to the ability of groups or individuals to contest control over political office. Competition implies more than simply political insecurity, or the possibility that those currently in power may, at some later date, find themselves removed from office. Although competition may create insecurity, it is the process of competition, the process by which different actors actively seek support from politically relevant constituents, that is of interest here. We assume that a government's hold on office depends on the continued support of some politically relevant group – what Bueno de Mesquita *et al.* (1999) refer to quite generally as the "selectorate" – and that competition occurs when more than one group or individual can attempt to garner the support of that selectorate. The actual strategies that candidates use can vary quite substantially across political systems. In democratic systems, competition for votes takes place through a variety of familiar means: candidates take positions on policy issues through speeches or votes; they take credit or assign blame for policy outcomes; they try to dole out benefits to potential supporters, through constituency service, pork-barrel politics, or other forms of patronage (esp., Mayhew 1974). In nondemocratic systems, competition generally has to take more subtle forms. Tullock (1989, ch. 2), for example, discusses the secretive process of building "subversive coalitions" large enough to overthrow a dictator.

As this example suggests, while competition is a necessary element of democracy, competitive or oppositional activity is not unique to such systems (e.g., Dahl 1973). There are, however, several features of political competition in democratic polities that make it particularly informative both to voters and to observers in foreign states. Four such features are crucial: it is public, legitimate, institutionalized, and informed. These features can be thought of as defining democracy for the purposes of this analysis.

Publicity

The first crucial element of democratic competition is that it takes place in a public manner, viewable by domestic and foreign actors alike. Candidates for office are clearly identifiable, and the competition for electoral support takes place primarily through public statements and actions. The open nature of competition in democratic polities means that the strategies and messages that parties use to attract political support are observable by foreign actors. Although it is possible to conduct international diplomacy in secret, away from the view of the domestic electorate, it is not possible to conduct democratic competition in secret, away from the view of other states. Hence, the interplay of parties in democratic systems generates information that is not necessarily available when competition is suppressed or takes place behind closed doors.

The media in a democratic polity play an important role in this process. Rules safeguarding media freedoms ensure that voices other than the government's can be publicized.[1] As a result, press coverage of political debates provides a cheap source of information not only for voters but also for foreign observers. Diplomatic dispatches often include summaries of press commentary, which are presented as indicators of popular sentiment regarding the issues at stake and the desirability of using force. Moreover, numerous studies of the media in democratic systems show that press coverage of international crises closely tracks the debate at the elite level (Bennett 1990; Sigal 1973; Alexseev and Bennett 1995; Cook 1994; Zaller and Chiu 1996). When

---

[1] Several authors have discussed the role of the media as it pertains to the democratic peace proposition (Van Belle 1997; Van Belle and Oneal 1998; Owen 1997, p. 46)

there is little conflict among official voices, the range of opinion that gets expressed both in news and editorials is relatively narrow and in line with the elite consensus. On the other hand, when there are conflicting voices at the elite level, a wider range of viewpoints is publicized. Thus, press coverage is highly sensitive to the underlying dynamic of political competition, making it an effective means by which consensus and discord among political parties are broadcast to outside observers.

Legitimacy

A second, and related, feature of democratic competition is that it is based on the idea that dissent is legitimate. Dahl (1966, p. xiii) considers one of the three great milestones in the development of democratic governance – along with the right to participate in elections and the right to be represented – to be "the right of an organized opposition to appeal for votes against the government in elections and in parliament." Democratic systems are based on the notion of a "loyal opposition," which means that dissent against the government and its policies does not imply disloyalty to the state. As a result, legal sanctions against dissent, while not impossible, are inherently suspect.

Speech and actions which take place in the context of official behavior – such as votes and statements made in a legislature – typically enjoy special protection. Consider, for example, the Alien and Sedition Acts, which were passed during a crisis between France and the United States in 1798. These laws went beyond prohibiting explicit acts of treason and could be interpreted as outlawing most criticism of the government and its policies (Smith 1956; Miller 1951). The US Constitution, however, explicitly protects members of Congress from prosecution for speeches made from the Floor. Consequently, the Alien and Sedition Acts could not apply to actions taken in Congress, and Republican lawmakers who opposed the government's policies used this protection to voice their dissent (Smith 1956, p. 127).[2] During the same period, as the Napoleonic Wars raged in Europe, Great Britain imposed draconian restrictions on public dissent, enacted press censorship, and suspended legal protections such as *habeus corpus*. In spite of this, opposition members of parliament who openly supported the French Revolution were not subject to these sanctions (Miller 1951, pp. 68–69, 110). Thus, as long as dissent takes the form of statements or votes within a legislative body, democratic states are constrained in their ability to mute it.

[2] See Chapter 8 for further discussion of this episode.

61

Institutionalization

The third quality of competition in democratic systems is that it is institutionalized, meaning that a fairly stable set of groups regularly competes for political office under a fairly stable set of rules. As a result, the adversarial relationship between government and opposition is not *ad hoc* and fluid, but rather an enduring feature of the political system. Not only does the identity of the competing parties remain relatively constant over time, but there is some expectation that their interaction is a repeated game that will continue into the future. In nondemocratic polities, by contrast, there are few, if any, rules regulating competition other than those that seek to stamp it out or keep it private.

Likewise, transitional systems, where the rules of the game and the identity of the key political actors are in flux, may create a good deal of uncertainty about how to interpret the signals coming from different sources. As Mansfield and Snyder (1995) have argued, countries making transitions to democracy may be dangerous and unpredictable. Their evidence suggests that the process of democratization can lead to belligerent foreign policies and an increased danger of war.[3] The mobilization of new demands and the fragility of institutions designed to aggregate those demands can unleash nationalist sentiments and create uncertainty about whether democratic norms of open competition and legitimate dissent will be respected and/or consolidated. Thus, the arguments in this book pertain to democratic polities in which policy and office, but not the fundamental rules and institutions, are contested.

Access to information

The final aspect of democratic competition that is central to this analysis is that the contending parties have useful information upon which to base their public strategies. For parties that control the government, this is an obvious statement; for parties in opposition to the government, it requires some justification. An important aspect of democracy is that those out of power are not excluded from the political process to the point that they have no information about public policy. Losing an election does not mean that a political party must suspend all activities. It is still free to gather information about policy, to gauge voter preferences, to make public statements in support or opposition to the government.

---

[3] It should be noted that several other researchers have contested these findings (e.g., Ward and Gleditsch 1997; Thompson and Tucker 1997).

As we saw in Chapter 2, information that is relevant in international crises includes information pertaining to the material outcomes of war, including the likelihood of victory and the expected costs, information about voters' willingness to trade off these costs for the good in question, and information about the likely political consequences of different crisis outcomes. Three factors in particular help opposition parties collect information about such matters.

Rotation in office. Because parties in a democratic system generally alternate in power, today's opposition may have been yesterday's government. Thus, all of the informational advantages that accrue to the government – such as control of the bureaucratic apparatus – may once have been at the disposal of the opposition. Opposition parties can thus have a high level of expertise and information about policy, especially when it pertains to attributes of the state that do not change much over the span of a few years. They are likely to be well informed about the state's resources and capabilities, as well as those of other states. Alternation in office also means that opposition parties have a core of foreign policy and national security experts who can advise them during crises.

It is also important to remember that, even though crises may arise with very little notice, the underlying disputes rarely emerge overnight. As the literature on "enduring rivalries" suggests, many militarized crises occur within the context of long-standing disputes that may predate the current government (e.g., Goertz 1993). As a result, the party that finds itself in opposition during any particular crisis could very well have been in government during some earlier stage in the dispute or even in some earlier crisis over the same issue. Many of the cases that we will consider in Chapters 6 and 7 have this quality. For example, the 1956 Suez crisis occurred during a Conservative administration in Britain, but the prospect of Egypt nationalizing the canal was considered by the previous Labour government after Iran nationalized the Anglo-Iranian Oil Company in 1951. The arguments that swayed Prime Minister Clement Attlee to reject the use of force against Iran were very similar to those used by the Labour opposition five years later: there was no US support for the use of force, and the United Nations charter, which enjoyed a good deal of respect among the British public, forbade unilateral action without the blessing of the Security Council (Kyle 1991, pp. 7–9). Thus, the very act of alternating in office ensures that those in opposition have information that is relevant to current policy debates.

Legislative institutions. Although opposition parties, by definition, do not control the executive branch of government, they generally do hold seats in a parliamentary body with legislative authority. As a result, they take part in the information gathering that is central to the legislative process, and they have access to resources for information collection. Unless the legislature is simply a rubber stamp for executive actions, members must have some access to policy-relevant information for debate and voting to be genuine. One institutional feature of democratic legislatures that can play an important role in this respect are specialized committees (Krehbiel 1991). In a cross-national study, Shaw (1979, p. 392) observes that, despite substantial differences in the structure and role of legislative committees across countries, all follow a rule of proportionality – in other words, party composition on committees tends to reflect the party composition of the overall body. This commitment to proportionality gives opposition parties access to whatever fact-finding and deliberative activities the committees undertake.

Party organizations. Finally, as we saw in Chapter 2, assessing the government's expectations about war requires some estimate of how voters will react to different outcomes – that is, what level of casualties they will tolerate, how much they value the objects at stake, how likely they are to base their voting decisions on the outcomes of a given crisis, and so forth. It is here that opposition parties are most likely to share the government's informational advantage over foreign states. A political party is more than simply a collection of like-minded individuals holding positions in the executive and/or legislature; it is also an enduring organization with connections to society at large. Even when in opposition, a party has ongoing contact with voters and interest groups.[4] After all, one of the major goals of an opposition party is to become the government, and thus one of the main activities it undertakes while in opposition is to figure out what political strategies will further that end. Parties exist to aggregate information about voter preferences, to anticipate the likely electoral effects of different strategies, and to articulate positions that they believe will be successful. If they did not, they would not last long. Hence, parties expend substantial time and resources attempting to learn about what voters want and how different policy outcomes will translate into support for the government and its opponents.

---

[4] The *Washington Post* of April 9, 1999 provides an interesting example of this process in action, reporting on a town meeting at which a Republican congressman sought his constituents' input on the air strikes that were underway against Yugoslavia.

In sum, competition in democratic political systems is not only public and institutionalized, but it takes place between actors who have information both about the nature of societal preferences and the likely effects of public policy. Together, these factors distinguish political competition in polities that are considered democratic from political competition in nondemocratic polities. Two kinds of oppositions generally operate in the latter: those which are part of the ruling group and those which operate, typically illegally, outside of the ruling group. The former are likely to have a good deal of information about government policies and incentives, and they may even have an appreciable chance of taking power. Competition within the ruling party, however, generally takes place in private, and there may be severe risks to publicly airing internal disputes. Although the outside world may get hints and suggestions of political debate, it cannot always rely on getting useful information from this source. Opposition groups that operate outside of the regime are unlikely to enjoy any of the features enumerated above, given that they are inherently illegitimate, have no institutionalized route to power, and are likely to have restricted access to useful information about what the government has done or intends to do.

Within democratic systems, these four distinguishing features exist to ensure representation and accountability domestically. The unintended effect is that whatever voters can observe can also be observed by decision makers in foreign states. The demands of publicity inevitably link communication at the domestic level with communication at the international level: a democratic government cannot speak to its voters without also permitting foreign states to listen in. In nondemocratic systems, by contrast, this link between the domestic and international realms can be severed. The government can speak to its selectorate in private, away from foreign eyes.

Opposition parties and international crises

What impact does public competition have on behavior and outcomes in international crises? Addressing this question inevitably forces us to think about the role of opposition parties in these events. In doing so, we do not deny that the government remains the most important actor in the state; after all, the party that controls the executive has control over foreign policy decisions, including the decision to make and carry out threats of force. Nonetheless, the existence of a publicly active opposition with access to information and a legal right to publicly compete for political support is what systematically distinguishes democracies from nondemocracies. To understand how democratic politics plays out in international crises, we must get a sense for the role these parties play, the strategies available to them, and their motivations.

Though the role of opposition parties in international crises has received only scant systematic attention,[5] three broadly different perspectives are apparent in the existing literature. None, as we will see, does justice to this topic. The most common theories see opposition parties as "yes men" who are strongly motivated to support the government's position in international crises. Arguments to this effect take several different forms. A substantial literature on the so-called "rally around the flag" effect suggests that dissent is unlikely in times of crisis due to social psychological dynamics that lead to increased domestic cohesion in time of crisis (e.g., Coser 1956; Mueller 1973; Russett 1990, ch. 2). According to this view, international threats generate a surge of patriotism and increased popular support for the executive. Under these circumstances, opposition politicians may experience the same emotional response, or they may make a political calculation to mute their criticism of government policies, lest they risk bucking the popular tide and being seen as unpatriotic. A related argument along these lines is that, in crisis situations that arise quickly, opposition politicians generally lack basic information about the situation. Because they are reluctant to dissent in the face of uncertainty, they have little choice but to go along with the government (e.g., Waltz 1967, p. 275; Brody and Shapiro 1989, p. 90). Some have also suggested that parties have incentives to reach a "partisan truce" in the area of foreign policy, with each agreeing to support the other when in opposition so that it can have a free hand when it becomes the government at some future date (Gowa 1999, ch. 3). Together, these views suggest that there might be a norm of nonpartisanship in the area of foreign policy, which dictates that domestic actors bury their differences when dealing with an external foe. Politics, in Senator Arthur Vandenberg's famous words, stops "at the water's edge."

Bueno de Mesquita and Lalman (1990, 1992) paint a different picture of the role of opposition parties. In their view, the opposition in democratic systems serves as a low-cost alternative to the party in power.

---

[5] For a general study of political opposition and foreign policy, see Hagan (1993). For other recent works on this topic, see Levy and Mabe (1998), Bueno de Mesquita *et al.* (1999), and Gaubatz (1999).

Though a purely passive, nonstrategic actor in their model, the opposition's implied role is to exploit popular dissatisfaction in the event that the use of force leads to a losing or costly outcome. The opposition thereby makes the resort to force particularly risky for elected governments, and institutions promoting competition systematically increase the potential political costs of waging war. Thus, while the existence of an opposition may signal to other states that the government has higher than average costs for war, the model does not permit variation in such signals from case to case.

Yet a third set of arguments suggests that opposition parties have incentives to take ambiguous positions on risky issues, such as the use of force in international crises (e.g., Page and Brody 1971; Zaller 1992). When there is uncertainty about how the public will evaluate the outcome of a crisis, an ambiguous stance allows a candidate to hedge his bets. A now infamous example of this strategy in action was the position of then Governor Bill Clinton on the Persian Gulf War. When asked his views shortly after Congress voted to authorize the use of force, Clinton told a reporter: "I guess I would have voted with the majority if it was a close vote, but I agree with the arguments the minority made." Asked again during the 1992 presidential campaign – long after the war was concluded successfully and at surprisingly low cost – his position was less equivocal: "I supported the Gulf War."[6] The opposition might also adopt an ambiguous stance by remaining silent during the crisis.

All of these arguments have some truth to them. As general characterizations of opposition parties' motivations, however, they run afoul of an important empirical observation: there is wide variation in the strategies that opposition parties adopt during international crises. The argument that opposition parties have incentives always to support the government overlooks the fact that these parties have on many occasions publicly opposed their government's threat or use of force. The argument that oppositions serve to harness discontent with the use of force overlooks the fact that parties in opposition often advocate the use of force as fervently, and at times more fervently, than do parties in power; hence, they do not always present an effective alternative on this dimension. And the argument that opposition parties should remain silent or ambiguous is called into question by numerous cases in which they have taken clear positions for or against.

---

[6] For a discussion of both statements, see, for example, a report in the *Los Angeles Times* of July 31, 1992.

We will encounter many examples of this variation in the following chapters. In general, the stance of the opposition can be classified into two broad categories: support or opposition to the use of force. There is no doubt that support – often outspoken, but sometimes tacit – is the most common response when the government has issued a threat. In Chapter 6, for example, I examine cases in which democratic states attempted to deter attacks on protégés; in twenty-six out of thirty-one such cases, the government's deterrent threat received the support of the opposition. Nevertheless, opposition to the use of force is not so unusual as to be a trivial curiosity. In the United States, the general tendency toward bipartisanship during the Cold War should not lead one to conclude that this pattern is a necessary or general feature of democratic politics. Indeed, there has been dissent over the use of force in many prominent crises: the Republicans strongly opposed the 1799 quasi-war with France, the Federalists opposed the War of 1812, many Whigs opposed the threats against Mexico in the lead-up to the Mexican–American War, the majority of Democrats voted against authorizing the use of force against Iraq in 1991, and most Republicans publicly opposed Clinton's threat to invade Haiti in 1994 and the airstrikes against Yugoslavia in 1999.

The evidence is similar from other major democratic countries. In Britain as in the United States, there have been many crises in which the opposition supported the government in a bipartisan fashion. But British history also provides numerous cases in which the main opposition party publicly opposed the threat or use of force, some of which we will consider in more detail in later chapters. In 1897, the Liberal Party strongly opposed the government's effort to coerce Greece into withdrawing from Crete. In 1899, Liberals opposed the threats against South Africa which led to the Boer War. In 1920, the Labour Party threatened a general strike when the government considered intervention in the Russo-Polish War. And in 1956, Labour vociferously opposed the threat of military action in the Suez crisis.

In France, the existence of parties along a wide ideological spectrum means that the country has rarely experienced complete unanimity in international crises. But dissent has not been isolated to extremist parties. During the 1930s, for example, successive French governments faced opposition to the threat of force from parties or factions on the center-left and center-right. It was only as the danger from Nazi Germany became increasingly hard to deny that opposition to the use of force, though it did not vanish, moved exclusively to the ideological extremes (Werth 1939; Micaud 1943).

If this observed frequency of dissent does not seem impressive, it is crucial to point out that there are substantial selection effects at work. As we will see, when conditions are such that opposition parties would have incentives to oppose the use of force, governments often have incentives to refrain from making threats, anticipating both the domestic and international responses. We do not observe, for example, the vocal dissent of the Republican Party when President Franklin Roosevelt threatened to wage war against Japan in the event of an attack on Western colonies in East Asia. Fearing isolationist sentiment in the United States, Roosevelt could not make public threats to this effect. In early 1941, he instead resorted to private warnings and engaged the British and Dutch in "secret" military talks which he hoped would soon leak to the Japanese (Sagan 1988, pp. 331–33). Likewise, we can only glimpse the wave of popular dissent in Britain and France that would have followed a decision by those governments to confront Hitler over his move into the Rhineland in March 1936. Both governments felt constrained by public opinion to avoid strong threats in this case. In France particularly, the prospect of elections in the near future made the government hesitant to respond forcefully. A similar pattern is evident in the British government's decision to renounce the use of force against Rhodesia in 1965.[7] In short, many potential cases of dissent are "off the equilibrium path" – we do not observe them because the government avoided taking actions that would have generated domestic opposition.

It is important to point out that, in all of these cases, opposition to the use of force arose, or was anticipated to arise, during crises – that is, prior to the onset of war in those cases which escalate to that point. It is during this period – when threats to use force are being weighed and interpreted – that the variation in opposition strategies is necessary to influence states' information and beliefs. Thus, I do not explicitly consider cases in which opposition emerged during the course of a war, such as during the Vietnam War. The possibility of such dissent influences crisis decision making indirectly, by shaping actors' expectations about the outcome and costs of a potential war, but it does not add to the signals available during crisis bargaining.[8]

Even when the opposition party chooses to support the government's threats, we see this support expressed in different ways and to different

---

[7] See Chapter 7 for a more complete discussion of these cases.

[8] Of course, bargaining does not end once a war starts, and a natural extension of the work here is to consider how domestic political factors influence states' assessments during wars (see, e.g., Goemans 2000; Wagner 2000).

degrees. In some cases, the opposition takes a more hawkish position than the government, arguing for more forceful measures and greater intransigence in bargaining. During the 1964 presidential campaign, Republican candidate Barry Goldwater was even more hawkish on Vietnam than was President Lyndon Johnson (e.g., Herring 1986, pp. 121–23). Similarly, in the crises over Czechoslovakia and Poland, the Labour opposition in Britain was stronger in its support for war than was the government. Support may also be given tacitly or guardedly. During the 1898 Fashoda crisis, Sir William Harcourt, an anti-imperialist Liberal, swallowed his distaste for the possibility of war against France long enough to declare that the matter was "in the hands of responsible and capable men, to whom the fortunes of this country are entrusted" (Gardiner 1923, p. 470). In yet other cases, support for the government in a crisis may also be coupled with criticism for the policies which led to the crisis in the first place. Republicans rallied behind President Truman's decision to send forces to Korea, but they tempered their support with charges that Truman was partly responsible for the war due to his weak policy toward China (Caridi 1968, ch. 2). Thus, opposition parties have historically exhibited a wide variety of political strategies.

Given this observation, we can dismiss the argument that there are binding norms of patriotism or nonpartisanship that constrain the opposition to rally behind the government in times of crisis. This is not to deny that such norms exist; on the contrary, opposition leaders who choose to support the government often appeal to them in explaining their actions. On the other hand, those who choose to oppose the government's actions in a crisis often take shelter behind a different norm: the idea that democracy is best served when the opposition can offer a free and independent critique of the government's policy. During the Suez crisis, for example, opposition leader Hugh Gaitskell justified his party's dissent with an appeal to democratic principles. His comments to the House of Commons are worth quoting at some length:

> In a free democracy, differences of opinion on matters vitally important cannot and should not be suppressed. Issues of this kind must be argued out; argued, of course, with a due sense of responsibility. I wish to make it plain that, far from opposing the Government for opposition's sake, we have always recognised that there are moments, in international affairs particularly, where restraint by the Opposition is clearly enjoined . . .
>
> But restraint of this kind must never be carried so far as to involve the suppression of differences of vital importance. On such cases it is

the duty, not only the right, of the Opposition to speak out loudly and
clearly.   (*GB, Parl. Deb.* 5s, 558: 16)

A similar argument was made by those in the United States who
deplored the insistence on bipartisanship during the Cold War.
Following the American intervention in the Dominican Republic,
Senator William Fulbright declared: "Insofar as it represents a genuine
reconciliation of differences, a consensus is a fine thing; insofar as it represents the concealment of differences, it is a miscarriage of democratic
procedure" (quoted in Collier 1991, p. 117). Even Vandenberg, the archi-
tect of bipartisanship in the early Cold War, conceded that foreign policy
is "a legitimate subject of partisan conflict if there is deep division"
among the public (quoted in Crabb 1957, p. 205). Thus, two contradictory norms appear to exist, and opposition parties can appeal to either
in announcing their policy position.

The argument that international crises unfold too quickly to provide
time for information gathering, debate, and dissent also fails to hold in
general. Prominent cases like the Korean War notwithstanding, "bolts
from the blue" – instances in which an external threat demands an
immediate decision about the use of force – are the exception, rather
than the rule. We can see this by looking at the duration of crises
reported in the Correlates of War data on Militarized Interstate Disputes
(MIDs). Since we will encounter these data extensively in Chapter 5, a
full description will wait until then. Briefly put, the MID data set provides information on 2024 crises in the period 1816–1992, where a crisis
is defined as an event in which at least one state directs a militarized
action against another state, and where militarized action can take the
form of a threat, display, or use of force. The data confirm that crises generally do not unfold with a degree of rapidity that forecloses debate.
Among crises that did not escalate to war, the median duration was 25
days, with a mean of 122 days.[9] Among those that did escalate to war,
the median pre-war duration was 59 days, with a mean of 140 days.[10]
Cases like the Korean War, in which the crisis and war started on the
same day, represent just one extreme. At the other extreme is the crisis
that became the Mexican–American War, which festered for almost
three years before the outbreak of war. As we have seen, the time

[9] In some cases, the coders could not identify exact start and end days, but they did estimate a minimum and maximum duration. The results reported refer to the estimated
minimum duration.
[10] The latter duration can be determined by merging the MID data with the data on international wars provided by Singer and Small (1994).

involved is clearly sufficient to permit the emergence of informed dissent.

Indeed, such observations have led to a revision of the basic rally-around-the-flag story. Brody and Shapiro (1989) show that the rally effect is not automatic and that much depends on how opposition elites react. They argue that these figures are often reluctant to criticize the government in the first few days of a crisis, in part due to the difficulty of gathering information at short notice. Dissent may emerge, however, after this initial period. Brody and Shapiro (1989) show that criticism by the opposition generally means that the president does not get the expected rise in popularity, a result they attribute to the effect of dissenting information sources on how the public evaluates presidential conduct.

On what basis, then, do parties select their strategies during international crises? Obviously, the variety of motivations behind any such choice is potentially quite large: national interest, partisan interest, personal bias, patriotism, fear, etc.[11] It is quite possible that choices are influenced by more than one consideration and by a different mix in each case. Moreover, the public statements of political actors provide only a meager guide to their underlying motives. Most debates about foreign policy, especially when considering questions of war and peace, use the language of national interest. Governments generally justify decisions to use or refrain from force in terms of the public good. When supporting the government in its threats, opposition leaders invoke the national interest and the virtues of patriotism and domestic unity. When dissenting, they speak of the evils of war and the meager value of whatever is in dispute. Rarely do politicians admit that more venal or particularistic considerations are at play. To the extent that domestic political considerations are openly invoked, politicians emphasize their desire to respect public opinion.

To build a general theory about the impact of democratic politics on crisis behavior, we have to make some simplifying assumptions about parties' motivations. In doing so, of course, we cut away much of the complexity of real life, as theory always does. The choice of assumptions is not, however, entirely arbitrary. In particular, good assumptions meet at least three criteria: they should be plausible empirically; they should

---

[11] See Levy and Mabe (1998) for an effort to disentangle some of the motives behind Republican opposition to the quasi-war with France and Federalist opposition to the War of 1812.

lead to interesting theoretical insights; and the theory upon which they are built should generate hypotheses that are empirically confirmed. The views of opposition parties discussed above all flounder on the first point because they suggest a consistency in behavior that we simply do not observe.

In this book, I assume that politicians select strategies to further their political interests. They try to anticipate how different policy positions will affect their future electoral prospects and act in a manner that maximizes their chances of holding office. A fundamental assumption underlying this analysis, then, is that political actors, whether in government or in opposition, are *office-seeking*. Their choice of strategies in international crises is primarily driven by expected voter reaction (Key 1961). I say "primarily" rather than exclusively, though, because the arguments of this book do not require that politicians only value holding office. As I show in Chapter 4, the basic results regarding the informational effects of democratic competition are robust to a richer set of motivations. Nevertheless, the pursuit of office generates the fundamental dynamic that drives all the results here. Because of the centrality of this assumption in what follows, we must establish that it is empirically plausible.

Political incentives in international crises

Assuming that politicians seek office is a common and relatively uncontroversial starting point in models of domestic policy making (e.g., Mayhew 1974). By making this assumption in an argument about international crises, however, we run afoul of a long-held conventional wisdom. It is common to argue that voters are poorly informed and inattentive when it comes to foreign affairs, and they are more likely to base their voting decisions on issues that are closer to home, such as the state of the economy (e.g., Almond 1950; Cohen 1963). As a result, the argument goes, elections tend not to be influenced by international outcomes. If this is true, then it makes little sense to assume that politicians are motivated by electoral concerns when choosing strategies in international crises. Given this conventional wisdom, it is worth addressing this question: Are international crises politically meaningful?

There are several reasons to answer this question in the affirmative. First, it is important to distinguish international crises from other areas of foreign policy. By definition, crises are situations in which the use of force is a distinct possibility. As a result, these tend to be rather visible and salient events. Even if it is true that voters generally ignore events in other parts of the world and less prominent aspects of their own country's foreign policy, crises command greater attention. Even Almond, who is closely associated with the conventional wisdom mentioned above, acknowledges that, "When foreign policy questions assume the aspect of immediate threat to the normal conduct of affairs they break into the focus of attention and share the public consciousness with private and domestic concerns" (1950, pp. 70–71).

The salience of crises is evident in opinion polls which ask Americans to name the most important problems facing the country. Since World War II, the percentage of respondents listing some foreign policy issue as most important has varied from a high of 72 percent, in the wake of the Cuban Missile Crisis, to lows of about 1–2 percent, during the period of détente and at the end of the Cold War (Smith 1985). Figure 3.1 shows how this percentage has varied from 1946 to 1992.[12] The figure also shows, for each month in this period, the number of militarized crises the United States was involved in at the time, where crises are as defined in the MID data set.[13] Two conclusions emerge from this analysis. First, the overall salience of foreign affairs has been quite large in some periods, especially when international tensions were high. Indeed, Smith (1985, p. 265) sees in these numbers a "hegemony of foreign affairs" during the early Cold War. Second, the public is clearly aware of its government's participation in international crises: concern about foreign affairs rises and falls in lock-step with US involvement.[14]

Additional evidence to this effect is provided by the Pew Research Center for the People and the Press, which tracks public interest in major news stories (Kohut 2000). In the period 1986–2000, the Iraqi invasion of Kuwait and the dispatch of US troops to Saudi Arabia in August 1990 was one of the most watched events, with 66 percent of Americans saying that they were following the story "very closely." Three other

[12] The responses are all from Gallup polls. Smith (1985) provides the data through February 1984; the rest come from Public Opinion Online, various dates. The "foreign affairs" category includes all responses referring to danger of war, the arms race, and specific international events; foreign trade and energy concerns are not included in this category. Because multiple responses per participant were allowed, all numbers were scaled to make the total add up to 100 percent.

[13] For the purposes of this graph, each crisis in which the United States made at least a threat to use force is counted equally. This technique might understate the importance of some events, such as the Korean War; nevertheless, a simple count of ongoing crises is sufficient for present purposes.   [14] The bivariate correlation between the two is 0.55.

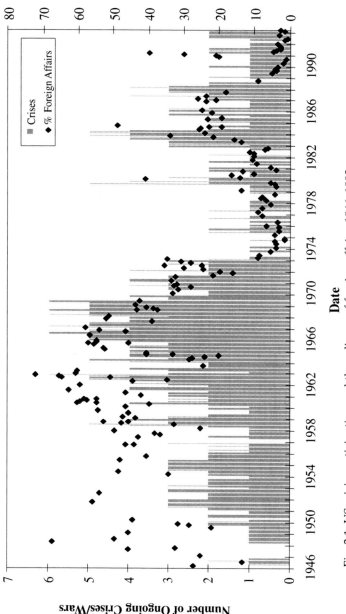

Fig. 3.1 US crisis participation and the salience of foreign affairs, 1946–1992

Sources: Crisis/war participation is from Jones, Bremer, and Singer (1996). Gallup poll data through February 1984 are from Smith (1985), thereafter from Public Opinion Online, various dates.

uses of force were not far behind: the invasion of Panama in 1991 (60 percent), US air strikes against Libya in 1986 (58 percent), and the air campaign against Yugoslavia in 1999 (43 percent). Thus, large portions of the electorate pay attention to crises and wars. Predictably, more arcane foreign policy issues received less attention. For example, the debate over whether to expand NATO to include Poland, Hungary, and the Czech Republic was very closely followed by only 5–6 percent of Americans. Given the visibility of and attention paid to international crises, it is not unreasonable to assume that these events have an impact on voters' evaluations of political actors.

Indeed, there is a growing body of evidence that wars and other foreign policy outcomes do have a significant impact on electoral fortunes. In a large, cross-national study, Bueno de Mesquita and Siverson (1995) show that governments that wage war are more likely to be removed from office if they lose or if the costs of war are very high than if they win at low cost. Goemans (2000) reports that, of the democratically elected leaders who took their countries to war, 45 percent of the winners remained in power two years after the war, while none of the losers did. Cotton (1986) confirms these findings in the case of the United States, showing that long, costly wars decrease the expected vote share of the incumbent president. Finally, Gaubatz (1999) provides indirect evidence of the connection between elections and wars by showing that democratic leaders tend not to get involved in wars late in their electoral cycle – i.e., when an election is nearing. If democratic leaders did not expect wars to have political repercussions, it is unclear why there would be such a pattern.

Less systematic attention has been paid to the impact of nonwar crisis outcomes on a government's political survival. Nevertheless, there is evidence from studies of the United States suggesting that foreign policy performance affects the evaluation of political candidates. Aldrich, Sullivan, and Borgida (1989), for example, review several works establishing links between foreign policy and election outcomes in the United States. These are most clearly evident in the effect of the Vietnam War on President Johnson and President Nixon and the role of the Iranian hostage crisis on President Carter's election defeat. Hurwitz and Peffley (1987), Nincic and Hinckley (1991), and Nincic (1992, ch. 4) present evidence suggesting that perceptions of foreign policy performance indirectly affect presidential elections by influencing voters' overall approval of candidates. Moreover, anecdotal evidence points to the potentially important role of crisis outcomes on leaders' political fortunes. British Prime Minister Anthony Eden resigned from office in large part due to dissatisfaction with his handling of the Suez crisis. Similarly, French Premier Joseph Caillaux was forced to resign in 1912 amid charges that he had conceded too much to Germany in the Agadir crisis.

All of the preceding evidence suggests that the outcomes of international crises and wars have an impact on a government's ability to stay in power. This means that, to the extent that political leaders are motivated by the desire for reelection, office-seeking behavior should carry over into the realm of crisis decision making.

Can we say the same thing about opposition parties? On this point, Regens, Gaddie, and Lockerbie (1995) offer the most useful results. They studied the electoral effects of voting for or against a declaration of war in the United States. Using data from three cases with useful variance – the Mexican–American War, World War I, and the Persian Gulf War – they show that representatives who voted against the first two of these wars were significantly less likely to be returned to office in the following election. In large part, this effect was driven by self-selection: those who opposed the wars were more likely to retire or seek alternative offices compared to those who supported the wars. In the case of the Mexican–American War, the retirement rate among dissenters was three times greater than the retirement rate among supporters. In the case of World War I, dissenters retired at twice the rate of supporters, and those who chose to face reelection received significantly lower vote shares, even after controlling for other factors. The Persian Gulf case exhibits both effects but only weakly, and none of the results for that case are statistically significant. Regens, Gaddie, and Lockerbie (1995) attribute this to the length of time between the end of the war and the 1992 election, as well as the effect of other intervening factors, such as the economy. Nevertheless, it is clear that Democrats suffered a prolonged period of low poll ratings as a result of their opposition to the war. Moreover, there is anecdotal evidence that the war had indirect ramifications on the 1992 presidential election. Senator Sam Nunn, previously a strong contender for the Democratic nomination, has said that his vote against the use of force scuttled whatever chances he had to mount a presidential bid (Pace 1996).

All of this suggests that candidates who oppose wars that turn out to be successful can pay a price at the polls. Moreover, the higher retirement rate among dissenters indicates that politicians believe this to be the case. This is an important point, one that is often lost in debates about the relationship between foreign policy on elections. Despite the conventional wisdom that foreign policy outcomes have no effect on voters' decisions, it is clear that *politicians do not act as if this were true* (Aldrich, Sullivan, Borgida 1989). Drew (1991), for example, describes how congressional Democrats agonized over how to vote on the Gulf War resolution. The great fear was being "caught on the wrong side of history" – that is, voting for a war that could turn out to be disastrous or voting against a war that could turn out to be wildly popular (Drew 1991, p. 86). The perception that this decision would have electoral implications later on was nicely expressed by one Congressional aide, who called the vote "a potential career-killer" (Drew 1991, p. 86; see also Zaller 1994a; Mueller 1994, pp. 96–97). Even though we now know that the 1992 elections were more heavily influenced by other factors, politicians concerned about reelection clearly could not and did not ignore the potential voter reaction to their performance at the time decisions were being made.

None of this is meant to imply that performance in international crises is the only factor that determines who will get elected at subsequent elections. Such a claim would be patently absurd. But these arguments do suggest that, to the extent that politicians are motivated by the desire to hold office, they should be expected to choose strategies in international crises with an eye toward their electoral repercussions.

How do these incentives affect parties' choice of strategies? For the government, reelection concerns motivate it to deliver favorable outcomes and to avoid fighting losing and/or costly wars (Fiorina 1981). Given this mandate, the government's approach is similar to that depicted in Chapter 2. Assuming that the electorate prefers more of the disputed good to less, then the government in the challenging state is more likely to be reelected if it gets concessions from the target than if it maintains the status quo or backs down from a threat. As long as we continue to interpret the value of war as determining where the war outcome ranks relative to these other outcomes, then the basic form of the government's strategy is unchanged. For the opposition party, the office-seeking motivation creates a more complicated problem. Whereas the government's mandate is clear – deliver good outcomes – the opposition must decide whether it is better to support or oppose whatever the government chooses to do.

In thinking about what motivates opposition parties, it is important to distinguish between public and private opinions. It is not hard to explain why, for example, opposition elites might be against waging war. They may consider the costs to be too high relative to the stakes, or they might be ideologically opposed to war or to war against certain kinds of adversaries or for certain kinds of ends. Indeed, antiwar sentiment both at the elite and mass level requires little explanation. What does require explanation is the decision to make opposition to force a political issue – that is, to give speeches opposing the threat of war, to engage in open debate with the government over the wisdom of using force, to vote against legislation authorizing or funding military action, etc.

This is particularly so given that, except in rare instances, opposition parties are not in a position to veto the government's decisions. By definition, these parties do not have the executive authority to control whether or not a threat to use force is carried out. It is true that in presidential systems that permit divided government, such as the United States, the opposition party might control the legislative branch giving it some say over the declaration of war, the appropriation of funds, and/or conscription. In practice, however, this kind of authority has not amounted to formal veto power. In the United States – where the legislature's constitutional jurisdiction over war and peace is most clearly established – neither Congress's right to declare war nor its power over the purse have given it an effective veto over presidential decisions to use force (Fisher 1995). One study notes that, between 1789 and 1989, Congress declared war on only five occasions, but the president used military force over 200 times (US Congress 1989). Moreover, while budgetary authority gives Congress the ability to withhold funds from a military operation, it has generally been unwilling to do so once troops are deployed. The two most prominent cases in which Congress cut off funds for a military operation, the Vietnam War and the 1993 intervention in Somalia, came only after those operations were well underway.

If the opposition party cannot veto a resort to force which it does not like, what role does its dissent serve? I argue that opposition parties publicly oppose the use of force for the same reason that they publicly oppose many policies that they are unable to stop: in order to present voters with an alternative. Opposition parties by their nature seek to highlight and exploit the government's failings in order to convince voters that they would be better off with a change. While this strategy does not amount to a formal veto, it may stay the government's hand in another way: by influencing the political calculus of war and peace.

When the opposition publicly opposes a military action, it seeks to place the entire political risk on to the governing party. Thus, Federalists repeatedly referred to the War of 1812 as "Mr. Madison's War" in order to emphasize the fact that they had voted against the conflict. Whigs opposed to the Mexican–American War derided it as "Jimmy Polk's War" (Bailey 1974, p. 257). Similarly, during the 1956 Suez crisis, newspapers aligned with the opposition Labour Party referred to the conflict as "The Government's War" and "Eden's War" (Epstein 1964, pp. 160–61). More recently, Republicans opposed to the US-led airstrikes against Yugoslavia in 1999 resorted to the same language, labeling the conflict "Clinton's War" (Martinez 1999, p. 1038). The effect of such arguments is to make the matter a partisan affair – to emphasize that while the governing party takes ownership of the conflict the nation need not. In adopting such a stance, the opposition distances itself from the government's policy and, by implication, the ultimate outcome.

The dissent of the opposition can also make force riskier for the government by encouraging cleavages in the electorate. Studies of public opinion show that people are highly responsive to cues they receive from elites (Brody and Shapiro 1989; Brody 1991; Zaller 1992, 1994b). Unity of opinion at the elite level tends to generate a similar unity at the mass level. As a result, when the opposition supports the government in a crisis, the latter enjoys a certain amount of political cover because the electorate is inclined to be supportive as well. On the other hand, when the opposition opposes the government, it tends to polarize public opinion. Voters who are dovish to begin with may amplify their opposition to force when they receive cues to that effect from politically legitimate elites. Thus, if large segments of the electorate are likely to follow the opposition party in its dissent, this strategy can generate a political payoff for the opposition and increase the political risks to the government.

Given this, it makes sense to infer that opposition parties have the strongest incentives to oppose the use of force when they expect that war will not play well with domestic audiences. The desire to unseat the government gives the opposition incentives to try to capitalize on antiwar preferences in the electorate. By going on record as opposed to the conflict, the opposition politicizes the issue and positions itself to exploit the outcome in the next election. Roger Brown confirms that this was the thinking of many Federalists in 1812. Since they believed that the country's prospects in war were sufficiently bad, they decided that the politically expedient move would be to vote against it: "They believed the temporary evils of war a price worth paying when it meant defeat of political adversaries . . . But to reap the benefits war would bring, Federalists must of course go on record as opposed to the conflict"

(Brown 1971, p. 175). More recently, House Republican whip Tom Delay urged his colleagues not to "take ownership" of the US action over Kosovo by approving a resolution authorizing the air strikes. It was suggested at the time that the purpose of this strategy was to avoid "complicity in defeat" (Dewar and Eilperin 1999).

Clearly, this motivation does not extend to all crises, however. The opposition must choose its battles wisely. There is no benefit in presenting an alternative to a policy that is popular or widely regarded as successful. Thus, opposition parties who have reason to believe a threat of military action will be successful and/or popular have incentives to publicly support those actions. Such a stance permits the opposition to appear patriotic rather than partisan, but there are also political benefits in doing so. At the very least, supporting the government lets the opposition avoid being caught on the wrong side of the (expected) success – whether diplomatic or military. The evidence presented by Regens, Gaddie, and Lockerbie (1995) and the anecdotal evidence from the Gulf War suggest that politicians perceive costs to opposing conflicts that are seen as successful. In addition, the absence of disagreement among the parties can diminish the electoral potency of the issue, thus depriving the government of potential benefits. In their study of the 1968 US election, Page and Brody (1972) found that voters' positions on Vietnam had very little influence on their voting decision; the reason, they argue, is that voters generally perceived little difference between the candidates on this matter and so had to base their vote on other issues. By adopting a "matching strategy," the opposition can try to remove the issue from political contention. Even if the government's policy leads to a desirable outcome, the perception that opposition would have delivered exactly the same outcome can rob the matter of its electoral salience.

Variation in opposition strategies is thus a natural result of variation in expectations about war. The office-seeking motivation gives opposition parties incentives to support or oppose the use of force depending upon their expectations about how the electorate will evaluate the crisis outcome. Of the two strategies, opposing force is the riskier one, in the sense that it is associated with the higher variance in payoffs. By taking a stand against the government's threats, the opposition puts itself in a good position to exploit a failure, but it also magnifies the political impact of a foreign policy success. The Federalist Party experienced both of these extremes as a result of its opposition to the 1812 war. The early campaigns of the war went quite badly, and in the elections of 1812 and 1814, Federalists exploited the discontent to mount their most impressive electoral gains in decades (Hickey 1989, pp. 100–05, 232). Indeed, the war breathed new life into a party that had been on the brink of extinction (Livermore 1962, ch. 1). This revival was temporary, however, because the US victory at the Battle of New Orleans, though it came after a peace treaty had been signed and ratified, allowed Republicans to redefine the outcome as a victory. In the aftermath of the war, Federalists were branded as unpatriotic and blamed for prolonging the conflict. By the elections of 1816, the Federalists were once again in decline, prompting one historian to declare the party "the most conspicuous casualty of the War of 1812" (Turner 1971, p. 299; see also Mueller 1994, pp. 108–10). Hence, opposing the government in an international crisis entails considerable political risk. It is perhaps no wonder that dissent is the rarer of the two stylized strategies we are considering here.

Conclusion

None of this is meant to imply that electoral considerations are the only factor that comes into play when parties choose strategies. In general, they are part of the mix of motivations. During the war over Polish independence, for example, the British Labour Party opposed the threat of intervention against the Soviet Union in part because of its ideological sympathy for the communist revolution there. But it also knew that its position was politically potent because broad sections of the British public were weary of war and had no appetite for more fighting. The fact that the government knew this too helps to explain why it ultimately chose not to intervene (White 1979, pp. 41–44). Similarly, the French Right opposed the use of force against Germany during the Rhineland and Czech crises in part because of its ideological hatred of the Soviet Union. But its position also grew from the general antiwar mood in France and the understanding that the country's military preparations were insufficient for confronting Germany (Micaud 1946). Again, these were the same considerations that stayed the government's hand in these cases.

The above arguments suggest that the opposition's strategy should be correlated with its expectations about how a potential war will be received by the electorate and hence correlated with the government's own evaluation of war. The opposition generally has greater political incentives to support the threat of force the better it expects the outcome to be. On the other hand, when the opposition expects that the threat or use of force has weak support in the electorate, it has incentives to capitalize on that fact by giving voice to those concerns.

The fact that opposition parties can and sometimes do dissent has two crucial implications. First, it creates a mechanism by which the government's political constraints are revealed. Because opposition parties have incentives to oppose force when they expect war to be politically unsuccessful, they make it more difficult for the government to conceal or misrepresent its weakness. Second, the possibility of dissent makes support meaningful. If, as the "rally around the flag" hypothesis suggests, opposition parties were motivated by patriotism or fear always to support the government in a crisis, then that strategy would convey no information. The fact that opposition parties dissent under some conditions, however, means that their support is informative: at the very least, it reveals that the conditions which motivate dissent are not present.

The opposition party's incentives mean that its strategy can generate additional information beyond what is available when the government is the lone voice of the state. Ultimately, of course, how these signals influence behavior and outcomes in international crises depends not only on the opposition party's own choices, but on the strategic interplay of all the actors in the game. Chapter 4 puts together the building blocks laid out here to develop a new model of crisis bargaining which will allow us to explore this interaction.

4 Domestic competition and signaling in international crises

This chapter merges the arguments from the previous two by showing how domestic political competition affects crisis outcomes through the signals sent by rival parties. It combines the basic crisis bargaining game from Chapter 2 with a simple model of two-party electoral choice. In doing so, it moves away from the unitary state assumption by breaking down one of the rival states into two strategic actors: a governing party and an opposition party. These parties vie for the support of the electorate through their public actions in the international crisis – in particular, the government's decision whether or not to threaten force and the opposition's decision to support or oppose such a threat. Because these actions are observable, they reveal to the rival state information about the government's underlying political incentives and, hence, its willingness to wage war.

The model shows how the government's decision to use threats, the rival state's response, and the probability of war are influenced by public competition. Introduction of an opposition party creates two effects. First, the opposition party can lend additional credibility to a government's threats when it chooses to publicly support those threats in a crisis. The decision to support the government reveals that there are political incentives to carry through on a threat to wage war. Hence, the opposition can bolster the government's signal with a "confirmatory signal" of its own. Second, the existence of an opposition party forces the government to be more selective about the threats it makes. When the outcome of a war is expected to be unfavorable, the opposition has incentives to try to capitalize on this fact by giving voice to domestic unease about the use of force. A strategy of dissent positions the opposition party to take advantage of a poor international outcome, and it also signals to the target state that the government may not be willing to carry out its threat. Because the target state is more likely to stand firm in the face of an opposed threat, outright bluffing is riskier. As a result, a government that faces a domestic competitor has less opportunity to misrepresent its preferences and constraints. The dilemmas associated with asymmetric information – and the danger of war – are consequently mitigated.

Underlying this analysis is the insight that was developed informally in Chapter 3: competition between actors within the state generates information for actors outside of the state. All of the results derived here stem from a key assumption that parties within democratic polities are engaged in a competitive relationship with one another, a conflict that is driven by the pursuit of office. Office-seeking motivations, at their extreme, generate a zero-sum conflict between government and opposition, since whatever increases the probability that one holds office must decrease the corresponding probability for the other. As we will see, it is this conflict that makes the parties' interaction so informative.

This chapter explores the relationship between domestic competition and international crises through a series of models. In the basic version, political parties are assumed to be purely office-seeking, in the sense that they care only about how the international outcome influences their probability of election. I start with this assumption, not because I believe it fully captures the motivations of parties in the real world, but rather to establish the theoretical relationship between competition at the domestic level and signaling at the international level. Once this relationship is developed in its starkest form, we can then see how a richer set of assumptions about party motivations modifies the initial logic. In particular, I explore two variants of the model that directly address the issue of party motivations. First, I consider the effect of policy preferences. If the opposition party represents dovish or hawkish constituents, does its position on the use of force still reveal information about what the government, which may represent different constituents, will do? Second, I look at the role of national welfare concerns, which tend to mitigate the conflict between the government and opposition. Can a shared interest in maximizing the international outcome align the parties' preferences to the point where the opposition's signals no longer convey additional information? I show that modifying the game to permit policy preferences or national welfare concerns does not alter the core results, as long as the parties continue to place sufficient weight on their desire to hold office.

A bargaining model with a strategic opposition

To capture the effect of public competition on international crisis bargaining we amend the model presented in Chapter 2. Rather than treating both states as unitary actors, we decompose one state into two strategic actors – a governing party and an opposition party – and a nonstrategic actor – the domestic electorate. The parties take actions that both the electorate and the rival state can observe. These strategies, and the corresponding response of the rival state, determine the outcome of the international game. Since the parties are assumed to be office-seeking, their payoffs depend upon how the voters evaluate their performance in the crisis. This evaluation is based on the public positions taken by the parties in the crisis and the realized outcome. This section provides a formal description of the game and the voters' evaluation of the parties.

The international crisis

As before, the game is premised on the assumption that two states compete over the possession of some good. A crisis occurs when one state challenges the other for the good. Each then has an opportunity to stand firm or to back down, thus conceding the good to the other side. If both states choose to stand firm, the result is a war. The main innovation added here is that the challenger is decomposed into two strategic actors: the government and the opposition. Though the state itself is not an actor, it will be convenient at times to continue referring to this two-actor entity as the challenging state.[1] The government is assumed to have full control over foreign policy decisions. Thus, the decision to make a challenge and the decision to go to war are both made by the party in power. The opposition party cannot veto the choices of the government, but it can make a public declaration of its policy position – in particular, whether or not it supports the threat of force. The target state chooses its strategy after viewing the action of the government and the policy statement of the opposition.

The game begins with the government's decision either to maintain the status quo or to issue a public challenge. Any challenge includes an explicit threat to use force in the event that the demands are not met. Following the government's move, the opposition party announces its

---

[1] Below, I discuss the implications of democratic competition in the target state. With a few qualifications, all of the results derived here apply in this case as well.

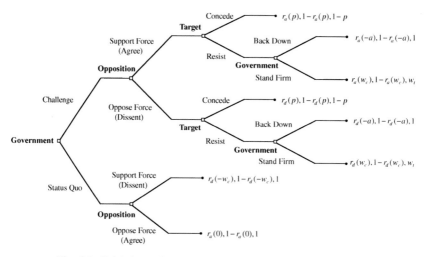

Fig. 4.1 Crisis bargaining game with a strategic opposition

policy stance. The opposition can either support or oppose the use of force. Notice that "Support Force" and "Oppose Force" refer to the opposition's position on the wisdom of using force – not its position on the government's policy. Of course, if the government makes a challenge, then supporting force is the same as supporting the policy. When the government chooses the status quo, support for force represents dissent from the government's policy. It will be useful to label the opposition's strategies "Agree" and "Dissent" to indicate that party's position relative to the government's.

In the event that the government chooses to accept the status quo, the game ends after the opposition's move. In the event of a challenge, and after the opposition makes its policy declaration, the target decides either to concede some share of the good or to resist the challenge. If the former, the game ends peacefully. If the latter, then the government faces a choice between backing down and standing firm. The former implies that the target retains the good and the game ends peacefully, while the latter leads to war. Figure 4.1 presents the extensive form of this game.

There are four possible outcomes at the international level: status quo, the target concedes, the challenger backs down, and war. We continue to assume that the value of the good is one and that the target possesses the good in the status quo. Concessions by the target implies that a share of the good that reflects the states' relative probabilities of victory in war, p, is transferred to the challenger. Since the government and opposition are assumed to be office-seeking, they do not value the international outcomes directly; instead, their payoffs are determined by the electorate's evaluation of their performance, which will be described below. The target, on the other hand, is treated as a unitary state, so its payoffs depend solely on the international outcome and are exactly as laid out in Chapter 2. Thus, the target gets a payoff of 1 if the government chooses the status quo or backs down from its challenge, $1-p$ if it makes concessions in response to a challenge, and w_t if the game ends in war.

As before, the game involves two-sided incomplete information: each state is uncertain about the other's expected costs from war. We generate this condition by assuming that nature randomly selects c_c and c_t from independent distributions over the ranges $[0, \bar{c}_c]$ and $[0, \bar{c}_t]$, respectively. Based on the arguments made in the previous chapter, we assume that the opposition party shares the government's advantage over the rival state when it comes to information about the state's political and military attributes. Hence, both the government and the opposition observe the selection of c_c, while the target knows only the probability distribution from which this term is drawn. Similarly, the target observes the selection of c_t, but the government and opposition know only the corresponding distribution.

The electorate's evaluation

The parties in this model are assumed to be office-seeking, so their payoffs depend upon how the outcome influences their probability of election at some future date. A complication that becomes evident in considering how voters respond to different outcomes is that the relationship between public opinion and party strategies is a reciprocal one. On the one hand, office-seeking candidates try to anticipate the likely electoral effect of different strategies and so choose positions that they expect will enjoy public support (e.g., Key 1961; Zaller 1994a). On the other hand, how the public evaluates policy options and outcomes can depend upon the messages that they receive from government and opposition elites. When voters have low knowledge levels about the issues in question – which is the norm in the area of foreign policy – they take cues from their leaders. Studies have shown that public support for the government in international crises and even assessments of the government's success or failure depend upon the level of consensus or discord at the elite level (e.g., Zaller 1992, 1994b; Brody

1991; Brody and Shapiro 1989). This simultaneity makes it difficult to capture the relationship between voter evaluations and party strategies in all its complexity.

Rather than modeling the voters' decision-making process, we rely on a simple set of assumptions that seem reasonable given the empirical patterns described in Chapter 3. The first is that voters prefer governments which deliver favorable outcomes to those which deliver unfavorable outcomes. Hence, the government's probability of reelection should improve as the outcome it achieves in the international crisis improves. With respect to the opposition, it makes sense to assume that voters reward opposition parties that either support successful policies or oppose unsuccessful policies, and they punish parties that oppose successful policies.

Parties seek to maximize their probability of election. For any international outcome, x, we let $r_a(x)$ denote the probability that the government is reelected in the event that the opposition agreed with the government's policy, and we let $r_d(x)$ denote the probability that the government is reelected in the event that the opposition dissented.[2] Naturally, $1 - r_a(x)$ and $1 - r_d(x)$ are the corresponding probabilities that the opposition will be elected. Given the set-up of the game, x can take on one of four values: 0, if the status quo prevails; p, if the target state makes concessions; $-a$, if the government makes the threat and backs down; and w_c, in the event of war. Because the electorate rewards the government for good outcomes, we assume that r_a and r_d are both increasing in x; thus, the better the international outcome is, the higher is the probability that the government will be reelected. We further assume that the election probability is more sensitive to the international outcome if the opposition dissented than if it agreed with the government's position. This assumption reflects the intuition that dissent tends to politicize the crisis, highlighting the parties' differences on the issue and thereby increasing the electoral salience of the outcome. A strategy of agreement, by contrast, mutes the differences between the parties and diminishes the electoral salience of the outcome. We thus assume that, while both r_a

---

[2] While other factors, such as the state of the economy, also affect that probability of election, we do not need to capture them explicitly in the model. To the extent that these factors are not a function of the crisis outcome, any contribution they make to the parties' expected utilities is constant for all choices and hence can be left out. To the extent that these factors do depend on the crisis outcome – say, if war has a significant effect on the state of the economy – they are already captured implicitly in terms like the expected value for war.

and r_d increase with x, r_d increases more rapidly; in formal terms, $\frac{\partial r_d}{\partial x} \geq \frac{\partial r_a}{\partial x}$ for all x.[3]

This second assumption means that, if a challenge leads to a good outcome – for example, the target makes concessions or the state fights a victorious, low-cost war – then the government's probability of reelection is higher if the opposition opposed the threat than if the opposition supported the threat. Put another way, the opposition is punished for opposing threats that turn out to have favorable results. On the other hand, if the outcome is unfavorable – for example, the state fights a costly war – the government's probability of reelection is higher if the opposition supported threat than if the opposition dissented. The latter strategy puts the opposition in a better position to exploit bad outcomes for political gain. In sum: if the outcome of a challenge is good, the opposition party is better off having supported the threat than having opposed it, and if the outcome is bad, the opposition party is better off having opposed the threat than having supported it. This reflects the intuition, discussed in Chapter 3, that the opposition party wants to avoid being "on the wrong side of history" (Drew 1991, p. 86).

One issue that is unclear is how we should treat the electoral implications of the status quo and, in particular, the effect of the opposition's stance in this instance. We observe empirically that opposition politicians may criticize governments which fail to take forceful action in a crisis. A recent example is then-candidate Bill Clinton's criticism of President George Bush during the 1992 election for failing to stop the war in Bosnia. Clearly, there is little risk to the opposition in calling for the use of force when the government has no intention of doing so. This is a form of cheap criticism: the opposition tries to score political points by portraying the government as weak without facing any risk that it will be held accountable for its proposed alternative. Since the non-use of force may entail acquiescence to an unfavorable outcome, the opposition tries to suggest that it would have prevented that outcome – without exposing itself to the political danger of actually doing so. In the Bosnia example, Clinton tried to exploit dissatisfaction with the ongoing bloodshed, fully aware that the alternative policy he was advocating would not be tested. The cheap nature of such criticism is all the

---

[3] The assumption that this relationship holds for x is actually more stringent than we need. All that is necessary for the following results is that the relationship hold at least weakly for all $x > -a$ and that $r_d(p) > r_a(p)$ – that is, the government benefits more from concessions if the opposition opposed the threat than if it supported the threat.

more evident given Clinton's turnabout on Bosnia shortly after coming into office (Gow 1997, pp. 202–22). On the other hand, we observe that the threat of opposition criticism can color the government's evaluation of the status quo. For example, President Johnson was particularly motivated to take escalatory actions in Vietnam because he wanted to defuse criticism from Republican challenger Barry Goldwater during the 1964 election campaign (Herring 1986, p. 122).

In what follows, we will leave open the possibility that there are conditions under which the opposition can score political points by advocating force after the government selects the status quo. We do this by assuming that the electorate gives some credence to the opposition's criticism and evaluates it on the basis of its own expectations about war. In particular, assume that the electorate has an unbiased expectation about its value for war, w_c. If the opposition dissents after the government selects the status quo, then the government's probability of reelection in this case is $r_d(-w_c)$, and the opposition's probability of election is $1 - r_d(-w_c)$. We further assume that $r_a(0) = r_d(0)$. Together, these assumptions mean that, if the electorate expects to do well in war (i.e., $w_c > 0$), the opposition can make electoral gains by opposing the government's inaction. Conversely, if the electorate expects to do poorly in war (i.e., $w_c < 0$), then the opposition is better off supporting the government's decision to forego a threat. As it turns out, these assumptions have little affect on the basic game. Whenever the state's value for war is sufficiently high that the opposition could profitably criticize the government's inaction, the government is motivated to make a challenge anyway. When we turn to the game in which parties have distinctive policy preferences, this kind of criticism will emerge in some equilibria.

Solution to the bargaining model

Since the goal of this chapter is to explore how the introduction of a strategic opposition affects the dynamics of crisis bargaining, the central focus is on comparing the equilibria of the game proposed above with those of the game in Chapter 2, in which the government was the lone strategic actor. We can thereby see how behavior and outcomes change when the challenging state shifts from a polity in which competition is suppressed to one in which opposition parties openly compete for political support. The formal solution to the model is presented in Appendix B. Here I present the main results.

Characterization of equilibrium strategies

The equilibrium strategies of the government and the opposition are described by a set of cutpoints along the continuum of possible types. As before, the government's strategy is defined by two such cutpoints, which partition the possible types into three ranges. Let k_{gov} and b denote values in the range $[p - \bar{c}_c, p]$, with $k_{gov} \geq b$. These cutpoints have the same meaning as they did in Chapter 2. Thus, if w_c exceeds k_{gov}, then the government makes the challenge and stands firm at the final node. If w_c falls between k_{gov} and b, the government makes the challenge but backs down in the face of resistance. If w_c is lower than b, the government selects the status quo.[4]

When the game includes an opposition party, there is an additional cutpoint describing its strategy. Let k_{opp} denote a value in the range $[p - \bar{c}_c, p]$ such that an opposition of type w_c uses the following decision rule in response to a government challenge: if w_c exceeds k_{opp}, the opposition supports a threat to use force, and if w_c is less than k_{opp}, the opposition opposes a threat to use force. It is shown in the appendix that $k_{opp} \geq k_{gov}$, implying that the opposition supports only genuine challenges, but does not support all such challenges. When the government chooses the status quo, the opposition supports force if and only if $w_c > 0$ – in other words, if it can impose political costs on the government by criticizing its inaction. As we have seen, however, the government always makes a challenge under these conditions, so this criticism is never observed in equilibrium.

As can be seen in Figure 4.2, these cutpoints divide the continuum of possible types into three or four regions, depending on whether or not the game includes an opposition party. When there is no opposition party (4.2a), the government's two cutpoints partition the continuum into three ranges: one in which the government issues a genuine challenge, one in which the government bluffs, and one in which the government selects the status quo. The inclusion of an opposition party (4.2b) introduces an additional cutpoint, which partitions the range of genuine challenges into those supported by the opposition and those opposed. For reasons that will be clear shortly, we can refer to the former as "confirmed" challenges.

Since the strategy of the government in this game is similar to that described in Chapter 2, there is no need to dwell on the underlying

---

[4] Though types in this range never have to make a choice between standing firm and backing down, their off-the-equilibrium-path strategy is to back down.

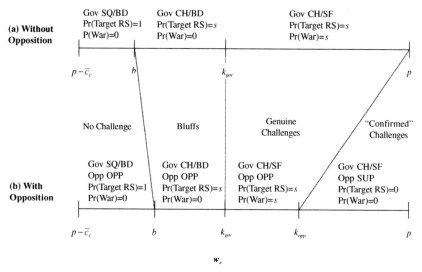

Fig. 4.2 The effects of the opposition party on strategies and outcomes

Note: BD = Back Down, CH = Challenge, Gov = Government, Opp = Opposition Party, OPP = Oppose Force, RS = Resist, SF = Stand Firm, SQ = Status Quo, SUP = Support Force.

intuition: those with high expected value for war are more likely to make the challenge, but there is some bluffing in equilibrium because of the temptation that exists to exploit private information. What explains the opposition party's strategy? Once the government has made a challenge, the choice of the opposition boils down to a decision either to "match" the government by supporting the threat – thereby sharing credit or blame for the eventual outcome – or to oppose the threat. Clearly, as the expected payoff from war goes down, the attractiveness of supporting the challenge decreases: the opposition prefers to distance itself from a threat that could result in either an unpromising war or a humiliating retreat. On the other hand, as the payoff from war increases, the opposition would rather support the threat in the hope of neutralizing the political impact of the affair and perhaps getting some credit for the (expected) favorable outcome.

The fact that the opposition's cutpoint, k_{opp}, is higher than the government's cutpoint, k_{gov}, implies that the opposition will sometimes oppose a threat to use force even though the government is willing to carry out such a threat. This does not reflect greater "dovishness" on the part of the opposition but rather a reluctance to match the government unless the credit that comes from doing so is sufficiently high. We will see shortly that, by supporting the challenge, the opposition can increase the probability that the target will concede. Because the government's reelection chances are highest when the rival state concedes, however, the opposition has incentives to pursue an "irresponsible" strategy: opposing the threat and gambling that the international outcome will be unfavorable (Gaubatz 1998). Drew (1991, p. 87) describes similar logic at work prior to the Gulf War: "Some Democrats reasoned that, either way, this would be Bush's war – if it was politically successful, he would get the credit, and if it wasn't he would get the blame – so there was more percentage in voting against it." Presumably, the calculus would have been different had these Democrats been sure that war would be a raging success, but *ex ante* concerns about the costs of the war gave them reason to distance themselves from the government. This incentive goes away when the state's expected payoff from war is relatively high; in this case, all possible outcomes from the government's challenge are sufficiently attractive to the electorate that the opposition prefers to hop on board.

How does the rival state respond to these signals? The target's equilibrium strategy is a function of its beliefs, which in turn depend upon the actions taken by the government and opposition. Since the target only gets to move if the government makes a challenge, two possible signals are of interest: a supported threat and an opposed threat. The key question facing the target upon viewing these signals is: what is the probability that the government will stand firm in response to resistance? In other words, what is the probability that the challenge was made by a government of type $w_c \geq k_{gov}$?

As noted above, the opposition only supports genuine challenges. Thus, the support of the opposition unambiguously signals that the government will fight in the event of a refusal. Given this, the target knows that it faces a stark choice between conceding the good or waging war: there is no chance that the government will back down. Since its payoff from conceding, $1-p$, is always greater than its expected value for war, the target always concedes in this case. If, on the other hand, the opposition opposes the challenge, then the target is left uncertain about whether the threat was genuine or a bluff. Recall from Figure 4.2b that both kinds of threats may be opposed by the opposition. If $k_{opp} > w_c \geq k_{gov}$, then an opposed threat is still genuine: governments in this range will stand firm in response to resistance. Governments for which $k_{gov} > w_c \geq b$ also make opposed threats, however, and these are bluffs.

As a result, the target faces some ambiguity regarding the government's true type. It can always concede a share of the good and ensure a payoff of $1-p$. Resisting the challenge, on the other hand, leads to a gamble: there is some chance that the government is bluffing and will back down, but there is also some chance that the threat is genuine and resistance will lead to war. Because war is only a possibility and not a certainty, some types of target find it optimal to take the gamble and resist the challenge. The uncertainty generated by the opposition party's dissent thus means that more types of target are willing to resist than are willing to do so when the opposition supports the government. The probability that the target will resist when the opposition opposes the threat is consequently greater than the probability that it will resist when the opposition supports the threat. As we saw, the latter was 0, so, if we let s denote the former, this intuition implies that $s > 0$.[5]

The effect of the opposition party

We can now address the central question of this chapter: how do behavior and outcomes change as a result of the public competition in the challenging state? What happens to the equilibria when we go from a game without an opposition party to one in which an opposition makes informed public statements? The shift from a game without an opposition to one with an opposition entails two important changes. First, the opposition party can increase the credibility of some challenges by publicly supporting the use of force. When the challenger's expected value for war is sufficiently high (i.e., $w_c > k_{opp}$), a strategic opposition has political incentives to back the government's threat to use force. In doing so, the opposition essentially confirms that the government is serious about carrying through on the challenge. The impact of this signal derives from the fact that opposition is engaged in a competitive interaction with the government and only has reason to support the government if its expected value for war is sufficiently high. *Thus, while the government may have incentives to bluff, the opposition has no incentive to collude in a bluff.* The target state

---

[5] Obviously, the prediction that the rival state never resists supported threats is unrealistic empirically. In Schultz (1998), I show that a positive probability of resistance can be generated by assuming that the good in dispute is indivisible. As with any comparative-static exercise, what matters is not the absolute probability of any outcome, but how the probability of the outcome changes across different conditions. The key result here is that the probability of resistance is lower when the opposition supports the threat than when it opposes the threat.

interprets a supported threat as a credible threat and will consequently concede. We refer to this finding as the "confirmatory effect" because the opposition's support confirms the credibility of the government's signal. Because of this effect, the existence of an opposition party permits states with high resolve to reveal that fact more reliably than when the government is the lone voice of the state.[6]

The second change that results from the introduction of a strategic opposition is that the government's willingness to bluff decreases. Notice from Figure 4.2 that the cutpoint b shifts to the right when the opposition party is added to the interaction, meaning that the range of types which bluff in equilibrium shrinks. The intuition underlying this result is straightforward. Just as the opposition's support can increase the credibility of a threat, the opposition's dissent casts doubt on whether the challenge is genuine. If the government were to leave its strategy unchanged, the target would want to resist opposed challenges more often. In equilibrium, however, the government compensates by bluffing at a lower rate; formally, b increases. As a result, domestic opposition does not increase the probability of resistance relative to the case in which no opposition party exists. Instead, the adjustment is made by the government, which becomes more selective about making threats and less inclined to engage in bluffing behavior. We will refer to this finding as the "restraining effect."

What does all this imply for the probability of war? There are three ways to think about this question: the probability of war for different types of challenger, the probability of war *ex ante*, before the game even starts, and the probability of war given that a challenge has been issued. War occurs in the model whenever the government makes a genuine challenge – that is, a threat which it is willing to carry out – and the rival state resists. Hence, there is only a nonzero probability of war when $w_c >$ k_{gov}, because any threats made by types which fall below this cutpoint would not be carried out. Given that a genuine challenge has been made, the probability of war is the same as the probability that the target resists.

---

[6] Interestingly, the opposition can play this role even when the government's challenge generates no audience costs. When $a = 0$, the government can costlessly make challenges regardless of its type, since the worst possible outcome, backing down and getting zero, is the same as choosing the status quo. Because of this, the government's strategy conveys no information. Elsewhere, however, I present a proof showing that the opposition party still sends informative signals in this case, as its decision to support or oppose still partially separates genuine threats from bluffs (Schultz 1998, pp. 842–43). This suggests that the existence of a second information source can compensate for the government's inability to send costly signals.

Using the notation introduced above, this probability is zero when the opposition supports the threat and s when the opposition opposes the threat or when there is no opposition party. Thus, for types which fall in the range $[k_{opp}, p]$, the probability of war is lower in the game with a publicly active opposition than it is in the game without one.

This result implies that the introduction of an opposition party decreases the *ex ante* probability of war – that is, the probability of war prior to nature's selection of w_c and w_t. Because the danger of war is reduced in the highest range of w_c, the expected probability of war across the entire range also falls. This result is driven by the fact that the probability of resistance by the rival state is the same (s) when there is an opposition party that opposes the government's threat as it is when there is no opposition party. Thus, while types in the range $[k_{opp}, p]$ see their probability of war decline with the introduction of competition, those in the range $[k_{gov}, k_{opp}]$ have the same probability of war in both versions of the game.

How does public competition affect the conditional probability of war given that a challenge has been made? On this point, the results are ambiguous, because there are two countervailing effects. Once a challenge is issued, a peaceful outcome can come about in one of two ways: either the target concedes a share of the good, or the government backs down from the challenge. As we have seen, adding an opposition party to the game increases the probability of the former, on average, since the rival state is less likely to resist those challenges which are publicly supported by the opposition. On the other hand, introducing competition also makes the government less likely to make challenges which it does not intend to carry out. Given that a threat has been made, the probability that the government will back down in response to resistance is lower in the game with an opposition than in the game without an opposition. Thus, governments that face domestic competition are less likely to have their challenges resisted but more likely to stand firm in the event of resistance; governments unconstrained by public competition are more likely to have their challenges resisted, but they are also more likely to have been bluffing in the first place. Which effect dominates is unclear and depends upon the actual distribution of types.

Extending the basic model

The model, of course, rests on a number of simplifying assumptions, many of which could be relaxed or changed. The central question in evaluating the assumptions is not whether or not they are realistic, but whether or not they lead to interesting insights and testable predictions. Still, considering extensions or modifications of the model can serve two purposes. The first is to determine how robust the main results are to a richer set of assumptions. That is, do the main comparative-static results still hold when we introduce new complexities in the model? The second purpose is to determine whether we gain additional insights and predictions by changing some of the initial assumptions. Will modifications and extensions of the model uncover additional relationships? In the sections that follow, I consider four extensions that serve both of these purposes:

(1) What happens if the democratic state is the potential target of the dispute rather than the potential challenger?

(2) What happens if the dissent of the opposition party increases the expected costs of war by hampering the state's war-fighting ability or by undercutting public support for war?

(3) What happens if the parties have distinct policy preferences over the use of force or cater to constituents with different expectations about war? In particular, how does the game change if policy preferences or heterogeneity in the electorate induce hawkish or dovish biases in the parties?

(4) What happens if the parties value the international outcome independent of its effect on their reelection chances? In particular, how does the opposition's influence change as national interest concerns align its preferences with those of the government?

The first two variations entail slight alterations in the structure of the game and can be dealt with briefly and informally. The second two relax the assumption that parties are purely office-seeking and permit us to explore how robust the results are to a richer conception of party motivations. Because the office-seeking assumption was central to the core results, I will treat these extensions at greater length.

Democracies as targets

There is nothing about the basic results presented here that depends upon the assumption that the democratic state is the first mover in a crisis. Hence, both the restraining and confirmatory effects apply in situations in which democracies are called upon to respond to the threats of others. Because the basic logic of the game is similar in this case, there is no need to go through the formal exercise of modeling it.[7] However, two insights emerge from this exercise.

The first arises from the observation that target states generally have less leeway to bluff than do challengers. Whether or not bluffing makes sense for the target depends upon the credibility of the challenger's threat. If it is highly likely that the threat is credible, then the target has little to gain by bluffing: the challenger is probably committed to carrying out the threat, and a bluff has little chance of working. Thus, under some conditions, no target – democratic or otherwise – will want to resist a challenge if it does not intend to stand firm at a later stage. Clearly, when these conditions hold, the informational effect of competition is attenuated. The external constraints on misrepresentation are so great that the internal constraints generated by democratic politics have no additional bite. Hence, democratic targets should be associated with the effects identified with democratic challengers above, but to a lesser degree and not under all conditions.

The second insight that arises is that, all other things equal, democracies make more attractive targets than do nondemocracies. The additional information provided by the opposition party creates opportunities for a challenger to engage in probes that it might not initiate against a nondemocratic target. In particular, a state that challenges a democracy can bluff "conditionally" – issuing a threat that it will carry out in the event it observes domestic dissent but which it will not carry out if it observes unified support. Because a challenger facing a democratic target knows that it will be able to better discriminate genuine resistance from bluff, there is less danger in probing such a target. We will see this quite clearly in the analysis of the 1936 Rhineland crisis in Chapter 7. Germany's move into the Rhineland was a gamble based in large part on the expectation that France and Britain would not respond militarily; indeed, despite the beliefs of some that Hitler would back down if confronted, neither country had the domestic political support to meet his bluff with one of their own. Democracies also make good targets because the dangers of unwanted war are lower. Since democratic governments

---

[7] To understand the impact of competition in the target state, the basic game structure has to be modified so that the target has an additional move, after the challenger's decision to stand firm. Giving the target a second chance to maintain its resistance or make concessions renders the target's initial decision informative and hence generates the same kind of signaling dynamics that surround the challenger's initial move in the basic game. Simply adding an opposition to the target in the basic game would have no effect, since the target has no opportunity to engage in misrepresentation.

are better able to signal their determination to fight, there is less danger that the challenger will misestimate the target's resolve and stumble into a war it does not want. All this suggests that the introduction of public competiton increases the probability that a state will become the target of a challenge.

Domestic opposition and the costs of war

In a very important way, the basic model assumes that the political costs of war depend upon the opposition party's strategy. When the opposition opposes the use of force, the electoral risks to the government increase. A bad war outcome becomes even worse politically since the opposition is well positioned to exploit it. Nonetheless, there are at least two additional ways in which the opposition's dissent can increase the expected costs of fighting. First, in presidential systems – in which different parties may control the executive and legislative branches – a condition of divided government means that the opposition may be able to do more than simply make policy statements. As noted in Chapter 3, control over the legislature rarely gives the opposition an actual veto over the use of force. The dissent of the legislative majority party may, however, make war less attractive in expectation. For example, the opposition party's control over funding provides a channel for public dissatisfaction with war to exert some influence over its conduct – as Democratic control of the US Congress eventually did in the case of Vietnam. If the government expects domestic political opposition to undermine its war-fighting effort in this way, then the value it places on war might decrease, at least in expectation. The opposition's stance might also influence the costs of war through its effect on the electorate's evaluation of the international outcome. As discussed earlier, a large literature suggests that public opinion is heavily dependent upon the cues it receives from politically legitimate elites. When there is discord at the elite level, the electorate tends to polarize as well, as people tend to adopt the position of the party with which they identify (esp., Zaller 1992). Consequently, dissent from opposition elites can draw away public support for the president in a crisis, potentially increasing the costs of war in expectation (Brody and Shapiro 1989). In extreme cases, the opposition's dissent and the public reaction it engenders may directly hinder the state's war-fighting ability. For example, when the British government was contemplating intervention in the 1920 war between Poland and the Soviet Union, the Labour Party threatened to lead a general strike that would have disrupted industry and shipping (White 1979, pp. 41–44).

Fortunately, all the results discussed here remain unchanged if we introduce these considerations, which can be done in a straightforward manner. Assume that, if the opposition opposes the use of force, the state's expected costs for war increase by some amount, $\Delta > 0$. Thus, the expected outcome of a war supported by the opposition remains $w_c = p - c_c$, while the expected outcome of a war opposed by the opposition is $w'_c = p - c_c - \Delta$. This change has no effect on the basic form of the equilibrium depicted in Figure 4.2. All that happens is that the cutpoints of the government and opposition party shift to the right. The confirmatory effect remains as long as there are still some conditions under which the opposition will support force (i.e., $k_{opp} < p$), and the restraining effect is enhanced because the range of types willing to make a challenge shrinks (i.e., b increases).

This amendment to the model introduces elements of the institutional constraints story in an interesting way. Rather than assuming that the costs of war always tend to be higher in democratic states, it suggests that higher costs of war might arise endogenously from the opposition's strategy – and therefore not in every case. Moreover, this take on the institutional constraints argument leads to a different conclusion about the effect of democracy on the reaction of the other state. In basic institutional constraints view, democratic institutions "signal" that the state tends to have higher than average costs for war (Bueno de Mesquita and Lalman 1992). We saw in Chapter 2 that such a signal can increase the probability of resistance by the target by raising doubts about the government's willingness to carry out its threat. Here, the mechanism that generates these additional costs – the dissent of the opposition party – is transparent to the other state. Thus, whether or not the government is particularly constrained in any given case is something which the rival state can observe. Because the confirmatory effect is still operative, the overall result of open competition is to decrease, rather than increase, the expected probability of resistance. As we will see, the empirical evidence in the next two chapters is more consistent with this prediction.

Hawks and doves: the effects of policy preferences

In the basic model, the parties are treated as being completely identical, except for the fact that one happens to be in government and the other does not. The opposition appears to be more dovish than the government since it is less likely to advocate the use of force, but this is entirely due to the fact that it is out of office, not to any inherent difference between the parties. If the opposition were to become the government at some later date, it would act exactly as the previous government had acted. In reality, however, political parties may be very different from one another in the ideologies or policy packages they typically promote. In the area of foreign policy, we can often identify parties and politicians as being relatively hawkish or dovish, depending upon their general attitudes toward the use of force. In this section, I amend the model to take such policy preferences into account.

Systematically different attitudes toward the use of force could arise in two ways. First, parties might have different ideologies. Some parties might be motivated by nationalistic, imperialistic, and/or militaristic ideas, while others adhere to pacifism, anti-imperialism, cosmopolitanism, and the like. Such ideological leanings might translate into a preference over policies, not simply outcomes. That is, militaristic actors might get some utility from advocating the use of force, beyond whatever utility they derive from the actual outcome. Pacifists, on the other hand, might prefer to oppose force on principle, even if they believe the war could be easily won. The second possible source of differences might be the interests of the parties' core constituents. If the costs and benefits of war fall unevenly across the electorate, and if the parties derive their support from groups with systematically different payoffs from war, then these differences could generate distinctive policy preferences.[8] Dovish parties might be distinct from hawkish parties because they derive their support from groups in the electorate which tend to get lower benefit from international goods and/or incur higher costs in the event of war. Especially in electoral systems with proportional representation, the incentives to cater to different segments of the electorate can be strong.

It is useful to consider the implications of these kinds of biases, because policy preferences should weaken the informational content of parties' signals. Say, for example, the opposition party is extremely dovish, in the sense that it always takes a principled position against the use of force, regardless of whether or not it believes war would be militarily and politically successful. Obviously, nothing can be learned from this party's strategy: since it always opposes the use of force, its signal does nothing to separate types with high value for war from types with low value for war. The same would be true of an extremely hawkish opposition that always supports the use of force – again, regardless of

---

[8] See Morgan and Bickers (1992) for evidence that parties care about the support of their core supporters when contemplating the use of force.

the state's type. The opposition party sent informative signals in the basic game because its incentives and the government's were inextricably linked. Both, after all, were trying to please the same representative voter. Distinctive preferences over policy weaken that link, meaning that the opposition's strategies may generate less information about the government's political constraints.

Does this consideration undermine the logic of my argument? The answer is no, and this section briefly outlines why. In particular, I amend the model to permit the parties to be relatively hawkish or dovish. I then show that the basic results derived above still hold, with only minor modifications. The main results in this section echo those of Calvert (1985), who argues that information sources with known biases can still be useful. The intuition behind this conclusion is that biased actors can reveal information if they sometimes act contrary to their known preferences. For example, if a hawkish defense secretary says that, according to his information, the foreign threat is great and defense spending needs to be high, we might be understandably skeptical of that signal. The advice is, after all, consistent with the actor's known preference for greater defense spending. If, on the other hand, that same person says that defense spending could safely be cut, this message has a great deal of credibility – more so, in fact, than if the same assessment were made by somebody with less obvious biases (Krehbiel 1991, p. 83). A biased actor thus has the ability to convey information through "surprise" signals that go against expectations.

In the same way, parties with known policy preferences can still send useful information in some cases. Dovish parties are expected to oppose threats to use force, so, when they do so, their dissent is less informative than that of the purely office-seeking party considered above. However, when parties that are generally dovish support the government's threats, it sends a strong signal that those threats enjoy widespread support. After all, when even the doves like the idea of using force, there is good reason to believe that threat is genuine. The same logic applies for parties with hawkish biases. A hawkish opposition might back the use of force even if the government's expected value for war is low. In that case, the support of the opposition no longer signals that the threat is genuine. When the same party opposes threats to use force, however, the credibility of the threat is seriously undermined. Hence, parties with policy preferences can still send informative signals, but they do so under a more limited set of conditions. As long as the policy preferences are not so strong that doves *always* oppose force or hawks *always* support force, then the basic effects of competition identified above still hold.

There are several ways to capture policy biases in the game. The simplest is to assume that parties get some additional benefit from advocating their preferred policy position – opposing force in the case of doves and supporting force in the case of hawks. This benefit might arise from ideology and principle, or it might reflect a desire to cater to segments of the electorate which, for ideological or material reasons, have distinctive preferences over the use of force.[9] Formally, let α denote how hawkish or dovish the opposition party is relative to the government. The payoffs of the game are identical to those above, with one exception: if the opposition party supports force, then its payoff is increased by α. Thus, $\alpha > 0$ implies a hawkish opposition that is particularly motivated to support force, while $\alpha < 0$ implies a dovish opposition that has special incentives to oppose force. The magnitude of this parameter determines how intense these policy biases are relative to the office-seeking motivation. The case of $\alpha = 0$ corresponds to the "neutral" opposition of the basic game. Though we could introduce a policy bias in the government in the same manner, it is better not to in order to keep the comparative-static analysis clean. The question here is not how the government's hawkish or dovish preferences influence the way the game is played; instead, we want to know how hawkish or dovish preferences influence the value of the opposition's signal. Thus, we use a neutral government as the basis for comparison and vary the bias of the opposition party.

Notice the effect of this change on the relationship between the parties' payoffs. In the original game, there is a perfect negative correlation in their payoffs, reflecting a condition of complete conflict. With the introduction of a policy bias in the opposition, this correlation weakens. Hence, the incentives of the opposition say less about the incentives of the government once the opposition is responding to its individual policy bias in addition to their shared electoral concerns.

The solution to this modified game is quite similar to that of the basic model. Rather than work through it in full detail, then, I will simply sketch the main results.[10] First consider what happens when the opposition is relatively dovish. Figure 4.3 depicts the effect of this change. Panel (a) shows the equilibrium cutpoints for the case in which there is

---

[9] Alternatively, we might assume that parties care about the support of different groups of voters who place different values on the disputed good or expect different costs from war. Under certain assumptions, the results of such a model are identical to those derived here.
[10] See Appendix B for proofs of the equilibria depicted here.

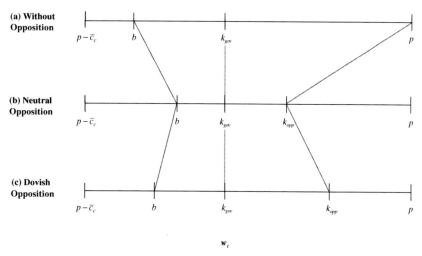

Fig. 4.3 The effects of a dovish opposition party

no opposition party; panel (b) shows the equilibrium cutpoints for the case of the "neutral" opposition discussed in the previous model – that is, the case in which $\alpha = 0$. Panel (c) shows the equilibrium cutpoints when the opposition is dovish, or $\alpha < 0$. As expected, the dovish opposition party opposes force more often than does the neutral opposition. Moving from panel (b) to panel (c), k_{opp} shifts to the right, meaning that the range of types for which the opposition is willing to support force decreases. Moreover, k_{opp} increases as α decreases. Thus, as the opposition party becomes more dovish, the chances that it will support a threat get smaller.

Intuition suggests that, when a dovish party opposes the use of force, this signal should be less informative than when an opposition party with no such bias adopts the same stance. Indeed, this is precisely what happens. As k_{opp} increases, the range of types which are consistent with a strategy of opposition grows, and the target state is less able to discriminate genuine threats from bluffs. Because of this, the government is now free to bluff more often, and the cutpoint b moves back to the left. When α gets sufficiently negative, k_{opp} equals or exceeds p, meaning that there are no possible types for which the opposition is willing to support force. In this extreme case, the dovish opposition conveys no information, and the game is identical to the one with no opposition party.

As long as this condition is not met, however, the existence of the opposition party with dovish preferences has the same basic effect as did the neutral opposition discussed above. As long as there is some chance that the opposition party will support the use of force, more information is revealed with the opposition than without. When the dovish party is willing to support force, this strategy unambiguously signals that the threat is genuine. In other words, the confirmatory effect identified above is still present. The probability that the target resists is lower in this case, and, as before, the expected probability of war *ex ante* is also lower. The restraining effect remains as well. The government is less likely to bluff when there is a dovish opposition than when there is no opposition. Thus, although a relatively dovish opposition affects the magnitude of the effects derived earlier, it need not eliminate them altogether.

What happens when the opposition party has hawkish preferences? This case is more complicated because much depends on the relative values of the parameters in the model. Rather than describe all the possible combinations and equilibria, I will instead highlight some interesting cases. Not surprisingly, hawkishness tends to have the opposite effect from dovishness. For some values of α greater than zero, the cutpoints move inward, towards k_{gov} – that is, relative to the case of a neutral opposition, k_{opp} is lower, and b is higher. This means that the range of types which are willing to support the use of force increases, and the government's willingness to bluff decreases. In terms of the probability of war, these changes have a beneficial effect. Recall that opportunism on the part of the purely office-seeking opposition induces a form of dovishness, or a willingness to oppose what the opposition knows to be genuine challenges. In these cases, when the state's expected value for war is in the middle range, the opposition has incentives to undercut the government, gambling that the outcome will be unfavorable. Introducing hawkish preferences partially counteracts this incentive. Given that a threat is genuine, the hawkish opposition is more likely to support it than is the neutral opposition. The confirmatory effect is thus strengthened.

This is not the only possible result of a hawkish opposition, however. Because such a party prefers to support force, it may do so even in cases when the government does not. When this is the case, then the support of a hawkish opposition becomes less meaningful, since it is a poor indicator of what the government intends to do. The equilibrium depicted in Figure 4.4 illustrates this possibility, which holds when α is sufficiently high that the opposition prefers to support force under most conditions. The cutpoints mean exactly what they meant before, but notice

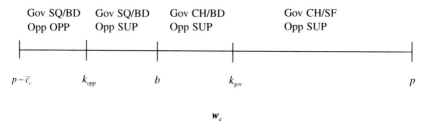

Fig. 4.4 One possible equilibrium with a hawkish opposition party
Note: BD = Back Down, CH = Challenge, Gov = Government,
OPP = Oppose Force, Opp = Opposition Party, SF = Stand Firm,
SQ = Status Quo, SUP = Support Force.

that the opposition's cutpoint, k_{opp}, is now lower than the government's cutpoint, k_{gov}. This implies that the opposition supports the government's threat regardless of whether or not it is genuine. The fact that k_{opp} is less than b means that the opposition even advocates force when the government chooses the status quo. Obviously, because the opposition supports the government every time it makes a challenge, this signal reveals no information about whether or not the government intends to stand firm. In this case, it is the strategy of opposing force that is unambiguous, clearly revealing that the government has very low expected value for war.

Thus, the basic results do not change fundamentally when we add policy biases, as long as these biases do not wholly eliminate variation in the opposition party's strategy. If there is some chance that the opposition party will act in an "unexpected" manner given its policy biases – that is, as long as there are conditions under which doves support the use of force and hawks dissent from the government's threat – then more information is revealed when there is an opposition party than when there is none. What this suggests is that the stance of parties with extreme policy preferences are likely to be discounted unless those signals run contrary to their known biases. During the Suez crisis, for example, US Secretary of State John Foster Dulles characterized France as "united in favor of military action," brushing off the dissent of the French Communist Party. Even though the Communists were the single largest party in the National Assembly, Dulles apparently felt that its opposition was driven by sympathy toward the Soviet Union and hence was not representative of the political pressures on the government. By contrast, he took the opposition of the British Labour Party – a more mainstream political party – as a serious indicator of the tenuous political support for the use of force in that country (US, Dept. of State 1990, p. 328).

As we just saw, the case of the hawkish opposition also predicts the two observations that our earlier model did not. In the equilibrium depicted above, there is some chance that the government will select the status quo and the opposition will advocate force, and there is some chance that the government will back down from a threat that had been supported by the opposition. Thus, we have improved the descriptive accuracy of the model and, at the same time, demonstrated that the results are robust even when our assumptions about party motivations are modified.

The public interest versus partisan interest: the effects of national welfare concerns

Finally, we consider what happens if political actors care not only about their electoral prospects but also about the welfare of the nation. To this point, government and opposition were assumed to value international outcomes only in so far as those outcomes influenced their chances of holding office at some future date. As we saw, these purely office-seeking motivations create a competitive dynamic that has important consequences for the government's ability to misrepresent or credibly reveal its preferences. Both the restraining effect and the confirmatory effect discussed above derive from the inherent conflict of interests engendered by competition for office.

Still, this is a highly cynical view of party motivations, one which assumes that political actors have no concern for the general welfare of the nation. This inattention to the national interest is particularly evident in the incentives of the opposition party, whose highest payoff in the model comes when the government fights a disastrous and costly war. Although it is true that, from the perspective of its electoral chances, this is the best outcome for the opposition party, there is also reason to think that opposition parties might not like this outcome under all circumstances. For example, a war that results in the elimination of the state or its annexation by foreign powers would deprive opposition politicians of their chance to hold office – and possibly of their lives. At a more general level, opposition figures are citizens of the state in addition to being politicians, and as such, they should place some value on the public interest in addition to their more narrow, partisan interest. To the extent that all politicians have such national welfare concerns, the conflict of interests between government and opposition is muted.

As with the policy preferences discussed above, there is good reason to think that introducing "public-spiritedness" will weaken the main results derived from the model with pure competition. In the extreme case in which parties care so much about the international payoff that government and opposition have identical preferences, the opposition's signals provide no additional information, and we are essentially back to the situation modeled in Chapter 2, where the state is a unitary actor. Thus, the strategies of a purely public-spirited opposition are as uninformative as those of a purely pacifist or militarist opposition; while the latter two always oppose or support the use of force, the former always mimics the government. As before, the interesting question is what happens in less extreme cases, when parties pursue both their electoral interest and the public interest. What happens when the opposition has "mixed motives," so that competition with the government is muted, but not eliminated, by some measure of shared concern for the national interest?

National welfare concerns can be captured in the model by assuming that parties' utility depends both on their probability of election and on the state's payoff from the international game. If we let x denote the latter, then

$$U_{gov} = \beta x + (1 - \beta)r(x), \text{ and}$$

$$U_{opp} = \beta x + (1 - \beta)[1 - r(x)],$$

where the β represent how much weight each party gives to the international outcome, and $r(x)$ equals either $r_a(x)$ or $r_d(x)$, depending upon the opposition's stance.[11] The case of $\beta = 0$ is identical to the model considered earlier, in which both parties are purely office-seeking; as a result, their payoffs are perfectly negatively correlated. As β increases from zero, the parties' shared preference for better international outcomes can induce a positive correlation in their payoffs, and in the extreme case of $\beta = 1$, their preferences are identical.

We can explore the effect of national welfare concerns by determining how the equilibrium cutpoints change as a function of β. The main results are depicted in Figure 4.5, with the formal proofs provided in

---

[11] To ensure that the resulting utility functions are well behaved, we have to introduce an additional assumption that r_d and r_a are concave functions. In practice, this means that the marginal electoral benefits diminish as the international outcome increases – or, alternatively, that the marginal electoral costs increase as the outcome gets worse. See Appendix B for details.

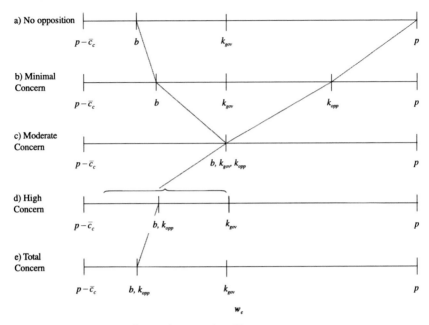

a) No opposition

$p - \bar{c}_c$ b k_{gov} p

b) Minimal Concern

$p - \bar{c}_c$ b k_{gov} k_{opp} p

c) Moderate Concern

$p - \bar{c}_c$ b, k_{gov}, k_{opp} p

d) High Concern

$p - \bar{c}_c$ b, k_{opp} k_{gov} p

e) Total Concern

$p - \bar{c}_c$ b, k_{opp} k_{gov} p

w_c

Fig. 4.5 The effects of national welfare concerns

Appendix B. Panels (b) through (e) show how the equilibrium strategies of the government and opposition change as β increases from zero through four different ranges. For comparison, panel (a) depicts the equilibrium cutpoints of a government without a publicly active opposition. In order to keep this comparison clean, the electoral and international payoffs have been scaled so that the strategy of a government without opposition does not depend on its level of concern for national welfare. Thus, all differences between the top panel and those below are due to the introduction of the opposition party, not the changing values of β.

The contrast between panels (a) and (b) is already familiar. It shows how the introduction of an opposition party reduces the probability of a challenge by the government (i.e., b increases) and creates a range of supported threats that the target state will not resist (i.e., those for which $w_c > k_{opp}$). Equilibria of this form exist not only when the opposition party is purely office-seeking, as it was above, but also for small values of β greater than zero. In this range, when national welfare concerns are relatively low, the basic form of the equilibrium – and all the core results – remain unchanged. As β increases beyond this low range, the restraining and confirmatory effects initially strengthen. Indeed, there is a range of moderate values for which the cutpoints of the government and opposition converge completely at k_{gov}, as shown in panel (c). When this happens, the government only makes genuine threats, and the opposition supports force whenever a challenge is made. The range of types in which the government bluffs – i.e., the interval $[b, k_{gov}]$ – and the range of types in which the opposition opposes genuine threats – i.e., the region $[k_{gov}, k_{opp}]$ – have disappeared. The reason for this pattern is that the opposition has lost its motivation to act irresponsibly. The purely office-seeking opposition has incentives to undercut the government's threat because one of the worst outcomes from the perspective of its electoral chances occurs when the government gets the target to concede a share of the good peacefully. Once the opposition places sufficient value on the national welfare, such foreign policy victories are no longer wholly undesirable, and the incentive to undercut the government in this way disappears. At the same time, the fact that $k_{opp} = k_{gov}$ means that, while the opposition is willing to support all genuine threats, it only supports genuine threats, not bluffs. Because opposition to force would unambiguously signal that a threat was not genuine, the government can no longer bluff in this equilibrium. Thus, moderate levels of concern for national welfare serve to magnify the confirmatory and restraining effects discussed above.

Once β increases beyond this level, however, these effects begin to break down. In particular, once the opposition places sufficient weight on the international payoff, there are conditions under which it would collude with the government in a bluff. That is, once β reaches a certain level, the interests of the government and the opposition are sufficiently aligned that the latter might support a bluff in the hopes of getting the target state to concede the good. Formally, this means that k_{opp} and b move below k_{gov}, as shown in panel (d). When w_c falls between k_{opp} and k_{gov}, any challenge by the government is a bluff, but the public interest in winning the good without a fight outweighs the opposition's electoral interest in exposing the bluff. The result is that the government has more leeway to bluff, because, in this range, there is a chance such a move will succeed. The cost, of course, is that the opposition's support no longer reveals unambiguously that the threat is genuine, since the opposition now supports both genuine threats and some bluffs. As the figure indicates, the model is ambiguous regarding whether b is higher or lower under these conditions than it is in the game without opposition. For the lowest values of β that fall in this range, a democratic government has less leeway to bluff than does a nondemocratic government. While the opposition is willing to support some bluffs, it will only do so if the bluff is very likely to succeed – that is, if the danger of resistance by the target is low. Because the rival state resists more the higher is the probability that a threat is a bluff, the opposition is only willing to go along with bluffs if they are sufficiently rare. Thus, in this range, the opposition still restrains the government to some degree. Moreover, while the opposition's support no longer confirms unambiguously that the threat is genuine, the government's constrained ability to bluff still leads to a lower probability of resistance relative to the case of no opposition.

For the highest values of β, however, these effects break down. Under some conditions which we cannot rule out without additional assumptions about the payoffs, the existence of an opposition might actually make bluffing more attractive and thereby increase the probability of resistance. Once $\beta = 1$, though, even this effect disappears. At this extreme, the interests of the opposition and the government are perfectly aligned, so that the former always mimics the latter, and its strategy reveals nothing. The equilibrium depicted in panel (e) is identical to the case of no opposition party, depicted in panel (a). Thus, once the competition is completely overwhelmed by the parties' shared desire to maximize the international outcome, the introduction of the opposition has no effect on the game. For all intents and purposes, the state speaks with one voice.

This exercise suggests two main conclusions. The first is that, unless the opposition places very high weight on the public interest, all of the effects associated with public competition which we identified above are still present. That is, even if the parties value national welfare in addition to their electoral prospects, the game with an opposition generates a lower rate of bluffing and a lower rate of resistance by the rival state than does the game without an opposition. Depending upon the values of the different parameters, these restraining and confirmatory effects might be weaker or stronger relative to the case of a purely office-seeking opposition. But, except in the highest range of β, they are always present relative to the case of no opposition. As with the introduction of policy preferences, the introduction of national welfare concerns modify the core results of the model, but they eliminate them only in the extreme cases.

The second conclusion is somewhat counterintuitive: From the perspective of the state's ability to prevail in international crises, having a highly public-spirited opposition is not necessarily a good thing. Recall that the confirmatory effect – the lower probability of resistance by the target state in the response to supported threats – derives from the conflict of interests between the government and the opposition. The opposition's signal is informative precisely because it has no incentive to collude in a bluff. Once the opposition party values the public interest in addition to its electoral interests, then it gains an incentive to collude in some bluffs. This gives the government greater leeway to bluff, but it also means that supported challenges are no longer as credible as they once were. As a result, the probability of resistance by the rival state can increase as β increases. Ironically, the greater the opposition values the public interest, the less useful it may become in furthering that interest.

Conclusion

In the conclusion to Chapter 2, I noted that the search for peace involves a search for credibility and that two things were necessary for the latter: constraints on the ability to engage in deception and/or mechanisms for ensuring that genuine threats are believed. This chapter showed how public competition between domestic actors can generate both of these effects. Credible information revelation and a lower probability of war result from the introduction of a second actor capable of sending informative signals and from the adjustments that the government has to make in the face of this. The existence of an opposition party makes possible what we have referred to as confirmatory signaling – that is, signals that enhance the credibility of certain threats by essentially verifying that they are genuine. As long as the opposition party places sufficient weight on its desire to hold office, the resultant conflict of interests between it and the government ensures that it will rarely collude in a bluff. Since the opposition generally supports the use of force only when the expected payoff from war to voters is sufficiently high, doing so serves as independent confirmation of the government's resolve.

At the same time, a government that has to contend with open competition makes adjustments in its strategies that also lend credibility to its threats. As we saw, public opposition to the use of force calls into question the genuineness of a threat. When the rival state views such opposition, it revises downward its estimate of the government's resolve. If the government were to leave its strategy unchanged, this would mean that, although supported threats were more credible than those made by a unitary, nondemocratic government, opposed threats would be less credible and hence resisted at a higher rate. In equilibrium, however, a democratic government lowers the rate at which it bluffs in order to preserve the credibility of opposed threats. As a result, supported threats are more credible than threats made by a nondemocratic government, and opposed threats are no less credible. Thus, the interaction between government and opposition generates both constraints on deception and mechanisms for bolstering the credibility of genuine threats. On average, then, democratic states challenge at a lower rate than do nondemocratic states, and their challenges are resisted at a lower rate. The probability that the dispute will become a crisis that eventually escalates to war is consequently lower.

All of these results depend upon an assumption about institutions and an assumption about party behavior. The institutional assumption defines the rules of political competition – in particular, that it takes place in public, so that the positions of contending parties are observable to foreign states, that it is unfettered by restrictions on dissent, and that parties out of power are not excluded from the political process to the point where they have no access to relevant information. The behavioral assumption is that political parties care about holding office – a motivation that generates a conflict of interests between those in power and those out of power. This conflict is necessary to ensure that the signals of the opposition party are informative. As we saw, distinctive policy orientations or concerns about national welfare water down this conflict and make the opposition's signals informative under a more limited set of conditions. However, as long as an appreciable element of office-seeking is present – that is, as long as policy preferences are not so extreme nor national welfare concerns so strong – then competition among political parties within the institutional framework of democracy mitigates the dilemmas and dangers of asymmetric information.

Considering a richer set of party motivations makes the game more complex but does not undermine the fundamental results. A question that arises from this exercise, though, is: how can we know which of the many panels in Figures 4.3 to 4.5 we are really in? What values of α and β generally hold in the real world? Do target states have reasonable enough estimates of these parameters to interpret the signals they receive? The answer to these questions is primarily empirical rather than theoretical, and the empirical validity of the model's predictions is the subject of the next three chapters. For now, though, we can at least make a *prima facie* case that national welfare concerns and policy biases are not so extreme that they eliminate meaningful variation in opposition parties' strategies. If opposition parties' concerns about national welfare were overwhelming, then we would not see instances of dissent. Instead, the government and opposition would always speak with one voice. Given that this is not true empirically, it is unlikely that β, the parameter describing the alignment of interests between government and opposition, is systematically close to one. Similarly, if hawkish or dovish biases were sufficiently intense, then we would not expect to see much variation in a given party's position from one crisis to the next. This too is contradicted empirically, as we will see over the next few chapters. While parties of the left do account for most of the cases of dissent identified here, many of the same parties have supported the use of force in other cases. Finally, do the targets of threats by democratic states interpret the signals in manner that is consistent with the argument presented here? This is one of the empirical questions to which we now turn.

Part II
Empirical analysis

What can we learn from the informational perspective on democracy developed in the preceding chapters? As noted at the outset of this study, interest in the democratic peace has generated a large number of studies exploring the empirical relationship between democracy and conflict behavior. Hence, any new perspective on this topic has to show that it generates new, previously unanticipated empirical regularities and that it provides a better accounting for these regularities than do existing theories. The purpose of this second part of the book is to do precisely that. The empirical tests probe the theory's predictions from two different levels of analysis. The hypotheses tested in Chapter 5 are at the level of regime type. They explore how the effects identified here influence the overall relationship between domestic institutions and observable crisis outcomes. While the crisis game can play out in many different ways depending upon the exact circumstances, domestic institutions pattern behavior in ways that generate effects "on average." The statistical tests seek evidence of such effects over a large number of observations. The hypotheses tested in the two subsequent chapters are at the level of strategies. Using a mixture of statistical and historical analysis, they explore how the strategies of government and opposition within democratic states influence one another and decision makers in other states. Thus, while the tests in Chapter 5 focus on the differences between democracies and nondemocracies, those in Chapters 6 and 7 focus on the differences between supported threats and opposed threats, unity and dissent.

5 Selective threats, effective threats: the initiation and escalation of international crises

The empirical analysis in this chapter centers around two effects which the informational perspective emphasizes: what I have referred to as the restraining and confirmatory effects. The restraining effect stems from the fact that governments that lack the ability to monopolize private information are less able to exploit information asymmetries through deception and bluff. Transparency and public competition mean that democratic governments face substantial constraints on their ability to make threats which they cannot or do not intend to carry out. The result, as we will see, is that governments so constrained are less likely to make militarized challenges against other states than are governments that have more leeway to engage in deceptive behavior.

The confirmatory effect goes hand in hand with this restraining effect. In the narrow sense in which we used this term in Chapter 4, the confirmatory effect stems from the existence of a second information source – the opposition party – whose interests conflict with those of the government. This second signaler can credibly confirm the genuineness of the government's threat and thereby increase the likelihood that the rival state will back down. At a more general level, the confirmatory effect stems from the fact that, if a government is constrained from bluffing, then the threats which it does choose to make are more likely to be genuine than are the threats made by a government not similarly constrained. As a result, the target of a challenge from a democratic state should be less likely to resist than should the target of a threat made by a nondemocratic state. Moreover, the two effects combined lead us to predict that democratic states are less likely to initiate crises that end in war or to be the targets of such crises. Thus, the restraining and confirmatory effects operate together to produce the pattern foreshadowed by the title of this chapter: selective threats, effective threats.

This chapter uses the theoretical model to derive six predictions relating regime type to three dependent variables: the probability that a state will initiate a challenge against another, the probability that the target of a challenge will choose to resist or take steps to escalate the crisis, and the probability of war. It then tests these hypotheses using data sets that cover 170 states from 1816 to 1984 and include information on roughly 1800 international crises. The main results are strongly supportive of my theory and especially those predictions dealing with the effect of democracy in potential or actual challengers. In particular, I estimate:

(1) Holding everything else constant, if a country switches from a nondemocracy to a democracy, the probability that it initiates a militarized challenge decreases by a third to a half; the probability that it becomes the target of such a challenge generally increases, as much as doubling in some cases.

(2) Threats made by democratic initiators are 30 percent less likely to be met by militarized resistance than threats by nondemocratic initiators. This reduction is equivalent to what happens if the initiator switches from a minor to a major power.

(3) If a country switches from a nondemocracy to democracy, the probability that it initiates a crisis that then escalates to war decreases by roughly 40 percent to 60 percent.

Not only are these findings consistent with my theory, but they cannot be adequately explained by the alternative perspectives considered here.

From theoretical model to empirical predictions

In this section, I use the theoretical models developed in the previous chapters to derive testable hypotheses regarding the effect of domestic political institutions on crisis behaviors and outcomes. After first spelling out the main predictions of my argument, I then briefly sketch out how these differ from the predictions of the institutional constraints and normative approaches. Though the purpose of this chapter is not to falsify these other approaches, it is necessary to ensure that the results cannot be accounted for by the causal mechanisms they highlight.

The informational perspective

The main results of the informational perspective were developed in Chapter 4. Consider first the probability that the challenger will initiate a threat. Democracy in the potential challenger decreases the *ex ante* probability of a challenge. This follows from the fact that democratic governments have a harder time bluffing given the incentives that opposition parties have to oppose threats that rest on weak political support. Because nondemocratic governments do not face this same constraint, probability of a challenge from a democratic state is less than the probability of a challenge by a nondemocratic state, all other things being equal. This suggests:

> **Hypothesis 1:** Democratic institutions decrease the probability that a state will initiate a challenge.

We also saw that democratic states can make attractive targets because of their constraints. Potential challengers know that democratic targets cannot as easily resist a bluff with a bluff, so the expected value of challenging a democracy is higher than the expected value of challenging a nondemocracy. The caveat here is that the regime type of the target influences the game under a more limited set of conditions than does the regime type of the challenger because the latter has greater strategic flexibility. Thus, this relationship, and all others dealing with democracy in the target, is predicted to hold only weakly. This suggests:

> **Hypothesis 2:** Democratic institutions (weakly) increase the probability that a state will be the target of a challenge.

Next consider the probability that a target state will resist given that it has been challenged. We saw in Chapter 4 that a threat supported by the government's domestic adversary is more credible than a threat sent by the government alone. As a result, the target state is less likely to resist a supported threat made by a democratic government than it is to resist either an opposed threat made by a democratic government or a threat made by a nodemocratic government. In Chapter 6, we will use a smaller data set to examine more closely the distinction between supported and opposed threats; there, we can show that the threats made by democratic governments enjoy a higher success rate primarily when they are supported by major opposition parties. Here, we simply make a statistical prediction: because there is some probability that a democratic government's threat will be supported and because that support lowers the probability of resistance relative to what nondemocratic challengers encounter, the probability of resistance must be lower, on average, for democratic challengers. Thus,

> **Hypothesis 3:** The targets of threats by democratic states are less likely to resist than are the targets of threats by nondemocratic states.

What if the target is democratic? Just as the restraining effect reduces the probability that a democratic challenger will issue a threat, so too does it reduce the probability that a democratic target will resist a challenge by force. Whereas nondemocratic targets may have occasion to bluff in response to a threat, democracies have less leeway to do so. Again, recognizing that regime effects may be less pronounced when looking at targets, this suggests:

> **Hypothesis 4:** Democratic targets are (weakly) less likely to resist threats than are nondemocratic targets.

Finally, we saw that the *ex ante* probability of war is lower when the challenger is democratic. Recall that the probability of war equals the probability that a challenger will make a genuine threat multiplied by the probability of resistance. Since we have assumed that democratic and nondemocratic governments do not differ systematically in the distribution of types, the first term is the same for both kinds of polity. What differs is the probability of resistance, which is lower, on average, for democratic challengers. Hence,

> **Hypothesis 5:** Democratic institutions lower the probability that a state will initiate a crisis that escalates to war.

The important thing to point out about this prediction is that it deals with the *ex ante* probability of war, *not* with the probability of crisis escalation given a challenge. On this point, the informational argument is ambiguous.

Similar logic applies to the target. Because democratic targets are less likely to resist threats, and because their resistance generally sends a more credible signal of resolve, the danger of war should be lower in this case. Thus,

> **Hypothesis 6:** Democratic institutions lower the probability that a state becomes the target of a crisis that escalates to war.

Alternative theories

The institutional constraints perspective suggests that democratic governments incur higher costs of war, on average, than do their non-democratic counterparts. As we saw in Chapter 2, a plausible way to capture this approach within the crisis bargaining model is to assume that democratic states expect to incur some additional costs of war. The derivation of this model and the resulting comparative-static predictions were discussed in Chapter 2 and depicted in Figure 2.4, so I will simply reiterate the results laid out there. If democracy increases the costs of war, then, all other things equal, a democratic government is less likely to initiate a crisis and more likely to become the target of a challenge. Thus, the informational and institutional constraints arguments make identical predictions regarding the effect of democracy on the probability of a challenge. The two perspectives also agree that democratic targets should be less likely to resist threats.

Where the two differ most dramatically is in their predictions about the response of the target when challenged by a democracy. The institutional constraints argument suggests that democratic leaders face risks in waging war that their nondemocratic counterparts do not. If so, then this effect should figure into the expectations of the target state, raising doubts about a democratic challenger's willingness to carry through on the threat if the target were to resist. The threats of a democratic leader are inherently more suspect than threats of a leader who is not similarly constrained from waging war; as a result, targets are more likely to resist the former than the latter.

Finally, as we saw in Chapter 2, the influence of the challenger's regime type on the *ex ante* probability of war is ambiguous. Although an increase in the costs of war does make the challenger less likely to be in a position to make a genuine threat, the higher rate of resistance by the target can counteract this effect. Thus, the institutional constraints perspective does not seem to make a clear prediction in this case. With respect to the target's regime type, the model suggests that higher costs of war do indeed lower the probability of war by reducing the target's motivation to resist.

The normative perspective argues that democracies enjoy a special relationship engendered by norms of mutual respect and nonviolence. Because of its emphasis on *shared* norms and values, this approach emphasizes the absence of conflict in dyads in which both states are democratic. While some in this tradition have suggested that liberal norms impel democracies to challenge nondemocracies (Doyle 1986) and others have suggested that autocratic states like to exploit democracies (Russett 1993), this perspective offers no strong and consistent claims about what happens when we introduce democracy in one state but not the other. Hence, unlike the predictions made above, those of the normative perspective deal with the effects of democracy in both the potential challenger and the target. The arguments of this school are unambiguous that shared democracy should decrease the probability of a challenge and the probability of war. With respect to the

Table 5.1. *Comparing the predictions of three perspectives on democracy*

| Outcome | Informational | | Institutional Constraints | | Normative |
	Challenger	Target	Challenger	Target	Challenger & Target
Challenge	−	+	−	+	−
	(Hypothesis 1)	(Hypothesis 2)			
Resistance	−	−	+	−	−
	(Hypothesis 3)	(Hypothesis 4)			
War	−	−	+ / −	−	−
	(Hypothesis 5)	(Hypothesis 6)			

probability of resistance, we find no explicit mention of this dependent variable in this literature, but we can nonetheless deduce a plausible hypothesis. A central tenet of this perspective is that liberal states consider the demands of fellow liberal states to be legitimate, in the sense that they flow from the will of the people. It follows that the probability of resistance should be lowest when the crisis involves two such states. Moreover, in the actual operationalization of this dependent variable, we will focus particularly on the incidence of militarized resistance – that is, responses by the target that tend to escalate the crisis militarily. Given that normative theory identifies a norm against violent conflict resolution, it is again plausible to deduce that this theory predicts a lower probability of resistance when both target and challenger are democratic.

Table 5.1 summarizes the comparative-static predictions of the three different perspectives. Entries in the table show, for each perspective and each observable outcome, how the predicted probability of the outcome changes when the challenger and/or target becomes democratic. The first thing that is evident from this table is that the probability of resistance is an excellent dependent variable for discriminating between the informational and institutional constraints perspectives and, to a lesser extent, for discriminating between the informational and normative perspectives (Schultz 1999). Whereas the informational story developed here predicts that democratic challengers should enjoy a lower probability of resistance, the institutional constraints argument suggests the opposite. Moreover, the informational theory predicts that democratic challengers enjoy a lower probability of resistance regardless of the

regime type of the target, whereas the normative perspective only anticipates such an effect when the target is also democratic. This distinction
between monadic and dyadic effects gives us leverage for distinguishing
between the normative and informational theories with other dependent
variables as well. Although both of these theories predict that democratic
states are less likely to make challenges, the normative argument suggests that this effect is only evident in jointly democratic dyads. The
informational perspective, on the other hand, predicts a general restraining effect that is not conditional on the regime type of the target. The
same is true of the *ex ante* probability of war.

Of course, lurking in the background of all of these predictions is the
null hypothesis associated with realist theory: that domestic institutions
have no systematic effect on international outcomes. In addition to providing this null hypothesis, realism also suggests alternative factors that
should explain variation in our dependent variables – in particular,
states' power and strategic interests. All of the empirical models will
include a battery of variables designed to control for and assess the
influence of these factors.

Democracy and the initiation of international crises

The data used for testing these hypotheses come from several pre-existing data sets that are widely employed in the quantitative study of international relations. Most of the data were collected under the auspices of
the Correlates of War (COW) project, which has produced a number of
data sets on interstate conflicts and wars, national capabilities, and
formal alliances. The second major data source is the Polity project,
whose codings of regime characteristics have become a standard in the
discipline. Together, these data sets provide information on over 170
countries for the period 1816–1992. Hence, they permit tests using a
large number of countries and across a long period of time.[1]

The data used for creating the dependent variables come from COW's
Militarized Interstate Dispute (MID) data set, as described by Gochman
and Maoz (1984) and Jones, Bremer, and Singer (1996). MIDs are events
in which at least one state took militarized action against at least one

---

[1] Much of the work merging the various data sets was done with the aid of *EUGene:
Expected Utility Generation and Data Management Program* (version 1.19), created by Bennett
and Stam (2000). I am very grateful to them for creating this marvelous resource and for
their help in using it.

other state, where such action can take the form of a threat, display, or actual use of force. To be classified as a MID, the militarized action has to be authorized by the government of a state, clearly directed at another state, and public in nature (Jones, Bremer, and Singer 1996, pp. 169–70). The events described in the data set range from large-scale wars to minor, often obscure, incidents. They include all interstate wars, all the prominent crises short of war – such as the Cuban Missile Crisis, the Berlin blockade, the Agadir crisis, etc. – as well as many events that are largely unknown because they did not escalate to any appreciable level of force. This wide coverage is desirable from the standpoint of our tests, since we are interested in all cases in which states used threats of force, regardless of how prominent or how severe the ensuing crisis eventually became. The MID data set gives us the full population of such events. This set contains information on 2042 disputes in the period 1816–1992; once the availability of other data is taken into account, the tests in this chapter cover 1785 disputes in the period 1816–1984.

The dependent variable: crisis initiation

Tests of hypotheses 1 and 2 require a dependent variable indicating the probability that a state initiates a crisis against another. In creating such a dependent variable, we need to take into account several considerations. For each pair of states, we are interested in how their respective regime characteristics affect the likelihood that one will challenge the other in a given time period. Because there is no *a priori* criterion for determining which state in a dyad is the challenger and which is the target, we have to allow for either state to make a challenge against the other in any given time period. The appropriate unit of analysis, therefore, is the "directed dyad," or uniquely ordered pair of states. In a directed dyad set-up, we distinguish between the dyad Britain–France and the dyad France–Britain, since, in each time period, either state could choose to challenge the other. The second consideration is that, since most of the independent variables are coded annually, the same should be true of the dependent variable. Thus, each observation corresponds to a "directed dyad-year." This means, for example, that we have one observation on the Britain–France directed dyad for each year in which both states were members of the international system and one observation on the France–Britain dyad for each of those years as well. This set-up permits us to model the probability of a challenge by any state against any other in every year as a function of the relevant independent variables.

Using the MID data set, we create the variable INITIATE$_{ijt}$ which indicates, for each directed dyad-year, whether or not state i initiated a crisis against state j in year t. Details on how this coding was determined are given in Appendix C.[2] One issue that we have to be wary of in this and subsequent tests is that not all crisis initiations take place by one state against one state. In a number of cases, there is more than one state on the initiating and/or target side. The proportion of such cases is rather small: only 139 disputes out of 1785, or 8 percent. Once the MIDs are rendered as dyads, however, they account for almost 20 percent of dispute dyads. These multilateral disputes introduce non-independence among observations. For example, in the 1936 crisis over the remilitarization of the Rhineland, Germany is coded as initiating a MID against both France and Belgium; it is implausible that the decision to initiate against France was independent of the decision to initiate against Belgium. While there is no perfect way to deal with this problem in this context, we can perform tests to determine whether multilateral MIDs unduly influence the results. In particular, for each MID, we can identify the state on each side with the greatest military capabilities. Following Dixon (1994), we can then collapse each MID into a bilateral affair by restricting our attention to the dyad containing the most powerful states on each side, coding INITIATE as missing in the other dispute dyads.[3] I will discuss the results of this exercise below.

The independent variables: defining democracy

The main independent variables in all regression models are those which indicate, for each state in each observation, whether or not that state was democratic. The problem of how to arrive at such a coding is not a trivial one, as evidenced by the ongoing debate in the democratic peace literature over how states should be classified (e.g., Russett 1993; Ray 1995; Layne 1994; Oren 1995). Although the difference between democracies and autocracies is obvious at the extremes – no one would contest that the United States was democratic in 1950 and the Soviet Union was not – there are gray areas in the middle. Democracy is, by its nature, a multifaceted phenomenon. States that have all of the qualities we associate with democracy – free and regular elections, unfettered competition, civil and political rights, extensive franchise, etc. – are easy

---

[2] See Appendix C for additional considerations in the coding of this variable.

[3] In the tests on the other dependent variables, I will deal with multilateral MIDs by throwing them out of the sample entirely. In this context, however, the rarity of crisis initiations argues for keeping multilateral MIDs in some form.

to classify, as are states that have none of them. States possessing some but not all of these qualities, on the other hand, leave room for debate. This ambiguity has been particularly salient in this literature because how one treats borderline cases has important consequences for the claim that there have been no wars between democratic states. Was Spain a democracy in 1898? If so, the Spanish–American War is a war between democracies. Was Germany democratic in 1914? If so, then World War I is a glaring exception to the democratic peace. The persistence of this debate is due in large part to the fact that the democratic peace first rose to prominence as an empirical claim, rather than as an implication of a theory. Once the claim had been made, it was only natural for critics to find ambiguities in the coding of certain cases.

When testing deductive theory, the preferred way of proceeding is first to specify the causal mechanisms underlying a hypothesized relationship and then to code the independent variables in a manner that best captures the concepts identified by the theory. The theory developed here suggests that the main consideration is whether or not a state's political institutions permit stable and open competition for political office. There must be toleration, and indeed recognition, of parties or factions that do not currently control the government, institutions that make it possible for those parties to displace the current governing party, and some expectation that such displacement might happen. These conditions are necessary for the payoff structure assumed in Chapter 4 to be appropriate. Recall that these specifications reflect the fact that the government and opposition are engaged in a zero-sum game: anything that increases the probability that one will win office necessarily decreases the corresponding probability for the other. This assumption requires that these probabilities be relatively elastic, not fixed due to institutional restrictions. Moreover, the assumption that the parties are sensitive to voter reaction at some future election requires that the polity be sufficiently stable that this future election, the rules under which it will take place, and the main parties or factions that will contest it, are reasonably predictable. Finally, opposition parties must have access to resources that permit them to gather information about state policy and voter preferences. All of these features are generally associated with democracy but need not, on their own, make a polity democratic by ideal standards. Rather than argue over this ideal standard, or attempt to classify states according to it, I will instead code states according to whether or not they possess the characteristics identified by the theory.

The data used for creating a coding based on these criteria come from *Polity III: Regime Change and Political Authority*, a data set which contains information on regime characteristics for every state in the international system over the period 1800–1994 (Jaggers and Gurr 1996; see also Gurr, Jaggers, and Moore 1989). For each state in each year, the data set codes the state's political system along a number of dimensions, including competitiveness and openness of executive recruitment, the regulation and competitiveness of political participation, the degree of constraints on executive decision making, and so forth.

Given the theory's emphasis on public contestation, two sets of variables stand out as particularly germane: the competitiveness of executive recruitment and the regulation and competitiveness of political participation. The first variable records the mechanism by which executives are chosen – that is, are they elected through a competitive process or selected by hereditary succession, designation, or rigged elections? A coding also exists for dual executives – such as in constitutional monarchies – in which one is chosen by heredity and the other by election (Gurr, Jaggers, and Moore 1989, pp. 10–11). The second set of variables, those measuring the regulation and competitiveness of political participation, captures the degree to which competition for office is institutionalized and the extent to which alternative preferences can be pursued. Polities range from those in which all oppositional activity is suppressed to those exhibiting stable competition between political groups (*ibid.* 1989, pp. 17–19).

Using these variables, a polity was coded as "competitive" if it met two criteria: (1) the executive was chosen through competitive elections, including cases of dual executives in which one executive was selected in this manner, and (2) competition was characterized by "relatively stable and enduring political groups which regularly compete for political influence at the national level" (*ibid.* 1989, pp. 17–19).[4] A listing of the countries that received this designation, along with the years in which they qualified, is provided in Appendix C. Countries were coded as noncompetitive if their executive was selected by heredity or rigged elections, if competition for political office was restricted or suppressed,

---

[4] In terms of the Polity III data set, these criteria mean that XRCOMP was coded as 2 or 3 and PARREG was coded as 2 or 5. Although it was not obvious how to deal with cases of dual executives, these were coded as competitive polities for the purposes of the tests reported below. Tests were performed coding countries with dual executives as noncompetitive, and many of the results dealing with regime type increased in magnitude and significance.

or if competition was not institutionalized in stable patterns. In what follows, I will continue to use the terms "democracy" and "nondemocracy" as shorthand expressions for states with and without competitive political institutions.

Additional independent variables

In addition to the regime indicators, the regression models include a number of independent variables designed to control for other factors which are known or suspected to affect the propensity of states to initiate crises. A further elaboration of these variables, along with data sources and coding rules, can be found in Appendix C. In brief, all regression models include two sets of additional control variables. The first set captures the absolute and relative power of the states in the dyad. The military power which each state can bring to bear influences both the amount of interaction between those states and the expected outcome of war. A high level of military capabilities and resources is a strong predictor of crisis and war involvement (Bremer 1980, 1992; Small and Singer 1982). States with the ability to project power globally tend to define their interests globally, and hence their opportunity to get into conflicts with others increases. In addition, the relative balance of military power in a dyad also influences the states' expected value for war going into a crisis. These factors are captured in three different ways:

(1) *Power status*: Using a conventional distinction between major and minor powers, three dummy variables indicate whether or not the initiator and/or target were major powers.

(2) *Balance of military capabilities*: A continuous variable indicates how balanced the military capabilities of the two states were.

(3) *Initiator's share of capabilities*: A continuous variable indicates the share of dyadic military capabilities possessed by the potential initiator.

Standard realist arguments and previous findings make two predictions about the effect of these indicators on crisis initiation. First, the weaker state in the dyad is less likely to initiate a crisis than is the stronger state, suggesting that the probability of crisis initiation should increase with the initiator's share of capabilities and major power status. Second, conflict is more likely in relatively balanced dyads than in unbalanced dyads.[5]

---

[5] Though there has long been a debate among realists as to whether conflict is more likely in balanced or unbalanced dyads, the vast weight of empirical evidence suggests that balance is a strong predictor of crisis and war onset (see, e.g., Bremer 1992, 1993).

A second set of variables captures the similarity of strategic interests and potential sources of conflict within the dyad. These are measured in three different ways:

(1) *Territorial contiguity*: A dummy variable indicates whether or not the states shared a land border or were separated by less than 150 miles of water.

(2) *Similarity of alliance portfolios*: A continuous variable indicates how similar the two states' alliance portfolios were, a proxy for the similarity of strategic interests in the dyad.

(3) *Status quo evaluations*: For each state, a continuous variable measures the similarity of that state's alliance portfolio with that of the most powerful state in the system (Great Britain until 1945, the United States thereafter), a proxy for the state's satisfaction with the international status quo.

Numerous empirical studies have shown that territorial contiguity is a strong predictor of crises and wars (e.g., Vasquez 1995; Bremer 1992). Moreover, realist arguments suggest that dissimilarity of strategic interests and dissatisfaction with the status quo should increase the likelihood of initiating crises (Gowa 1999; Schweller 1996; Lemke and Reed 1996).

Estimation technique

A central difficulty in testing the restraining effect is that any such test requires good controls for factors that are exogenous to the theory. The crisis bargaining models used throughout this book are predicated on the assumption that there exists some good over which the two states have some dispute. As a theoretical matter, it is no stretch to posit the existence of a dispute: unless states have identical preferences, there is always something about which they can disagree. As an empirical matter, however, we know that some pairs of states have more divergent interests – and hence the potential for more serious disputes – than do others. During the late nineteenth and early twentieth centuries, Germany and France had incompatible claims regarding their common border, claims that generated a number of crises and wars between the countries. During the period of American westward expansion, the United States had severe conflicts of interest with Mexico, Spain, and Great Britain, all of which led to the brink of war or beyond. On the other hand, the United States and Canada, during most of this century, have had few disagreements so severe that the use of force could be considered a viable option. Likewise, Lebanon and Paraguay, by virtue of their vast separation and small size, have had nothing to contest between them. This variation in the degree to which states' interests conflict creates a complication for any empirical test of the restraining effect, which, like all comparative-static predictions, rests on the caveat that all other things must be equal.

While all statistical tests depend upon adequate controls, this problem is particularly pressing when testing hypotheses on crisis initiation. While the theoretical result deals with the effect of regime type on the probability of a challenge per interaction, our data can only assess the effect of regime type on the probability of a challenge per year. The problem is that some pairs of states have very dense relationships with a high frequency of interaction, while others interact much less frequently on a small number of issues. Holding constant the probability that any given disagreement will lead to a crisis, there will be a higher probability of a crisis in the first dyad than in the second. Likewise, if there is some factor that dampens the probability of a challenge in the first dyad, the effect of this factor may not appear in the yearly data if we do not adequately control for the higher frequency of interaction.

Thus, if there is systematic variation in the level of conflict and the frequency of interaction within dyads, then separating regime effects from these other influences is problematic. Ideally, this variation would be captured by control variables like those discussed above. These variables are rather crude, however, and we have to admit the possibility that they leave some of the relevant heterogeneity across dyads unmeasured. If this unmeasured heterogeneity is correlated with regime type of one or both states in the dyad, then there is a danger of biasing our estimates of whether and how regime type matters.

The solution I employ here is blunt, but effective. I assume that the unmeasured heterogeneity across units can be captured by including "fixed effects" in the empirical model. This means that the models effectively include one dummy variable for every directed dyad in the sample. For example, there is a dummy variable called US–Britain that is set to one for all observations on this directed dyad and zero otherwise. If there are unmeasured factors which systematically affect the probability that the US challenges Britain, then this variable will pick up those factors. By including one such variable for every directed dyad in the sample, we can determine the effect of the states' regime type independent of these factors.

Because the implications of using the fixed-effects treatment may not be familiar to all readers, a more complete discussion and justification of this technique is provided in Appendix C (see also Stimson 1985; Green, Kim, and Yoon 2000). Several brief comments are worth making here. Because this technique uses dummy variables to pick up much of the variation across units, the estimates are heavily dependent upon variation across time in both the independent and dependent variables. For this reason, directed dyads which experienced no initiations – and thus exhibit no variation across time in the dependent variable – do not contribute to the estimates: they are effectively dropped from the analysis. Similarly, because the fixed-effect dummy variables pick up the effects of any factor that is constant over time in the dyad, these models tend not to attribute much causal importance to independent variables that change little from year to year. Because regime type is one such variable, the fixed-effect technique is very conservative with respect to our hypotheses. For example, if a potential challenger is democratic for the entire period, and it never makes a challenge against the potential target, this technique forces us to assume that the absence of conflict was due to unmeasured heterogeneity captured in the fixed-effect term, not to the challenger's regime type.

Finally, this method assumes that the heterogeneity across units is fixed over time. Unlike measures of power status, contiguity, or alliance portfolios, the dummy variable takes on the same value for all observations on the directed dyad. Thus, if there are factors that make Germany very likely to challenge France in one period, and these factors disappear at some later date, the Germany–France dummy variable cannot capture this change. One solution to this problem is to divide the entire sample into smaller subsamples. In doing so, we have to manage an important trade-off. On the one hand, because estimates obtained using this method are highly dependent upon variation over time in both the dependent and independent variables, there is a virtue in having long time series. On the other hand, the assumption that heterogeneity is fixed over time becomes less plausible the longer the period covered. Since methodological considerations do not dictate the optimal solution to this problem, I instead fall back on a theoretical rationale. Neorealist theory suggests that different international structures lead to systematically different patterns of conflict (Waltz 1979; Gowa 1999). This suggests that a good break point in the time series is in 1945, separating the multipolar structure of the pre-Cold War period from the bipolar structure of the Cold War.[6]

The regression models were estimated using a conditional logit model, which is similar to the familiar logit model for dichotomous dependent variables but is particularly well suited for the fixed-effects treatment (Chamberlain 1980; Hamerle and Ronning 1995). In brief, the conditional logit permits us to estimate the regression equation as if we included the fixed-effect dummy variables but without actually estimating coefficients for each of those variables.[7] As discussed in Appendix C, the fixed effects were initially introduced in two different ways. Dyad fixed effects assume that the unmeasured heterogeneity affects both states in the dyad equally; directed dyad fixed effects assume that the heterogeneity affects each state in the dyad differently. Specification tests showed that, in every model estimated below: (a) there was unmeasured heterogeneity across units, implying that the fixed-effect technique is justified, and (b) directed dyad fixed effects picked up additional heterogeneity that was not captured by dyad fixed effects. Hence, the results reported here use directed dyad fixed effects.[8]

Results

The main results are presented in Table 5.2. As mentioned earlier, the sample was divided into two time periods: pre-Cold War (1816–1945) and Cold War (1946–80). In the first sample, a complication arises in dealing with the years of general warfare associated with the two world wars. While the years 1914–18 and 1939–45 make up only 7 percent of years covered in the data set, they account for over 16 percent of all dispute initiations. There is good reason to believe that many of these

[6] An argument might be made that the pre-World War I period should be treated separately from the inter-war period (Gowa 1999). The difficulty this presents for the present analysis is that, prior to 1880, only three states (the United States, France, and Switzerland) were democratic and involved in at least one crisis (and France is coded as democratic for only two years in that period). Between 1880 and 1913 a number of additional states make the transition, but the number of years in which we can observe the effect of the shift are quite few. Hence, pooling the inter-war and pre-war periods not only provides greater variation on the main independent variables, since many more states shift to democracies in this period, but also permits us to explore a longer time series after these earlier transitions. Tests performed isolating the pre-World War I period confirm that the effects of regime type are less robust in this sample.

[7] The conditional logit was implemented using the logit function in Stata 6.0 (StataCorp 1999).

[8] All models also contain controls for time dependence suggested by Beck, Katz, and Tucker (1998). See Appendix C for details.

Table 5.2. *The probability of crisis initiation*

Variable	Pre-Cold War		Cold War (3)
	(1) World wars included[†]	(2) World wars excluded	
Regime Indicators			
Democratic Initiator	−0.49 (0.17)[c]	−0.48 (0.19)[b]	−0.79 (0.28)[c]
Democratic Target	0.39 (0.17)[b]	0.92 (0.22)[c]	0.09 (0.25)
Both Democratic	−0.83 (0.34)[b]	−1.13 (0.43)[c]	0.51 (0.36)
Power Indicators			
Major Power Initiator- Major Power Target	−0.07 (0.32)	−0.53 (0.39)	−0.86 (1.30)
Major Power Initiator- Minor Power Target	0.23 (0.21)	0.14 (0.26)	0.23 (1.23)
Minor Power Initiator- Major Power Target	−0.96 (0.29)[c]	−1.87 (0.48)[c]	−1.04 (1.12)
Balance of Capabilities	0.70 (0.28)[b]	1.29 (0.32)[c]	1.02 (0.49)[b]
Initiator's Share of Capabilities	−0.56 (0.46)	−0.87 (0.53)[a]	3.23 (0.94)[c]
Interest Indicators			
Contiguous	0.33 (0.26)	0.13 (0.33)	1.91 (0.52)[c]
Alliance Portfolio Similarity	−0.52 (0.15)[c]	−0.32 (0.25)	−0.64 (0.34)[a]
Status Quo Evaluation of Initiator	−0.13 (0.17)	−0.79 (0.28)[c]	−0.68 (0.39)[a]
Status Quo Evaluation of Target	0.12 (0.16)	0.46 (0.27)[a]	0.0039 (0.40)
χ^2	428.67[c]	163.19[c]	152.54[c]
Number of observations	22,904	15,033	10,082

Notes:
Estimates obtained using a conditional, fixed-effects logit model. Standard errors reported in parentheses. Coefficients on PEACEYRS cubic spline not reported (see Appendix C).
[†] Dummy variables for world war years included but coefficients not reported.
[a] $0.10 > p > 0.05$
[b] $0.05 > p > 0.01$
[c] $p < 0.01$

disputes were offshoots of the world wars and would not have taken place in their absence. To deal with this problem, tests were conducted in two ways. First, dummy variables were included to capture the years associated with World War I and World War II; these controls help capture the systematic increase in the probability of a dispute during these years. Second, the tests were also conducted excluding these years altogether. As is evident, the basic findings do not depend upon which treatment was used.

As predicted by hypothesis 1, the coefficient on "Democratic Initiator" is negative and significant at conventional levels in all models. The probability of crisis initiation clearly decreases when the potential initiator is democratic.[9] Hypothesis 2 also finds support in the data, as the coefficient on "Democratic Target" is consistently positive, though it is statistically significant only in the pre-Cold War sample. As noted earlier, the theoretical model gives reason to believe that the target's regime type influences the probability of a challenge under a more limited set of conditions than does the initiator's regime type. The insignificance of this coefficient in the Cold War sample may reflect the weaker relationship underlying this hypothesis.

The coefficient on "Democratic Target" is also sensitive to the presence of multilateral MIDs. As noted earlier, the fact that some MIDs involve more than one dyad introduces nonindependent initiations in several directed dyads. After collapsing these cases into bilateral events as described above, I re-ran all the estimations. The results are remarkably stable, with the exception of one: the effect of democracy in the target in the pre-Cold War period. This coefficient is the only one that moves by more than one standard error when multilateral MIDs are collapsed. The effect of this change is to cut the estimated coefficient by a factor of four when the world wars are included and a factor of two when they are not; in the former sample, the coefficient is no longer significant, while in the latter it remains significant at the 5 percent level.

---

[9] One concern that arises in tests using directed dyads is whether the observations on the two directed dyads in the same dyad should be treated as independent. Is the probability of a challenge by France against Britain in a given year independent of the probability of a challenge by Britain against France? If these probabilities are correlated due to factors that are in the error term of the regression, then our estimated standard errors may be wrong. Under the worst-case assumption that the error terms within the same dyad in the same year are perfectly correlated, we would multiply the standard errors by the square root of 2, reflecting the fact that we really have half as many independent observations (see, e.g. Rousseau *et al.* 1996, p. 518). The main result here, the negative coefficient on "Democratic Initiator," remains significant after this transformation.

The reason for this instability is that there are a few large MIDs during this period in which democracies are coded as the targets. Three MIDs alone – crises in 1886, 1896, and 1897 in which Greece was the target of threats by all or most of the major powers – generate seventeen initiations against democratic targets and account for over 10 percent of such observations. Thus, while there is still evidence that democracy increases the probability that a state will be the target of a crisis, the effect is overstated when multilateral MIDs are included. Below, when I estimate the predicted probabilities implied by these results, I will correct for this.

In the pre-Cold War sample, the coefficient on "Both Democratic" is negative and strongly significant. It is important to be clear that this is not necessarily evidence of a democratic peace effect in this period. In interpreting these results, recall that the effect of two democracies is given by the sum of the three regime coefficients, since all three regime variables score a one in this case. When this calculation is performed, we find that the effect of two democracies is statistically indistinguishable from the effect associated with a democratic initiator and a nondemocratic target. Thus, the effect of a democratic initiator on the probability of challenge does not depend upon the regime type of the target. What the negative coefficient on "Both Democratic" does tell us is that democratic initiators do not pick on democratic targets the way nondemocratic initiators appear to. One interpretation of this result is that nondemocratic initiators are better able to exploit the constraints operating on democratic targets, and they are thus more likely to initiate probes against such states. While suggestive, however, this result does not hold in both samples, once more suggesting that the regime type of the target has weak or inconsistent influence. In the Cold War period, the effect of two democracies is positive but insignificant, and we can again show that the estimated effect of a democratic initiator does not depend upon the regime type of the target. In all models, then, one pattern is remarkably stable: *The directed dyads with the lowest probability of crisis initiation are those in which the potential initiator has democratic political institutions, regardless of whether this is also true of the potential target.*

In addition to the sign and statistical significance of the regression coefficients, it is worth considering the substantive effects they imply. How does the probability of a challenge change when the potential challenger or potential target shifts from a nondemocracy to a democracy? Estimating this change is complicated by the assumption, captured by the fixed-effects treatment, that the baseline probability of a challenge is

Table 5.3. *Predicted probabilities of crisis initiation as a function of regime type*

Level of conflict	Nondemocratic initiator and target	Democratic initiator	Democratic target
(A) Pre-Cold War (world wars excluded)			
High	0.12	0.080	0.21
Medium	0.047	0.031	0.088
Low	0.018	0.012	0.034
(B) Cold War			
High	0.22	0.11	0.25
Medium	0.032	0.014	0.038
Low	0.0038	0.0017	0.0045

Note:
All independent variables other than the regime type were set at their means or modes. See text (fn. 10, p. 138) for a description of how the "levels of conflict" were determined.

systematically different across directed dyads. Because the logit model is nonlinear, this means that the effect of a regime change on the probability of a challenge is not constant, but rather depends upon the underlying level of conflict in the dyad. To deal with this, we calculate the marginal effect of a regime change for three types of dyads in the sample: one with "high" conflict, one with "medium" conflict, and one with "low" conflict.[10]

Table 5.3 reports the estimated probability of crisis initiation as a function of the initiator's and target's regime type for each of the two samples. All other independent variables are set at their means (for continuous

[10] The predictions for different levels of conflict were obtained as follows. First, the regression model was estimated using the standard logit model and including dummy variables for each dyad. Because most of the time series are rather long, the bias on the estimated coefficients on these fixed effect dummies is negligible. The mean and standard deviation of the estimated fixed effects were then calculated. A "medium" dyad is one whose estimated coefficient is at the mean; "high" and "low" dyads are those with estimated coefficients one standard deviation above or below the mean, respectively. The use of the term "medium" needs to be qualified by the recognition that dyads only enter the estimation if they have experienced at least one dispute. Hence, "medium" levels of conflict mean the average level of conflict among dyads that have experienced at least one MID, a level which is much higher than in the overall population. For those dyads that have no crises, there is no way to estimate how a regime change would affect the probability of a challenge.

variables) or modes (for discrete variables). For the pre-Cold War period, the predictions are based on the tests in which multilateral MIDs were collapsed in order not to overstate the effect of democratic targets.[11] It is clear from this table that the effects of a regime change in the potential initiator are consistently quite large. In the pre-Cold War sample, a change from a nondemocratic to democratic initiator causes the probability of a challenge to fall by one-third. In the Cold War sample, such a regime change cuts the predicted probability of a challenge roughly in half. Thus, the evidence in support of hypothesis 1 is substantively, as well as statistically, significant. With respect to the target's regime type, the magnitude of the effect depends upon the time period. In the pre-Cold War period, the predicted probability of a crisis increases 75–90 percent when the target switches from a nondemocracy to a democracy. In the Cold War period, such a switch leads to a more modest predicted increase of 15–20 percent; recall, moreover, that the underlying coefficient in this case was statistically insignificant. Thus, the evidence in support of hypothesis 2 is spotty but substantively large in the early period.

Alternative explanations

How do the alternative perspectives fare? As noted earlier, the predictions of the informational and institutional constraints perspectives substantially overlap when looking at this dependent variable, so it is difficult to evaluate the relative merits of these arguments using the tests reported here. Because the institutional constraints argument predicts the same pattern of outcomes, we cannot rule out the possibility that the results are a product of this alternative causal mechanism. The tests in the next section provide a more rigorous way to differentiate between the two.

It seems quite unlikely that the normative perspective accounts for the results. As we saw, the political institutions of the initiator have the most robust impact on the likelihood of a challenge, and this impact is not contingent on the regime type of the target. Thus, democracy in the initiator decreases the probability of crisis initiation regardless of whether the potential target is also democratic. An argument that democratic countries enjoy a special relationship that does not extend to autocratic governments cannot explain this result. This is not to imply that normative theory has been falsified. One can legitimately question whether the

---

[11] In the Cold War period, the predicted probabilities are virtually identical regardless of whether or not multilateral MIDs are collapsed.

indicators of democracy employed here – emphasizing institutionalized competition rather than the prevalence of liberal norms – are the most appropriate for capturing that theory. In addition, it is clear that the fixed-effect treatment is heavily biased against this approach. After all, if two states are democratic for an entire time period and they experience no MIDs, then that dyad is dropped from the sample: we simply assume that the absence of conflict is wholly explained by the unmeasured factors captured in the fixed-effect terms. Thus, these results should not lead us to reject the normative perspective, but they do suggest a pattern that cannot be accounted for by that argument. Something else must be going on to produce the effects we observe here.

Finally, in assessing the realist perspective, we need to differentiate between that theory's positive claims – those emphasizing the importance of military power and strategic interests – and its negative claim – that domestic political institutions have no systematic influence on international outcomes. The latter is clearly belied by the significant coefficients on the regime variables. The rejection of this null hypothesis is all the more striking given that the regression models were designed to be as sympathetic to that hypothesis as possible. The two core explanatory concepts of realism – power and interests – are captured in the models through a battery of control variables. Measures of relative power appear in two different forms. The variables that measure similarity of interests and status quo evaluation, while admittedly imperfect, are the best available. In addition, the fixed-effects technique controls for any other systematic factors which influence the outcome but which we cannot measure. As indicated earlier, this technique is biased against attributing causal significance to the regime variables, since these tend not to vary much over time. In short, the regression models make every effort to attribute outcomes to factors other than the regime variables. The fact that these variables have significant coefficients nonetheless strongly attests to their fundamental importance.

That said, realism's positive claims about the importance of power and interests are generally borne out by the analysis. The variables which measure the military balance, the similarity in states' alliance portfolios, their status quo evaluations, and territorial contiguity have explanatory power in all of the models.[12] Moreover, their estimated effects are consistent with the predictions of realist theory. In particular:

---

[12] Standard restriction tests show that these variables are collectively significant in all models.

(1) As the potential initiator gets weaker relative to the potential target, the probability of a challenge decreases. In the pre-Cold War sample, this effect is evident in the negative coefficient on the dummy variable indicating a minor power initiator and a major power target. In the Cold War sample, this effect is evident in the positive coefficient on the initiator's share of capabilities. The strong are clearly in a better position to challenge the weak than *vice versa*.

(2) Consistent with previous results, dyads in which power is more evenly balanced experience a higher probability of crisis initiation than do unbalanced dyads.

(3) An increase in the similarity of the states' alliance portfolios decreases the probability of a challenge. Thus, the more strategic interests the states share, the lower the likelihood of military conflict between them (Gowa 1999).

(4) An increase in the potential initiator's evaluation of the status quo – as measured by the similarity of its alliance portfolio with that of the lead state in the system – also decreases the probability that it will issue a challenge. This result fits with the realist argument about "revisionist states" and their propensity to start military conflict (see, e.g., Schweller 1996).

(5) Territorial contiguity – which captures the potential for conflict in the dyad as well as the degree of threat that states pose to one another – increases the likelihood of a challenge. This relationship is statistically significant only in the Cold War sample, but this is not surprising given that contiguity rarely changes over time, so most of its influence is picked up by the fixed effects.

In sum, realism's positive claims about the influence of power and interests on state behavior have merit; its negative claims about the lack of systematic influences at the domestic level do not. Realism is not wrong – only incomplete.

Democracy and the reciprocation of international crises

We now turn to the next set of hypotheses, those dealing with the target state's response given that it has been challenged. Hypotheses 3 and 4 collectively predict that the probability of resistance should be lower for democratic initiators and for democratic targets. To examine the conditional probability of resistance, we focus solely on dispute dyads.[13]

Dependent variable: crisis reciprocation

Testing these hypotheses requires that we code the dependent variable in a way that captures whether or not the target state chose to resist the initiator's challenge. One way to do so is to ask whether or not the target reciprocated that challenge with a militarized action of its own. That is, did the target take steps to escalate the crisis after the initial threat, or did it avoid a military response? A large proportion of militarized actions – roughly 50 percent – are not reciprocated, meaning that the target state or states did not even respond with a threat to use force. A lack of reciprocation does not mean that the targets did nothing in response to the initial threat, but it does suggest that they did not consider military escalation of the conflict to be in their interests. On the other hand, a willingness to reciprocate suggests that the target considered a military response potentially worthwhile. The decision to reciprocate is thus a plausible indicator of how genuine the target believes the challenge to be.

Using the MID data set, the dependent variable RECIP is coded as a one if the target of the dispute engaged in any kind of militarized action in response to the initiator's action. RECIP is coded zero if the target did not respond with at least a threat to use force.[14] Some prominent examples of unreciprocated crises include the 1891 USS *Baltimore* Affair between the United States and Chile, 1902 Alaskan boundary dispute between the United States and Great Britain, the annexation of Austria by Nazi Germany, and the Soviet invasion of Czechoslovakia in 1968. Not surprisingly, though, most unreciprocated MIDs are rather obscure. It would be a mistake to assume that they are therefore minor events, not worth including in the same class of interactions as full-scale wars or prominent, near-war crises. Their obscurity stems in large part from an *ex post* evaluation of how high they escalated or how close the participants actually came to war. As we have seen, such outcomes do not necessarily reflect *ex ante* expectations. A dispute may not escalate because the target believes that the initiator is willing to wage war and therefore

---

[13] Because our hypotheses deal explicitly with the conditional probability of resistance given a crisis, selection bias – which arises when trying to estimate unconditional probabilities using samples with nonrandom selection – is not a major problem for inference. See Schultz (1999) for a discussion of this issue.

[14] See Appendix C for details and further elaboration.

decides to defuse the crisis early on. In the 1902 Alaskan boundary dispute, for example, the British government was sufficiently convinced by President Theodore Roosevelt's threats that it accepted an arbitration panel with members clearly biased in the United States' favor (Penlington 1972). It is precisely such cases – in which the *ex ante* expectation of war leads to an outcome that falls quite short of war – that we must consider when exploring the credibility of threats.

Complications again arise due to the fact that not all disputes involve only a single dyad, raising the specter of nonindependence among observations. It is almost certain that probabilities of reciprocation are highly correlated among target states within the same dispute. Of the eighty-two MIDs in which there is more than one original target state, there are only eleven in which some target states reciprocated but others did not; in the rest of the cases, either all target states reciprocated, or none did. Moreover, in disputes with more than one initiating state, reciprocation takes place against all initiators or none. As before, there is no perfect way to deal with this problem, but we do have some methods for mitigating it. First, standard errors are corrected to take into account nonindependence among dyads in the same MID. Second, the regressions are run on the sub-sample of MIDs that involve only one state on each side; because observations in this sub-sample are independent of one another, these results serve to check whether the multilateral disputes have undue influence on the results.

Additional independent variables

The regression models include the same controls for relative power and interest similarity as above. The only exception is the variable measuring the degree of balance in the dyad; once the initiator has been identified, this variable would seem to have little relevance independent of the initiator's share of capabilities. Indeed, tests show that it is insignificant in all models, and its exclusion has no impact on the results. For the remaining variables, we can again generate plausible expectations about the direction of their impact from realist theory. In particular, we would expect the probability of reciprocation to decrease with the relative power of the initiator and to increase with contiguity, dissimilarity of interests, and the target's dissatisfaction with the status quo.

In this context, we also have an additional set of indicators that can help control for the value of the good in dispute. Typically, the initiating state's militarized action is accompanied by a demand to revise the status quo. These demands may involve a reallocation of territory, a shift in some policy, or a change in the target's regime type or government. If some kinds of goods are systematically more valuable than others, then the type of revision demanded by the challenger is a proxy for the value of the good in dispute. We might surmise, for example, that disputes over territory or the form of a country's government have higher stakes than disputes over policies. If so, then targets might be more willing to resist demands to revise the former than the latter. The MID data set codes states' demands according to whether they entail a revision of territory, policy, the target's regime type or government, or something else. For each of these four categories, a dummy variable was created indicating the type of revision sought by the initiator.[15]

Results

Before turning to the multiple regression analysis, it is worth getting a feel for the data through some cross-tabulations. The overall rate of reciprocation in the data set is 51 percent. This rate is fairly constant across time periods, with the exception of the disputes that took place during the two world wars. The probability of reciprocation was 35 percent for disputes that occurred during World War I and 28 percent for those that occurred during World War II. Clearly, target states were more selective about reciprocating disputes while these wars were under way. Because there is reason to believe that these periods are substantially different from the others, the MIDs that took place during the world wars will require special treatment in the following analysis.

Turning to a preliminary test of the hypotheses, Table 5.4 displays the observed frequency of reciprocation as a function of the initiator's and target's regime type. The results are based on the full sample of multi- and bilateral MIDs, excluding those that took place during the world wars. The evidence in these tables supports both hypothesis 3, which predicted that democratic initiators enjoy a lower rate of reciprocation, and hypothesis 4, which predicted that democratic targets reciprocate at a lower rate than nondemocratic targets. The frequency of reciprocation was 16 percent lower in crises initiated by democracies than in crises initiated by nondemocracies. Similarly, the frequency of reciprocation by democratic targets was 10 percent lower than the frequency of reciprocation by nondemocratic targets. Underneath each table, I report the

---

[15] All four dummy variables equal zero when the initiator made no revisionist demand, which happened in about 27 percent of the cases. These correspond to cases in which the initiator was seeking to prevent the target from changing the status quo. The results are not affected if these observations are dropped.

Table 5.4. *Observed frequencies of reciprocation by regime type*

	Initiator		Target	
	Nondemocratic	Democratic	Nondemocratic	Democratic
Not Reciprocated	46.8	55.3	47.2	52.7
	(592)	(220)	(513)	(274)
Reciprocated	53.2	44.7	52.8	47.3
	(672)	(178)	(574)	(246)
	Pearson $\chi^2 = 8.6^c$		Pearson $\chi^2 = 4.3^b$	

Notes:
[b] $0.05 > p > 0.01$
[c] $p < 0.01$

results of a Pearson χ^2 test, which assesses the null hypothesis that the probability of reciprocation is independent of regime type. In both cases, we can reject the null hypothesis at conventional levels.

We now consider the relationship between regime type and reciprocation through multiple regression analysis. As we will see, the inclusion of control variables lends additional support for hypothesis 3 but weakens the evidence in support of hypothesis 4. Since the dependent variable is dichotomous, estimates are obtained using a logit model. Four models were estimated. Because of concerns about MIDs that took place during the world wars, the model was estimated both including and excluding those observations; in the former case, dummy variables were included to control for any systematic effects associated with each war.[16] Because of the problems of nonindependence noted earlier, each sample was estimated twice: once using all originating dispute dyads and once using only bilateral disputes.[17] Table 5.5 displays the regression results.

[16] To determine whether or not there were other time period effects, dummy variables were included for the Cold War and pre-World War I periods. The coefficients on these variables were insignificant and indistinguishable from one another. The results reported below do not include these period dummies.

[17] When multilateral disputes are included, Huber-White robust standard errors were calculated in order to compensate for nonindependence among dyads within the same dispute. These were generated by using the "cluster" option to group dyads within the same dispute (StataCorp 1999, pp. 256–60).

Table 5.5. *The probability of crisis reciprocation*

Variable	All MIDs		Bilateral MIDs	
	(1) World wars included[†]	(2) World wars excluded	(3) World wars included[†]	(4) World wars excluded
Constant	0.10 (0.28)	0.55 (0.31)[a]	0.21 (0.31)	0.43 (0.34)
Regime Indicators				
Democratic Initiator	−0.22 (0.16)	−0.49 (0.17)[c]	−0.43 (0.18)[b]	−0.53 (0.19)[c]
Democratic Target	−0.08 (0.14)	−0.10 (0.15)	0.02 (0.16)	0.0019 (0.17)
Both Democratic	0.07 (0.31)	0.30 (0.33)	0.28 (0.34)	0.41 (0.36)
Power Indicators				
Major Power Initiator-Major Power Target	−0.15 (0.21)	−0.34 (0.21)	−0.28 (0.24)	−0.52 (0.25)[b]
Major Power Initiator-Minor Power Target	−0.10 (0.18)	−0.21 (0.18)	−0.32 (0.18)[a]	−0.40 (0.19)[b]
Minor Power Initiator-Major Power Target	−0.18 (0.21)	−0.02 (0.23)	0.07 (0.23)	0.05 (0.24)
Initiator's Share of Capabilities	0.03 (0.24)	−0.05 (0.25)	0.05 (0.24)	0.04 (0.25)
Interest Indicators				
Contiguous	0.57 (0.13)[c]	0.55 (0.14)[c]	0.54 (0.14)[c]	0.55 (0.16)[c]
Alliance Portfolio Similarity	−0.01 (0.19)	−0.21 (0.22)	0.05 (0.22)	−0.05 (0.24)
Status quo evaluation of initiator	−0.03 (0.21)	0.47 (0.25)[a]	0.34 (0.25)	0.54 (0.29)[a]
Status quo evaluation of target	−0.05 (0.20)	−0.67 (0.24)[c]	−0.47 (0.24)[b]	−0.72 (0.26)[c]
Revision Type				
Territory	0.55 (0.15)[c]	0.45 (0.16)[c]	0.34 (0.16)[b]	0.29 (0.17)[a]
Government	0.85 (0.33)[b]	0.59 (0.33)[a]	0.43 (0.35)	0.35 (0.36)
Policy	−0.98 (0.14)[c]	−1.10 (0.14)[c]	−1.18 (0.15)[c]	−1.27 (0.16)[c]
Other	−0.63 (0.45)	−0.60 (0.46)	−0.60 (0.60)	−0.51 (0.65)

Table 5.5 (*cont.*)

Variable	All MIDs		Bilateral MIDs	
	(1) World wars included[†]	(2) World wars excluded	(3) World wars included[†]	(4) World wars excluded
χ^2	207.48[c]	185.96[c]	186.31[c]	172.93[c]
% Correctly predicted	68.2	67.0	68.0	68.0
(% Modal outcome)	(51.1)	(51.3)	(51.2)	(50.8)
Number of observations	1768	1559	1329	1184

Notes:
Estimates obtained using a logit regression model. Standard errors reported in parentheses.
[†] Dummy variables for world war years included but coefficients not reported.
[a] $0.10 > p > 0.05$
[b] $0.05 > p > 0.01$
[c] $p < 0.01$

The first main result in this table is that the coefficient on "Democratic Initiator" is consistently negative, meaning that targets are less likely to reciprocate threats made by democratic states. Moreover, this result is statistically significant at conventional levels in three out of the four models; the only exception comes when the model is estimated on the full sample of MIDs, including those that took place during the world wars. Thus, the relationship predicted by hypothesis 3 is clearly evident in the data, except when the multilateral disputes associated with the two periods of general warfare are included in the sample. Given both the unusual nature of these periods and the complications of signaling in a multilateral environment, this exception should not be too troubling.

The evidence is less supportive of the hypothesis that democratic targets are systematically more selective when it comes to reciprocating challenges. Though a relationship to this effect was evident in the cross-tabulations in Table 5.4, the coefficient on "Democratic Target" is inconsistently signed and never significantly different from zero in the multiple regression analysis. This suggests that other control variables account for the relationship that was evident in the bivariate comparison. As noted before, the hypotheses relating to the regime type of the target were anticipated to hold more weakly, so the lack of support here is unfortunate but not damning. The tests in Chapter 6 will allow us to

Table 5.6. *Predicted probabilities of reciprocation*

Initiator–Target	Nondemocratic initiator	Democratic initiator
Major Power–Major Power	0.28	0.18
Major Power–Minor Power	0.31	0.21
Minor Power–Major Power	0.38	0.27
Minor Power–Minor Power	0.39	0.28

Notes:
Predicted probabilities were calculated using the coefficient estimates from Table 5.5, column 4. The predictions shown are for a contiguous dyad, a nondemocratic target state, and policy revision demanded. All other variables were set to their mean values for each power configuration.

revisit the question of how domestic institutions influence the use of threats by targets.

As before, we can show that the effect of a democratic initiator does not depend upon the regime type of the target. The coefficient on "Both Democratic" is consistently insignificant. Moreover, standard restriction tests confirm that the effect of a democratic initiator and nondemocratic target is equivalent to the effect of a democratic initiator and democratic target. Thus, *the lowest probability of reciprocation occurs when the initiator is democratic, regardless of whether or not the target is similarly democratic.* This finding is crucial not only because it supports the informational perspective and permits us to reject the realist null hypothesis, but also because it contradicts the prediction of the institutional constraints perspective and is entirely unanticipated by the normative approach.

To get a sense for the magnitude of this effect, we can calculate the change in the probability of reciprocation when the initiator changes from a nondemocracy to a democracy. To keep the comparison clean, we will assume in this exercise that the target is nondemocratic throughout. Since the logit model is nonlinear, the marginal effects of such a regime change depend on the value of the other independent variables. Table 5.6 reports the predicted probabilities of reciprocation for different power configurations, with all other independent variables set at their means or

[18] Because the initiator's share of military capabilities covaries strongly with the power status of the two states, the mean of this variable was recalculated for each of the four kinds of dyads. The same technique was employed when calculating means for the other continuous variables, though the differences in these cases were less pronounced.

modes.[18] In order to facilitate a comparison between the regime effects and the power effects, the predictions are based on the estimates from bilateral MIDs excluding the world wars (Table 5.5, column 4) because it is in this sample that the dyadic power relations have the most pronounced effect. As can be seen from this table, changing the initiator's regime type from nondemocratic to democratic leads to a 30 percent reduction in the probability of reciprocation. To get a more concrete feeling for this effect, notice that the probability of reciprocation is roughly the same when the initiator is a minor power and democratic as it is when the initiator is a major power and nondemocratic. Thus, if the initiator shifts from a nondemocratic to a democratic polity, the effect on the predicted probability of reciprocation is the same as if the initiator shifts from a minor to a major power. Clearly, domestic political institutions matter, and they do so in a manner that is consistent with the informational perspective.

Alternative perspectives

How do the alternative perspectives fare? As the foregoing discussion suggests, it is very clear that neither the institutional constraints, normative, nor realist approaches can account for the observed pattern of outcomes. The institutional constraints perspective predicts that the probability of resistance should be higher against a democratic initiator than against a nondemocratic initiator. This is clearly not the case; indeed, the opposite is generally true. The normative argument also fares poorly in these tests. We cannot discern any distinctive effect associated with shared democracy. Because of the small number of MIDs involving democracies on both sides, it may again be the case that shared democracy has an effect that the data do not permit us to find. Even given this generous interpretation, however, we can readily dismiss the possibility that the pattern observed here is driven by the causal mechanisms of this theory. After all, the most robust finding was that nondemocratic targets are less likely to resist democratic challengers than they are to resist nondemocratic challengers. The normative perspective does not anticipate such a result.

Finally, the statistically and substantively significant effects associated with the regime variables run counter to the realist claim that domestic political factors do not matter. Once again, this does not mean that neorealism adds nothing to our understanding of these events. The models show that several of the variables suggested by realist theory do influence the probability of reciprocation. In particular:

(1) Target states take seriously the power status of the initiator, as they are more likely to reciprocate threats made by minor powers than those made by major powers. Because these variables measure the distribution of power in the dyad, this effect is most evident in the models that focus on bilateral MIDs (Table 5.5, columns 3 and 4).

(2) Contiguity is positively correlated with reciprocation, and demands to revise territory tend to be resisted with higher probability than demands to change policy. Again, this points to the importance of territory as a source of conflict in international politics.

(3) Target states that are dissatisfied with the status quo are more likely to reciprocate, once again suggesting that "revisionist" states have a greater willingness to use force and risk escalation.

Still, a model based purely on indicators of power and interest does not tell the full story.

Democracy and the probability of war

Finally, we turn to the probability of war, the subject of hypotheses 5 and 6. Recall that these hypotheses deal not with the overall frequency of war participation but rather the probability that a state will initiate or become the target of a crisis that then escalates to war. In theory, there are two ways to estimate this latter probability. First, we could create a dependent variable analogous to the one measuring crisis initiation, indicating for each directed dyad-year whether or not the potential initiator initiated a crisis which then became a war. The difficulty with this technique is that such events are extremely rare; whereas there are roughly 1800 crises in our sample, only 66 of them escalated to war. Thus, estimating a model of initiations that lead to war using the fixed-effect treatment is impractical: too many observations are thrown out for lack of variation.

The alternative approach, which I employ here, is to take advantage of the following relationship: the probability that a state initiates a crisis that escalates to war is the product of the probability that it initiates a crisis and the probability of escalation conditional on initiation, or

$$\text{Pr(Initiate \& War)} = \text{Pr(Initiate)} \cdot \text{Pr(War | Initiate)}.$$

We have already seen that, holding everything else constant, a shift from nondemocratic to a democratic challenger lowers the probability of initiation. If we can now show that such a switch decreases, or at least leaves unchanged, the conditional probability of war given an initiation, then such evidence will be supportive of hypothesis 5. We have also seen that a shift from a nondemocratic to a democratic target increases the probability of initiation. To be consistent with hypothesis 6, the data must show that a democratic target lowers the probability of crisis escalation by a sufficient amount to outweigh this effect.

The dependent variable: escalation

The dependent variable for this test indicates, for each dispute dyad, whether or not the two states ended up at war. The MID data set records cases of interstate war, which are defined as military conflicts that are sufficiently severe that they result in at least 1000 total battle deaths (Jones, Bremer, and Singer 1996, p. 171). Again focusing only on dispute dyads, we code the variable WAR equal to one if both states in the dyad reached this level of conflict, something which happens in only about 4 percent of observations. The cases so coded constitute a familiar list of interstate wars. Cases in which crises initiated by democracies escalated to war include the Mexican–American War, the Spanish–American War, the 1897 Greco-Turkish War, the 1961 Sino-Indian War, and several wars between India and Pakistan. Notice that, because I have coded polities according to their competitiveness, and not according to an ideal notion of liberal democracy, there are some cases of war between countries that are both coded as democratic – for example, the 1965 and 1971 wars between India and Pakistan.

Because of the low frequency of events that meet the criterion for war, the tests in this section are also performed using a less restrictive coding of escalation. In about 25 percent of MIDs, the states ended up using military force against one another, but the conflict was not severe enough to generate 1000 battle deaths. Some of these events are quite minor, such as the so-called "Cod Wars" between Britain and Iceland in which the mutual use of force involved harassment of fishing boats. Other such events, however, include small border wars, such as between India and Pakistan over Kashmir, that do not rise to the level of full-scale war and cases in which one state was so superior militarily that the fighting that took place ended quickly, such as the US invasion of Grenada. Because the theoretical model says nothing about the intensity of the "war" that occurs after threats and displays of force have failed to settle the issue, it is not unreasonable to count these cases of mutual violence as instances of escalation. Thus, I created a second variable, FORCE, which indicates whether or not both states in the dyad used force. Notice that the full-scale wars constitute a subset of these events.

The problems of multilateral disputes discussed above also applies in the context, and the same techniques are used to deal with them. The problem of what to do with the world war periods also arises. In this context, however, the problem is particularly vexing because most of the cases of dyadic war that broke out during these periods have been lumped together. Thus, for example, no MIDs are coded as escalating to war during the period between August 1, 1914, and November 11, 1918. The reason is that, if a dispute arose during this period and lead to war, the event was coded as being part of the ongoing general war, rather than an independent event (Jones, Bremer, and Singer 1996, p. 176). For this reason, we drop entirely the MIDs that occurred between the start of each world war and its conclusion; notice that this rule leaves in the sample the MIDs that actually escalated into those wars.[19]

Results

To get a feel for the data, Table 5.7 presents simple cross-tabulations comparing the observed frequencies of WAR and FORCE as a function of the initiator's and target's regime types. In every panel, the frequency of the escalation is lower when the dispute involved a democracy on either side. The effects of democracy in the target are particularly striking, reducing the frequency of war by about two-thirds and the frequency of force by 25 percent. The Pearson χ^2 statistics, reported beneath each table, show that these effects are statistically significant below the 1 percent level. The reductions associated with a democratic initiator are less dramatic, and only when looking at FORCE is the effect even marginally significant. The weakness of these latter results is not too troubling, however, because the model was ambiguous when it came to the effect of democracy on the probability of war given a challenge.

We now turn to multiple regression analysis. All of the independent variables are the same as in the tests on the probability of reciprocation.[20] We again estimate the models using a logit regression. The results

---

[19] All of the results reported hold if the world war MIDs are included along with dummy variables for those cases. It is unclear what to make of estimates using this sample, however.

[20] In addition, a dummy variable was included to capture the generally lower rate of escalation in the Cold War period. The coefficient on this variable was negative and significant in both models.

Table 5.7. *Observed frequencies of escalation by regime type*

	Initiator		Target	
	Nondemocratic	Democratic	Nondemocratic	Democratic
No War	95.4	96.2	94.7	98.1
	(1210)	(384)	(1033)	(511)
War	4.6	3.8	5.3	1.9
	(59)	(15)	(58)	(10)
	Pearson $\chi^2 = 0.57$		Pearson $\chi^2 = 10.07^c$	
No Force	66.8	71.7	66.1	73.7
	(848)	(286)	(721)	(384)
Force	33.2	28.3	33.9	26.3
	(421)	(113)	(370)	(137)
	Pearson $\chi^2 = 3.29^a$		Pearson $\chi^2 = 9.49^c$	

Notes:
[a] $0.10 > p > 0.05$
[b] $0.05 > p > 0.01$
[c] $p < 0.01$

are presented in Table 5.8. The first two columns report the estimates obtained using WAR as the dependent variable, while the second two columns report the estimates obtained using FORCE. For each dependent variable, the model was run on both the full sample of MIDs and on the subsample of bilateral disputes. In all models, the signs on "Democratic Initiator" and "Democratic Target" are both negative. When WAR is the dependent variable, none of these coefficients is statistically distinguishable from zero; however, when we use the less restrictive FORCE variable, the regime effects are significant at conventional levels. The coefficient on "Both Democratic" is generally positive, and even significant at the 10 percent level in one model (column 4). What this suggests is that, when both states are democratic, the reduction in the probability of escalation is less than the sum of the reductions associated with democracy in the initiator and target individually. Indeed, in no case can we discern a statistically significant difference between the probability of escalation in jointly democratic dyads and that in jointly nondemocratic dyads, a result that may simply reflect the small number of crises between democracies. The most pronounced effects are thus monadic: democracy in either the initiator or target reduces the probability of escalation given a crisis, especially using a

Table 5.8. *The probability of escalation*

	WAR		FORCE	
Variable	(1) All MIDs	(2) Bilateral MIDs	(3) All MIDs	(4) Bilateral MIDs
Constant	−4.28 (1.01)[c]	−4.84 (1.35)[c]	−0.82 (0.47)[a]	−1.06 (0.49)[b]
Regime Indicators				
Democratic Initiator	−0.08 (0.46)	−0.11 (0.55)	−0.38 (0.19)[b]	−0.35 (0.21)[a]
Democratic Target	−0.46 (0.43)	−0.76 (0.66)	−0.36 (0.16)[b]	−0.39 (0.18)[b]
Both Democratic	0.09 (1.00)	1.19 (1.14)	0.47 (0.33)	0.69 (0.36)[a]
Power Indicators				
Major Power Initiator- Major Power Target	−0.17 (0.64)	−0.62 (1.02)	−0.63 (0.27)[b]	−0.57 (0.29)[b]
Major Power Initiator- Minor Power Target	1.01 (0.40)[b]	0.57 (0.47)	−0.10 (0.21)	−0.48 (0.22)[b]
Minor Power Initiator- Major Power Target	0.91 (0.59)	1.27 (0.66)[a]	−0.19 (0.26)	−0.27 (0.27)
Initiator's Share of Capabilities	−0.29 (0.68)	−0.15 (0.65)	−0.08 (0.28)	−0.07 (0.27)
Interest Indicators				
Contiguous	1.13 (0.34)[c]	1.05 (0.46)[b]	0.47 (0.16)[c]	0.40 (0.18)[b]
Alliance Portfolio Similarity	0.72 (0.57)	0.61 (0.68)	0.09 (0.24)	0.19 (0.27)
Status Quo Evaluation of Initiator	0.86 (0.64)	0.67 (0.96)	0.33 (0.28)	0.29 (0.33)
Status Quo Evaluation of Target	−0.60 (0.67)	−0.063 (0.83)	−0.47 (0.27)[a]	−0.26 (0.31)
Revision Type				
Territory	0.46 (0.36)	0.59 (0.51)	0.41 (0.16)[c]	0.25 (0.17)
Government	0.34 (0.59)	1.07 (0.73)	1.21 (0.32)[c]	1.16 (0.38)[c]
Policy	−0.30 (0.35)	−0.27 (0.53)	−0.81 (0.15)[c]	−0.95 (0.17)[c]

Table 5.8 (*cont.*)

	WAR		FORCE	
Variable	(1) All MIDs	(2) Bilateral MIDs	(3) All MIDs	(4) Bilateral MIDs
Revision Type (cont).				
Other	−0.02	—[t]	−1.83	−1.85
	(1.09)		(0.76)[b]	(1.01)[a]
χ^2	94.98[c]	55.60[c]	154.78[c]	134.84[c]
Number of observations	1559	1171	1559	1184

Notes:
Estimates obtained using a logit regression model. Standard errors reported in parentheses. A dummy variable for the Cold War period was included in both models; the coefficient is not reported.
[t] Other revision type perfectly predicts failure to escalate. Thus, the variable was dropped along with all observations in which it was coded as one.
[a] $0.10 > p > 0.05$
[b] $0.05 > p > 0.01$
[c] $p < 0.01$

broad conception of escalation that includes events that fall short of full-scale war.[21]

What do these results imply for the *ex ante* probability of war, which is the subject of hypotheses 5 and 6? We saw before that a shift to democracy decreases the probability that the state will initiate a crisis. Hence, the negative coefficients on "Democratic Initiator" provide the second piece of evidence needed to support hypothesis 5. When looking only at wars, we cannot rule out that democracy in the initiating state has no effect on the probability of crisis escalation, and we know that the true effect is more likely to be negative than positive. When we expand the definition of escalation to include cases of mutual violence, then our confidence that the effect is negative only increases. Combined with our

---

[21] It is interesting to note that other empirical tests on this dependent variable have similarly found weak or contradictory evidence that democracy has any significant influence. For example, Morgan and Campbell (1991) and Rousseau *et al.* (1996) show no or weak monadic effects of democracy on crisis escalation. Rousseau *et al.* (1996) and Dixon (1994) find that joint democracy lowers the probability that a crisis will escalate to force; Senese (1997), on the other hand, finds that democratic dyads are just as likely, and perhaps even more likely, to escalate to the use of force once involved in a crisis.

Table 5.9. *Predicted probabilities of war as a function of regime type*

Indicator of escalation	Nondemocratic initiator and target	Democratic initiator	Democratic target
(A) Pre-Cold War (world wars excluded)			
WAR	0.00071	0.00045	0.00061
FORCE	0.0064	0.0031	0.0084
(B) Cold War			
WAR	0.00010	0.000041	0.000057
FORCE	0.0065	0.0022	0.0055

Note:
The predicted probabilities are derived from the results in Tables 5.3 and 5.8, columns 2 and 4. All independent variables other than regime type were set at their means of modes.

earlier results, this evidence suggests that the *ex ante* probability of war does indeed decrease when a state becomes democratic: such a change decreases the *ex ante* probability of a challenge and, at the very least, does not increase the probability of escalation given a challenge.

Using the estimates from Table 5.8, we can calculate the predicted probability of escalation as a function of the initiator's regime type and combine them with the predicted probability of crisis initiation from Table 5.3 to obtain the predicted effect of a democratic initiator on the *ex ante* probability of war and force. The results are reported in Table 5.9. Recall that the predicted probability of initiation depends upon the baseline level of conflict in the dyad, as captured by the fixed-effect terms. To simplify the presentation, and because the magnitude of the changes associated with democracy is similar across these levels, we focus only on what was referred to above as "medium" dyads.[22] Again, different probabilities are predicted for each time period because of the way we estimated crisis initiation. Regardless of the time period, however, it is clear that a shift to a democratic initiator leads to a substantial reduction in the predicted probability of war – roughly, a 40 percent reduction in the pre-Cold War period and a 60 percent reduction during the Cold War. Of course, the large standard error on the underlying coefficient in the model of escalation means that we should treat this

[22] For this test, the means and modes of the other independent variables were calculated using the entire population, as in Table 5.3.

prediction with some caution. Nonetheless, the same basic result holds when we turn to the less restrictive coding of escalation, which generated more precise estimates. Based on this dependent variable, a shift to democracy in the challenger is predicted to decrease the *ex ante* probability of mutual force by 50 percent in the pre-Cold War period and 66 percent during the Cold War. This is strong evidence in support of hypothesis 5.

With respect to the target's regime type, the results are again spottier. Recall that democracy tends to increase the probability that a state will be the target of a challenge. Thus, for democracy in the target to decrease the *ex ante* probability of war, it must be the case not only that it decreases the probability of escalation given a crisis, but that it does so by a large enough amount to offset the higher probability of being in a crisis. The estimates from Table 5.8, in which the coefficient on "Democratic Target" is consistently negative, support the first half of this claim. To determine whether the magnitude of this effect is sufficiently large, we again calculate the predicted probabilities. The results are mixed. In the model of escalation using the strict definition of war, the coefficient on "Democratic Target," while insignificant, is quite large in magnitude; indeed, the coefficient estimate implies that democracy in the target cuts the conditional probability of escalation to war in half.[23] As Table 5.9 shows, the magnitude of this effect is sufficiently large to offset the increased rate of challenges against such states. When the target state becomes democratic, the *ex ante* probability of war is predicted to decrease 13 percent in the pre-Cold War period and 45 percent in the Cold War. Because the underlying coefficient in this case was insignificant, however, these point predictions come with considerable noise. Using the less restrictive FORCE variable, the effect of a democratic target on the conditional probability of escalation was statistically more robust but smaller, corresponding to a reduction of about 30 percent.[24] In the Cold War period, this reduction is large enough to decrease the *ex ante* probability of force by about 15 percent; in the pre-Cold War period, however, the higher rate of challenges against democratic targets meant that the *ex ante* probability of force was about 30 percent higher in these cases. Thus, while there is good evidence that democracy in the target decreases the

---

[23] Setting all other variables at their means or modes, the probability of escalation to war given a crisis is predicted to be 0.015 when the target is nondemocratic and 0.0070 when the target is democratic.

[24] The probability of escalation to force given a crisis is predicted to be 0.14 when the target is nondemocratic and 0.096 when the target is democratic.

Table 5.10. *Summary of results*

Hypothesis	Result
1. Democracy in challenger reduces Pr(Challenge)	1. Confirmed: Pr(Challenge) decreases 30–50 percent
2. Democracy in target increases Pr(Challenge)	2. Partly confirmed: Pr(Challenge) increases 75–90 percent in pre-Cold War period
3. Democracy in challenger reduces Pr(Resistance)	3. Confirmed: Pr(Resist) decreases 30 percent
4. Democracy in target reduces Pr(Resistance)	4. Not confirmed
5. Democracy in challenger reduces Pr(War)	5. Confirmed: Pr(War) decreases 40–60 percent
6. Democracy in target reduces Pr(War)	6. Partly confirmed: Pr(War) decreases in Cold War period

probability of escalation given a crisis, the evidence for hypothesis 6 is less impressive, both in terms of consistency and magnitude.

Conclusion

What have we learned? Table 5.10 summarizes the results for each of the hypotheses. As is clear, the predictions pertaining to the effect of democracy in the potential or actual challenger are most consistently supported. Democratic institutions: (1) decrease the probability of initiating a crisis; (2) decrease the probability of resistance; and (3) decrease the *ex ante* probability of war. In each case, we showed that these results do not depend upon the regime type of the target state, suggesting purely monadic effects of democracy. The predictions regarding democracy in the target were less consistently supported. While there is evidence that democracy increases the probability of being targeted by a threat, this result was statistically significant only in the pre-Cold War period. It was also true that the observed frequency of resistance was lower for democratic targets than for nondemocratic targets, but this effect disappeared in the multiple regression analysis. Finally, the evidence with respect to the *ex ante* probability of war was spotty.

Overall, these results support the informational argument developed here. The robust results supporting hypotheses 1 and 3 stand out because they provide strong, direct evidence of the main predictions of the model. The lower probability of challenges by democratic states is consistent with the restraining effect – the idea that, all other things being equal, governments constrained from bluffing issue fewer threats than do governments that are not so constrained. The lower rate of resistance against democratic challenges is consistent with the confirmatory effect – the idea that public competition can increase the credibility of some threats made by democratic governments. Together, these empirical results confirm the pattern hypothesized at the outset: selective threats, effective threats.

At the same time, these results contradict the predictions of the alternative theories in several places. Although the institutional constraints argument anticipates the lower rate of challenges by democratic states and the higher rate of challenges against these states, it does not predict the lower rate of resistance against democratic challenges. Indeed, the constraints argument suggests that we should have seen precisely the opposite relationship. Likewise, the normative argument predicts a special relationship among democratic states that simply is not evident in the data. The impact of democracy on the probability of challenges, the rate of resistance, and the likelihood of war is not dependent upon the regime type of the target. Given that the effects we uncovered are monadic, it is hard to see how they could be the product of shared norms that operate exclusively in jointly democratic dyads. Finally, while realism performed well in identifying the importance of power and interests in determining international outcomes, its negative claim that domestic variables have no systematic effect fares poorly.

That said, the tests performed here do not falsify these alternative perspectives for three reasons. First, the coding of the regime variables, though appropriate for testing the theory developed here, might not be the most appropriate for testing these other perspectives. A theory that points to the importance of political competition should be tested using independent variables that measure regimes along this dimension. Similarly, theories that emphasize decisional constraints, electoral insecurity, liberal norms, or the like, should be tested using independent variables that capture those features. Hence, it would be inappropriate to reject the institutional constraints and normative perspectives solely on the basis of the tests performed here. As noted above, the coding used here generates some wars between "democratic" states that liberal theorists would not so classify. Second, as mentioned before, the fixed-effects technique used when considering the probability of a challenge may be biased against the normative argument. The fixed-effect terms were included because there is reason to believe that there are systematic differences across dyads in the intensity and frequency of their underlying disputes. For testing the informational theory, it was crucial to look for regime effects while holding constant the conflict of interests in the dyad. To the extent that the normative argument sees the conflict of interests as endogenous to the countries' political systems, it is wrong to separate regime and interest effects in this way.

Finally, although the tests on the probability of reciprocation are powerful, they cannot rule out the possibility that the causal mechanisms of both the informational and institutional constraints perspectives are at work. Democratic institutions could serve two roles simultaneously: increasing the political costs of war and facilitating information revelation. As we saw in Chapter 4, if the constraints are introduced in a transparent manner – so that the target state can observe whether or not the government faces unusually high costs of war – then the probability of resistance is still lower on average. Hence, the institutional constraints argument can be made consistent with the evidence as long as it is supplemented with the informational effects identified here.

Admittedly, the empirical picture is less compelling when looking at the impact of democratic institutions in potential or actual targets. As noted before, the model predicts weaker relationships here because the strategic problem facing targets is somewhat different from that facing potential challengers. The latter have greater flexibility in choosing whether and when to make challenges. Because their opportunity to exploit informational asymmetries is more pronounced, so too is the effect of domestic institutions which influence their ability to do so. Targets, on the other hand, are more constrained by the imperatives of a crisis. Once challenged, they are closer to what Wolfers (1962) refers to as the "pole of compulsion," where the external constraints are more binding than internal ones. Given this, the weaker effects in this context are not entirely unanticipated. Still, we need not leave the matter here. Chapters 6 and 7 not only continue to explore the empirical implications of the theory, but they focus quite extensively on cases in which democratic states were targets. Thus, we have more opportunities to look for some of the effects hypothesized here.

6   Credibility confirmed: the implications of domestic support

Chapter 5 relied on the broad distinction between democratic and non-democratic regimes, and the hypotheses were derived by asking how a regime shift in one or both states affects the expected probability of various observable outcomes. In this chapter and the one that follows, we change the focus from variation in institutions to variation in strategies. After all, the institutions do not, on their own, generate the effects considered in the previous chapter. Rather, institutions structure the incentives of political actors within the state, and it is the actual choices made by these actors that determine crisis outcomes. The argument that democratic institutions influence the credibility of threats made in crises was built on explicit claims regarding the public actions taken by government and opposition parties, as well as the effect which those actions have on the beliefs of foreign decision makers. In order to determine whether or not these specific causal mechanisms underlie the correlations we just saw, we need to examine actual crises in greater depth. Does public competition between the government and opposition play out as predicted in the model? Do the parties' strategy choices make sense given their political incentives? Do foreign states pay attention to the resultant signals and act in a manner consistent with the theoretical model?

The model developed in Chapter 4 points to three broad patterns which are of particular interest here:

(1) *The government makes a threat, and the opposition supports it.* All other things being equal, these "confirmed" threats should have greater credibility than threats made by nondemocratic governments. The targets of such threats should be less likely to resist or take actions to further escalate the crisis.

(2) *The government makes a threat, and the opposition opposes it.* Opposed threats can be genuine, or they can be bluffs. From the perspective of foreign decision makers, open dissent by the opposition party calls into question the government's willingness and ability to carry out the threat. As a result, the rival state is more likely to resist such a threat than one which is supported by the opposition.

(3) *The government makes no threat, and the opposition opposes the use of force.* All states forego making threats when their expected value for war is sufficiently low; democratic governments, however, are especially reluctant to bluff given that the opposition party's stance makes it harder to do so successfully. Hence, the prospect of public dissent restrains a government that might otherwise try to misrepresent its constraints.

The purpose of this chapter and the one that follows is to explore these patterns empirically. Chapter 7 focuses on the second and third claims, looking at the effect of domestic dissent on both a government's decision to make threats and the way rival states react to those threats. This chapter tests hypotheses that arise from the first claim, focusing on the proposition that states which permit public competition for political office can generate more credible signals of resolve than can states in which competition is suppressed or private.

The logical basis for this proposition is what we referred to earlier as the confirmatory effect: the idea that a signal sent by two actors with opposing interests is more informative than a signal sent by one actor with known incentives to misrepresent its preferences. As we saw, the competitive interaction between governing and opposition parties means that, while the government has incentives to bluff in a crisis, the opposition generally does not have incentives to collude in a bluff. Instead, the opposition's electoral interests dictate that it should only support the use of force when it has good reason to believe that war would be politically successful. Thus, when the government's threats are publicly supported by its domestic adversaries, the resulting signal of resolve is more credible than a similar signal sent by a government that acts as the lone voice of the state.

This chapter explores the confirmatory effect in two different ways. First, it looks at a class of interactions which Huth (1988) refers to as "extended-immediate deterrence" crises. In such a crisis, a defender seeks to deter an attacker from using force against some valued protégé. A central argument in rational deterrence theory, and echoed in the models developed here, is that successful deterrence depends on the defender's ability to make a credible retaliatory threat – that is, to make the attacker believe that it would incur unacceptable costs if it were to carry out its challenge. If the confirmatory effect is real, then a democratic defender's ability to make a credible retaliatory threat depends not only on what the government does but also on the reaction of its domestic competitors. All other things being equal, a deterrent threat should be more likely to succeed if it is supported by the domestic opposition party than if it is greeted by public dissent. In addition, a democratic government that receives such support should be better able to signal its determination to resist the attacker than should a non-democratic government. The first section of this chapter uses Huth's (1988) coding of extended-immediate deterrence cases to test these propositions.

The remainder of this chapter then explores at much greater depth a single case from this population: the confrontation between Britain and France at Fashoda in 1898. As this case study will show, the logic of costly signaling and confirmatory signaling both play a major role in the outcome of this crisis, and democratic institutions made these signals possible to an extent that has not been fully appreciated by previous work on this crisis. This case also allows an explicit comparison of the theory presented here with the alternative perspectives we have been considering throughout: democratic peace theories in both their normative and institutional versions as well as neorealist theory. I will argue that an analysis of the case that focuses on the role of incomplete information and signaling provides a better account of what we observe than do these other approaches. Together, these analyses reveal both a statistical correlation that is consistent with the argument made here and historical evidence that the hypothesized causal mechanisms underlie this correlation.

Domestic support and success in extended-immediate deterrence crises

Crises of extended-immediate deterrence arise when one state seeks to defend a protégé against threats made by a third. Huth (1988, pp. 23–27) provides a list of fifty-six such cases in the period 1885–1985, a list which is reproduced in Table 6.1.[1] To be in this sample, the attacker must make an explicit threat to use force against the protégé, and the defender must make an explicit threat of retaliation. The outcome of the event is coded according to whether or not the defender's threat deterred the attacker. Deterrence is successful if the defender refused to capitulate to the attacker's demands and the attacker pulled back from its threat or engaged in only small-scale combat (involving fewer than 200 casualties). Failure implies either that the defender capitulated or that the attacker carried through on its threat with large-scale military force. We can use the success or failure of the challenger's deterrent threat as an indicator of how credible that threat was perceived to be.

The underlying game implied by this data entails an extra decisional step on the interaction we modeled in earlier chapters. In it, the attacker first decides whether or not to threaten the protégé, and the defender decides whether or not to issue a retaliatory threat. Both decisions have to be made in the affirmative for the case to enter the sample. Once the two threats have been made, each side has a chance to back down. If the attacker backs down, the result is a deterrence success. If the attacker does not back down, then deterrence has failed and the defender must either makes concessions or make good on its retaliatory threat. As discussed in Chapter 4, adding this step to the game and considering the effect of competition in the target (defender) state does not change the basic logic, though it can weaken it. The restraining and confirmatory effects should both be evident in such interactions, though they need not be evident in every case. Indeed, the results in Chapter 5 suggested only a weak relationship between the target's regime type and its propensity to reciprocate threats, suggesting that the restraining effect is weaker on targets than on challengers. The tests here will help determine whether or not a confirmatory effect is nevertheless apparent when looking at democratic targets.

---

[1] I note that Lebow and Stein (1990) raise objections to many of the codings in this data set. In an unpublished appendix to his book, Huth (1990), rebuts many of these criticisms and justifies his coding decisions. While I am persuaded that the data are appropriate for the purpose of my tests, I have deleted two cases as a result of this exchange. First, Huth (1990) concedes that the 1913 crisis between Serbia and Bulgaria (case no. 19 in the original data set) was not a case of attempted deterrence. Second, the 1971 Jordanian civil war (no. 51) has a number of ambiguities, both about the nature of the outcome and the identity of the participants. Although including this case has no impact on the results presented below, I have chosen to delete it to avoid these complications.

Table 6.1. *Cases of extended-immediate deterrence*

No.	Year	Defender(s)	Attacker(s)	Protégé	Outcome
1	1885	Britain/India	Russia	Afghanistan	Success
2	1885–86	Austria-Hungary	Bulgaria	Serbia	Success
3	1886	Britain	Greece	Turkey	Success
4	1894	China	Japan	Korea	Failure
5	1897	Britain/Turkey	Greece	Crete	Success
6	1898	Britain	France	Egyptian Sudan	Success
7	1902–03	United States	Germany	Venezuela	Success
8	1903–04	Russia	Japan	Korea	Failure
9	1903–04	United States	Colombia	Panama	Success
10	1905–06	Germany	France	Morocco	Failure
11	1905–06	Britain	Germany	France	Success
12	1906	Britain	Turkey	Egypt	Success
13	1908–09	Germany	Serbia/Russia	Austria-Hungary	Success
14	1911	Turkey	Italy	Tripoli	Failure
15	1911	Germany	France	Morocco	Failure
16	1911	Britain	Germany	France	Success
17	1912–13	Germany	Serbia/Russia	Austria-Hungary	Success
18	1913	Russia	Rumania	Bulgaria	Success
20	1913	Austria-Hungary	Serbia	Albania	Success
21	1914	Russia	Austria/Germany	Serbia	Failure
22	1914	Germany	Russia/Serbia	Austria-Hungary	Failure
23	1914	Britain/Russia	Germany	France	Failure
24	1914	Britain	Germany	Belgium	Failure
25	1921	United States	Panama	Costa Rica	Success
26	1922	Britain	Turkey	Greece	Success
27	1935	Britain	Italy	Ethiopia	Failure
28	1935–36	Soviet Union	Japan	Outer Mongolia	Success
29	1937	Japan	Soviet Union	Manchukuo	Success
30	1938	Japan	Soviet Union	Manchukuo	Failure
31	1938	Britain/France	Germany	Czechoslovakia	Failure
32	1938–39	France/Britain	Italy	Tunisia	Success
33	1939	Britain/France	Germany	Poland	Failure
34	1940–41	Germany	Soviet Union	Finland	Success
35	1946	United States	Soviet Union	Iran	Success
36	1946	United States	Soviet Union	Turkey	Success
37	1948	United States	Soviet Union	West Berlin	Success
38	1950	United States	China	Taiwan	Success
39	1950	China	United States	North Korea	Failure
40	1954–55	United States	China	Quemoy-Matsu	Success
41	1957	Soviet Union	Turkey	Syria	Success
42	1961	Britain	Iraq	Kuwait	Success
43	1961	United States	North Vietnam	Laos	Success
44	1961	Portugal	India	Goa	Failure
45	1961–62	Netherlands	Indonesia	West Irian	Failure
46	1964–65	Britain	Indonesia	Malaysia	Failure

Table 6.1 (*cont.*)

No.	Year	Defender(s)	Attacker(s)	Protégé	Outcome
47	1964–65	United States	North Vietnam	South Vietnam	Failure
48	1964–65	China	United States	North Vietnam	Success
49	1967	Egypt	Israel	Syria	Failure
50	1967	Greece	Turkey	Cyprus	Failure
52	1971	China	India	Pakistan Kashmir	Success
53	1974	Greece	Turkey	Cyprus	Failure
54	1975	Spain	Morocco	Western Sahara	Failure
55	1975	Britain	Guatemala	Belize	Success
56	1977	Britain	Guatemala	Belize	Success
57	1979	Soviet Union	China	Vietnam	Failure
58	1983	France	Libya	Chad	Success

Source: Huth (1988). Note that case nos. 19 and 51 have been dropped (see fn. 1, p. 164). Reproduced with permission.

Table 6.2 isolates the cases in which the defending state had a competitive polity, as defined earlier. For each such state, it indicates the stance of the opposition regarding the desirability of meeting the attacker's threat with a retaliatory threat. Thus, the entry under "Opposition" tells us whether the opposition party in the defending state supported or opposed the threat of force in this crisis. In cases in which there was more than one such party, the opposition was coded as opposing force if any major opposition party took that stance.[2] When more than one democratic country was listed as the defender, the stances taken by opposition parties in both countries were considered. In only one case – the 1938 Munich crisis (no. 31) – was the opposition's position different in the two countries. For the purposes of the following analysis, this case was split into two, one in which Britain was the defender and one in which France is the defender. All other cases with multiple defenders were treated as single cases in order to avoid introducing non-independent observations. Notice that, in two of these cases (nos. 5 and 23), the defending side includes a democracy and a nondemocracy. These cases were treated as having only the democratic defender, since the democratic state was coded as the lead defender both times.[3] Appendix D

[2] In some cases, dissent by minor or fringe parties was ignored.
[3] Splitting these cases to treat the two defenders separately would add one success and one failure to the cases with nondemocratic defenders, a change that would have no substantive effect on the following analysis.

Table 6.2. *Democratic defenders and their opposition parties*

No.	Year	Defender(s)	Attacker(s)	Opposition	Outcome
1	1885	Britain	Russia	Support	Success
3	1886	Britain	Greece	Support	Success
5	1897	Britain	Greece	Oppose	Success[a]
6	1898	Britain	France	Support	Success
7	1902–03	United States	Germany	Support	Success
8	1903–04	United States	Columbia	Oppose	Success
11	1905–06	Britain	Germany	Support	Success
12	1906	Britain	Turkey	Support	Success
16	1911	Britain	Germany	Support	Success
23	1914	Britain	Germany	Support	Failure
24	1914	Britain	Germany	Support	Failure
25	1921	United States	Panama	Support	Success
26	1922	Britain	Turkey	Oppose	Success
27	1935	Britain	Italy	Support	Failure
31a	1938	Britain	Germany	Support	Failure
31b	1938	France	Germany	Oppose	Failure
32	1938–39	France/Britain	Italy	Support	Success
33	1939	Britain/France	Germany	Support	Failure
35	1946	United States	Soviet Union	Support	Success
36	1946	United States	Soviet Union	Support	Success
37	1948	United States	Soviet Union	Support	Success
38	1950	United States	China	Support	Success
40	1954–55	United States	China	Support	Success
42	1961	Britain	Iraq	Support	Success
43	1961	United States	North Vietnam	Support	Success
45	1961–62	Netherlands	Indonesia	Oppose	Failure
46	1964–65	Britain	Indonesia	Support	Failure
47	1964–65	United States	North Vietnam	Support	Failure
55	1975	Britain	Guatemala	Support	Success
56	1977	Britain	Guatemala	Support	Success
58	1983	France	Libya	Support	Success

Notes:
See Appendix D for details on coding and sources.
[a] See text and Appendix D for a discussion of the coding of the outcome in
  this case.

contains additional detail on the codings and the evidence used to generate them.

The first thing to notice about this list is that domestic opposition to a deterrent threat is relatively rare; we observe it in only five of the thirty-one cases in which democratic states made retaliatory threats. It might be tempting to conclude from this observation that opposition parties are extremely reluctant to oppose the government when faced with an external challenge. On the face of it, this is evidence for some kind of rally effect. This interpretation, however, ignores the selection effects that can operate in this context. States only enter this sample as defenders if the government has chosen to make a retaliatory threat. The theory suggests – and the evidence in Chapter 7 will confirm – that a democratic government is reluctant to make threats when military and political conditions are such that the opposition party would have incentives to oppose them. Hence, cases in which attackers made an initial challenge but the government was unwilling to issue a deterrent threat – anticipating that the opposition party would undermine that threat – do not appear in the sample.[4] Since some instances in which the opposition party would have publicly opposed the use of force are selected out, it is not surprising that, in those cases in which the government did choose to resist the attacker, the opposition generally supported that decision.

The theory presented here has three implications that can be probed using this data. The first is that a democratic state sends a more credible signal of resolve when the opposition supports the government's threat than when the opposition opposes that threat. The second implication is that a threat made by a democratic government and supported by the opposition party conveys a more credible signal of resolve than would the same threat if made by a nondemocratic government. This logic suggests two hypotheses:

> **Hypothesis 7:** Democratic defenders are more likely to succeed if their deterrent threat is supported by the opposition than if it is opposed.

> **Hypothesis 8:** Democratic defenders whose threats are supported are more likely to succeed than are nondemocratic defenders.

Finally, the model showed that threats made by democratic governments and opposed by the opposition should be met with the same rate of resistance as threats made by nondemocratic states. This suggests

---

[4] Unfortunately, there is no comparable data set of threats to protégés that were not met with a deterrent threat.

Table 6.3. *Deterrence outcomes as a function of the opposition's stance*

	Opposition's Stance	
Outcome	Support Force	Oppose Force
Success	19	3
	(73%)	(60%)
Failure	7	2
	(27%)	(40%)
	Pearson $\chi^2 = 0.35$	

that there should be no statistically discernible difference between the probability of success for nondemocratic defenders and the probability of success for opposed democratic defenders. We will not present this as a formal hypothesis, because one cannot test the null hypothesis associated with it.

The first of these hypotheses is hard to test given the scarcity of cases in which the opposition dissented. Table 6.3 displays a simple cross-tabulation of the opposition's strategy and the outcome of the case. As this table shows, the observed probability of success was higher when the opposition supported the government's threat (73 percent) than when the opposition opposed force (60 percent). Standard statistical tests, however, suggest that we cannot reject the null hypothesis that there is no association here.[5] The weakness of this result rests in large part on the small number of observations involving opposed threats. It should be pointed out, however, that evidence from one of these cases, the 1897 crisis over Crete, lends support to my hypothesis, even though Britain's opposed threat is coded as having been successful. As I show in Appendix D, a strong argument can be made that the deterrent threat was not successful and, moreover, that domestic opposition shaped British policy and Greek perceptions in a way that contributed to this failure. This is the only case of "successful" deterrence in the data set in which the attacker (Greece) ended up at war with one of the defenders (Turkey) over the issue in question; moreover, Greece backed down only after having been defeated militarily in the war, not as result of

---

[5] The Pearson χ^2 test yields a p-value of 0.56. A Fisher's exact test, which is particularly useful when the expected frequency in some cells is low, leads to a similar conclusion.

Table 6.4. *Deterrence outcomes as a function of defender's type*

	Defender Type	
Outcome	Supported Democratic	Nondemocratic
Success	19 (73%)	11 (42%)
Failure	7 (27%)	15 (58%)
	Pearson $\chi^2 = 5.04^b$	

Notes:
[b] $0.05 > p > 0.01$

British threats. If this case is recoded as a failure, the success rate of opposed threats is only 40 percent, and the p-value on the Pearson χ^2 test drops to 0.15, which is still above conventional levels. As I note below, this recoding has more pronounced effect in the multiple regression analysis.

The evidence in support of hypothesis 8 is more robust. Table 6.4 presents a cross-tabulation showing how the outcome varied across these two types of defenders. The results are as anticipated. The probability of success is higher when the deterrent threat was made by a democratic government and supported by the domestic opposition (73 percent) than when it was made by an nondemocratic government (42 percent). A Pearson χ^2 test shows that the association between defender type and outcome is significant below the 5 percent level. The same result holds if we pool together nondemocratic defenders and opposed democratic defenders, whose combined frequency of success is 45 percent. Moreover, there is no discernible difference in the success rates between opposed democratic defenders and nondemocratic defenders.[6]

It is important to be clear that these results are not meant to imply that the stance of the opposition party is solely responsible for the success or failure of deterrence. The opposition's support, together with the government's own actions, sends a signal that summarizes information about the state's military and political attributes. We are focusing on

---

[6] Both Pearson's χ^2 test and Fisher's exact test fail to reject the null hypothesis of no association.

variation in opposition strategies, but there may also be meaningful variation in the governments' actions. For example, although the British government is coded as having made a supported threat in both the Fashoda and Ethiopian crises, the speed and tenacity with which it threatened France in the former contrast with the slowness and timidity of its threat against Italy in the latter. The tests concentrate on the signal sent by the opposition, not because the government's signal is unimportant, but because it is the existence of the opposition's signal that systematically differentiates democratic from nondemocratic defenders. Since the opposition's stance is driven by its expectations about the likely outcome and costs of war, all factors that play a role in this calculation – e.g., the state's military capabilities, the public's tolerance for costs, the value of the issues under dispute – are reflected in the signal. In equilibrium, when these factors suggest that war would be politically successful, the government has incentives to issue a genuine threat to use force and the opposition has incentives to support the threat. As long as some of the information about the defender's value for war was not available to the attacker at the outset of the dispute, then the attacker updates in response to these signals and acts accordingly.

How do we know, then, that the parties' signals revealed new information during the crisis and did not simply tell the attacker what it already knew? The case study presented below will demonstrate this process in the context of the Fashoda case. To make the argument more general, though, we rely on the logic developed throughout this book. In order to appear in this sample, the attacker must have decided to make the initial challenge. It is reasonable to assume that it would not have done so if it was certain from the outset that the defender would resist and the attacker would have to back down from its threat. If the attacker only selects challenges that it believes it has a chance of winning, then it must learn something new between the decision to make the challenge and the decision to back down. The actions of the government and opposition are crucial in signaling this new information.

To see this empirically, we can redo the previous analysis in a manner that controls for some observable indicators to which the attacker would have had access prior to its decision to make the challenge. Huth (1988) has collected data on a number of variables that capture both the balance of military capabilities and the importance of the protégé to the defender.[7] His analysis, together with Fearon's

---

[7] See Huth (1988, pp. 57–65) for a discussion of the data coding and sources.

(1994b) reinterpretation, suggests several factors that should be included in the empirical model: the short-term balance of military capabilities, which measures the ratio of forces which the defender and protégé could muster against the attacker within the first few months of a war; an indicator for whether or not the defender possessed nuclear weapons; an indicator for whether or not the defender and protégé were allied; a measure of how important trade with the protégé was to the defender; an indicator for whether or not the defender and protégé shared a border; and a measure of arms transfers from defender to protégé. If the theory developed here is correct, the effects of democracy and domestic support that we saw above should remain even after we take into account these factors that were common knowledge at the outset of the dispute.

We can use probit analysis to model the probability of deterrence success as a function of the defender's regime type, the stance of the opposition party in democratic defenders, and the controls for information that was available *ex ante*. The results are shown in Table 6.5.[8] The two models that were estimated are identical except in their treatment of the defender. The first model (column 1) includes a dummy variable that simply records the regime type of the defending state – i.e., whether or not it had a competitive polity. The second model (column 2) differentiates democratic defenders according to whether or not the opposition supported the retaliatory threat. The theory suggests that threats made by democratic governments are more credible than those made by autocratic government when those threats are supported by the opposition; when threats are opposed by the opposition, the probability of resistance by the receiving state does not vary with regime type. The second model permits a test of these predictions.

The results generally bear out these expectations. The estimates in

---

[8] As in Chapter 5, there is some concern about non-independence among some of these cases. For example, deterrence failures surrounding the outbreak of World War I are treated as four separate cases in Huth's (1988) sample (nos. 21–24). It is likely that the outcomes in these cases were not independent of one another. Similarly, the First Moroccan Crisis is broken into two cases (nos. 10–11), as is the Second Moroccan Crisis (nos. 15–16). As noted above, I also split the Munich crisis into two observations to deal with the different responses of the opposition parties in Britain and France. Finally, because of their proximity in time, it is possible that the two cases of British deterrence successes against Guatemala (nos. 55–56) were not wholly independent. Since the outcomes of individual cases within the same crisis are not independent, we need to correct standard errors to take account of this fact. As before, Huber-White robust standard errors were calculated, and observations within the same crisis were clustered together.

Table 6.5. *The probability of successful deterrence*

Variable	(1) Coefficient (standard error)	(2) Coefficient (standard error)
Constant	−1.65 (0.61)[c]	−1.70 (0.63)[c]
Democratic defender	0.82 (0.43)[a]	
Supported democratic defender		0.93 (0.45)[b]
Opposed democratic defender		0.41 (0.58)
Democratic attacker	0.29 (0.52)	0.26 (0.52)
Balance of forces	0.72 (0.30)[b]	0.79 (0.33)[b]
Nuclear defender	0.73 (0.53)	0.61 (0.55)
Defender–protégé allied	−1.10 (0.53)[b]	−1.18 (0.52)[b]
Defender–protégé trade	0.21 (0.10)[b]	0.21 (0.10)[b]
Defender–protégé contiguous	0.19 (0.44)	0.23 (0.44)
Defender–protégé arms transfers	0.086 (0.063)	0.091 (0.063)
χ^2	16.09[b]	17.17[b]
Percent correctly predicted	78.2	75.44
(Percent modal outcome)	(57.9)	(57.9)
No. observations	57	57

Notes:
Estimates obtained using a probit regression model.
[a] $0.10 > p > 0.05$
[b] $0.05 > p > 0.01$
[c] $p < 0.01$

column (1) show that deterrent threats by democratic defenders were more likely to succeed than those issued by nondemocratic defenders; however, the coefficient on "Democratic Defender," while correctly signed, is significant only at the 10 percent level. A more robust effect emerges in column (2), which differentiates between supported and opposed defenders. As predicted by hypothesis 8, threats made by democratic governments and confirmed through the support of the opposition are significantly more likely to succeed than are threats made by nondemocratic governments. The coefficient on "Supported Democratic Defender" is positive and statistically significant. Also as predicted, the success rate for threats made by democratic governments but opposed by domestic oppositions parties is not measurably different from the rate of success for threats made by nondemocratic governments. The coefficient on "Opposed Democratic Defender" is positive but statistically indistinguishable from zero. Unfortunately, the high variance on this coefficient once again means that there is also no statistically measurable difference in the probability of success between supported threats and opposed threats.[9]

To determine whether the coding of the 1897 Cretan crisis makes a difference to this analysis, I re-ran the regressions with that case coded as a failure. The results are similar to that above, except that the difference between supported and opposed threats becomes more pronounced. In particular, the coefficient on "Opposed Democratic Defender" is negative and statistically distinguishable from the coefficient on "Supported Democratic Defender" at the 10 percent level.[10] Moreover, with this coding, we cannot observe a statistically measurable advantage for democratic defenders until we differentiate them on the basis of the opposition's stance.

To summarize, then, we can establish two relationships with these data:

Pr(Success | Supported Democracy) > Pr(Success | Nondemocracy), and

Pr(Success | Opposed Democracy) ≈ Pr(Success | Nondemocracy).

Though these relationships would seem to imply that hypothesis 7 also holds – that is, Pr(Success | Supported Democracy) > Pr(Success | Opposed Democracy) – the small number of cases in which opposition parties dissented makes it harder to establish this result with great confidence. By re-coding one case whose history is consistent with my theory, some evidence of this relationship emerges. Of course, the fact that this result is sensitive to the coding of a single case only reinforces

---

[9] A Wald test of the hypothesis that the coefficient on supported threats and the coefficient on opposed threats are equal generated a χ^2 statistic of 0.96, which is not significant at conventional levels (p = 0.33).

[10] The Wald test yields a χ^2 statistic of 3.04, which has a p-value of 0.08.

the sense that these data do not permit a reliable test of the effects of domestic dissent. Hence, we leave this topic to Chapter 7.

This weakness aside, these results are consistent with the arguments made here. Support by the opposition party in a defender state is positively correlated with deterrence success, even after controlling for military capabilities and indicators of issue salience.[11] Dissent by the opposition party reduces the probability of success to a level comparable to that of nondemocratic defenders. There is thus reason to believe that the strategies of the government and the opposition signal additional information, beyond what was known to the attacker prior to its decision to make a challenge. The remainder of this chapter delves deeper into one case in which the predictions of the theory are correct. In the Fashoda crisis, the British government went to great lengths to send costly signals of its resolve, opposition parties unanimously supported the threat to use force, and the attacker, France, ultimately backed down. While the test presented here suggests a larger pattern that is consistent with the confirmatory effect, a more detailed analysis will show that the causal mechanisms associated with this effect were actually present in this case.

Fashoda revisited

The Fashoda crisis began on September 19, 1898, when an Anglo-Egyptian expeditionary army arrived at the village of Fashoda in the Upper Nile Valley and found it occupied by a small French force.[12] The meeting was the culmination of the two countries' "race" to the Upper Nile. The French band, lead by Jean Baptiste Marchand, reached Fashoda first, having come largely uncontested from the French Congo. The much larger British force, under Sir Herbert Kitchener, had been working its way south down the west bank of the Nile, fighting occasional battles against Dervish armies. Though Marchand and Kitchener

---

[11] The coefficients on the other control variables are in the expected direction given the discussion in Huth (1988), Huth and Russett (1988), and Fearon (1994b). The only result which might look surprising is the negative sign on the coefficient for the alliance variable. As Fearon (1994b) argues, however, attackers who challenge a protégé with known alliance ties to the defender must expect a high probability of resistance *ex ante*; hence, there is little additional information in the defender's *ex post* response.

[12] I relied on a number of historical sources in constructing this case study. Excellent accounts of the Fashoda crisis can be found in Langer (1951), Grenville (1964), Sanderson (1965), Bates (1984), Andrew (1968), Wright (1951), Riker (1929), Brown (1970), and Albrecht-Carrié (1970).

greeted each other with utmost civility, the meeting touched off a diplomatic crisis over the division of colonial rights in the Upper Nile. Britain had long claimed sole right to the region and had asserted several years earlier that it would consider any attempt by the French to occupy the Nile Valley as an unfriendly act. The French, for their part, never recognized Britain's unilateral claim and hoped that the showdown could lead to a new demarcation between French and British spheres. In the end, the French had to back down entirely: Marchand abandoned Fashoda unconditionally, and British dominance in the region was reaffirmed.

As an international crisis between two major powers in the volatile pre-World War I period, the Fashoda incident has received a great deal of attention in the literature on crisis bargaining and deterrence (Snyder and Diesing 1977; Lebow 1981; Bueno de Mesquita and Lalman 1992, pp. 81–84; Peterson 1996, ch. 4). As a prominent "near miss" between two democratic states, it has also generated interest among those studying the democratic peace (Russett 1993, pp. 7–8; Ray 1995, ch. 5; Layne 1994; Doyle 1997, pp. 290–91). Given all this attention, one might legitimately ask why yet another look at this crisis is warranted. The answer is that previous work on this crisis is incomplete, and it is incomplete in a manner that usefully demonstrates the value of the arguments made in this study. After all, to make the case that I have added something new to our understanding of international relations, it makes more sense to revisit a crisis that has been considered previously than to try to explain an event that has received scant prior attention.

In addition, this case is useful for considering the merits of different perspectives on democracy and war. Scholars from both the neorealist and democratic peace camps have considered the Fashoda crisis and declared it to be consistent with their views. Summarizing conventional interpretations of this case, Elman (1997, p. 34) writes that the outcome of the Fashoda crisis is "consistent with what both the democratic peace theory and neorealist balance-of-power theory would lead us to expect":

> Critics [of the democratic peace] contend that the crisis was resolved peacefully because of the balance of power – France was far too weak to contemplate military action against the British. By contrast, democratic peace proponents maintain that even though the military balance of power goes far in explaining why the crisis was resolved short of war, shared democratic values did play a part in moderating the conflict.

I will argue that the Fashoda case is not well explained by either balance of power or democratic peace theories and, indeed, clearly contradicts them in several places. I will then show how the logic developed here provides an explanation of this case that avoids the gaps and inconsistencies of the other approaches.

Shortcomings of neorealism and democratic peace theories

The neorealist argument is straightforward: France backed down because Britain was stronger (Snyder and Diesing 1977, pp. 123–24; Layne 1994). A simple review of the military balance serves as the basis for this conclusion (Marder 1940, pp. 320–21; Langer 1951, pp. 560–61). British forces greatly outnumbered the French at Fashoda. Marchand arrived at Fashoda with roughly 120 Sengalese troops. Kitchener, by contrast, arrived with 2000 troops and had the 20,000-strong "Grand Army of the Nile" not far behind. Britain also had the advantage at the strategic level. Its navy at the time was second to none. In terms of total tonnage, the British fleet was more than twice the size of the French fleet – over 900,000 tons compared to about 420,000 tons (D'Lugo and Rogowski 1993, pp. 67–68). In the Mediterranean theater, where most of the fighting would have occurred, Britain had 18 battleships totaling 239,450 tons, while France had 15 battleships with a tonnage of only 170,085. Moreover, Britain's navy was newer, better equipped, and better integrated than France's. The British Admiralty concluded that, in the event of war, France would not have "a ghost of a chance" – a conclusion which officials on the other side of the Channel generally shared (Sanderson 1965, p. 355; Langer 1951, pp. 561–62; Bates 1984, p. 158). Given Britain's clear and overwhelming military superiority, this argument runs, France had little choice but to back down.

The main problem with the neorealist story is that it cannot explain why the crisis happened in the first place, why it lasted almost two months, and why it escalated to the point at which war was considered imminent. The military balance described above did not appear overnight. British naval superiority had been a feature of European politics for some time. In 1895, when Marchand's mission to Fashoda was first approved, the British fleet was 780,000 tons compared to France's 310,000 tons – a ratio greater than that in 1898 (D'Lugo and Rogowski 1993, p. 68). Furthermore, every fact about the military balance cited above was just as true on September 19, 1898 – the day Marchand and Kitchener met – as it was on November 3, 1898 – the day the French cabinet decided to evacuate Fashoda. If the balance of power logic made this humiliating retreat a foregone conclusion, why did the French send Marchand to Fashoda in the first place, why did they not recall him as the prospect of a clash became increasingly clear, and, failing all that, why did they not defuse the situation quietly as soon as the meeting occurred, rather than allow it to escalate into a full-blown diplomatic crisis that would bring the countries to the brink of war?

The core problem with this argument is that it depends on factors about which decision makers had complete information at the outset of the crisis. Given the costliness of the event to French honor, to the government of Henri Brisson, and to relations between the two countries, it is not at all clear why France would have let the situation reach the point that it did if in fact the outcome was preordained and common knowledge. Under complete information, the costs of the crisis and the risk of war that it entailed would have been entirely preventable. The course of events that we observe only makes sense if whatever factors convinced France to back down at the end of the crisis could not have been foreseen at the beginning of the crisis – or indeed, three years earlier when the seeds of conflict were planted.

A balance of power story cannot provide these factors. As we just saw, the naval balance between England and France had been a fact of life for some time. The extreme mismatch of forces at Fashoda was less foreseeable at the time the Marchand mission was approved since Kitchener's army did not set its sights on Khartoum and the White Nile until early 1898. Given the small size of the French group that eventually took the fortress, however, there could have been no expectation that it would be able to hold out against any appreciable European force. After all, Marchand's mission was never designed to be military in nature; his purpose was primarily political: to assert French rights in the Upper Nile and to force an international conference to settle the issue once and for all (Sanderson 1965, ch. 12). The French had to know from the outset that, if a confrontation arose, Marchand would not be able to hold his own militarily.

From a balance of power perspective, the only meaningful consideration that could have changed during this period was the disposition of third parties – particularly Germany and Russia. There had been occasional conversations between the German and French governments in this period about the possibility of cooperating to check British expansion in Africa (Sanderson 1965, pp. 327–31). Though relations between the two countries were still quite sour a quarter of a century after the Franco-Prussian war, they were at times content to use each other against the British (Taylor 1950, p. 62; Langer 1951, ch. 15). Talks between the two came to naught, however, and, 1897–98 saw a brief reconciliation between Britain and Germany. After Kitchener won a major victory at Atbara in April 1898, Kaiser Wilhelm was one of the first to send his congratulations (Sanderson 1965, p. 325; Bates 1984, p. 144). Had the French been counting on German assistance in a showdown with Great Britain, this change in the balance of power would be the kind of unanticipated event which might explain the anomalies mentioned above. The drive to Fashoda could make sense *ex ante* but look regrettable *ex post*, once Germany's attitude changed (Bates 1984, p. 144; Brown 1970, pp. 84–85).

The problem with this explanation is that there is no reason to believe that the French were ever counting on the Germans to side with them in the event that Marchand's mission provoked a confrontation. Despite occasional talks, the long-time rivals could never get past their underlying hostility and particularly the dispute over Alsace-Lorraine. French diplomats even admitted to their German counterparts that open cooperation between the two countries was politically unthinkable given the attitude of the French public (Taylor 1950, p. 62; Sanderson 1965, pp. 327–31; Carroll 1931, p. 170; Brown 1970, pp. 75–76). Moreover, even if this shift in German attitudes accounts for the initial mistake of going to Fashoda, Germany's position was well known by September 1898, when the crisis began (Brown 1970, pp. 84–85).

Russia is the other third party whose involvement might have affected the balance of power. Despite its alliance with France, Russia had no intention of intervening against Britain in a war over Fashoda. From a practical standpoint, the Russian fleet was ice-bound from November to April, meaning that France's navy would have been at the bottom of the sea long before its ally could join the fray (Sanderson 1965, p. 355). More importantly, Russia did not consider Fashoda to be worth a war against Britain (Langer 1951, pp. 562–63). The Russian foreign minister, Count Muraviev, apparently told the French as much when he visited Paris on October 15, in the midst of the crisis. Again, had France been expecting assistance from Russia, this new information could account for the pattern of events: the French allowed the situation to develop into a crisis because they anticipated help from their ally; when they learned that such help would not be forthcoming, they looked for a way to back down.

As before, though, there is no evidence that French actions were shaped by an expectation of Russian assistance. Indeed, from early on, French decision makers seem to have resigned themselves to going it alone. In 1896–87, as Marchand was making his way to Fashoda, French Foreign Minister Hanotaux failed to raise the issue with the Russian government on several occasions. Sanderson (1965, p. 314) suggests that Hanotaux feared that a direct request would lead to a direct refusal, and "he was really well aware that he had nothing to hope for in this quarter." His successor, Théophile Delcassé, was reminded of Russia's indifference on this point when, one month before the crisis erupted, the tsar proposed an international conference on the limitation of armaments and said nothing about the ongoing dispute over Egypt – the one topic which France desperately wanted such a conference to address (*ibid.*, p. 327). It is clear that, going into the crisis, France could have expected little in the way of assistance from its ally. Muraviev's discouraging message only told the French what they already knew.

In sum, balance of power theory does not account for this case very well. Its deterministic view can not explain why France chose to challenge Britain in the first place, nor why the French risked war and political upheaval in a showdown which, if we are to believe this story, they were doomed to lose from the outset. Unless French decision makers blundered from start to finish, there had to be some uncertainty, some lack of information, which explains their actions. Neorealism, with its focus on relative military power and alliances, does not provide this essential element.

Theories of the democratic peace – in both their normative or institutional forms – fare no better. Whereas the neorealist story fails primarily by being incomplete, elements of the democratic peace story are directly contradicted by many aspects of the crisis. Consider first the normative argument, which posits that democratic states are motivated by shared liberal norms that mandate mutual respect for legitimate interests, a willingness to compromise, and a hesitancy to use or threaten force as a means of dispute settlement. Most of these expectations are not borne out. The British position was entirely unyielding – to the point that Prime Minister Salisbury refused even to call discussions between the two countries "negotiations." Intransigence was backed by a willingness to threaten war, a step the cabinet took on October 28, when it ordered the mobilization of the fleet. British public opinion was more nationalistic than liberal. As Sir William Harcourt noted, "We shall either see the submission of France which will be popular or a war with France which will be more popular still" (Koss 1981, p. 381).

While much of this has been noted before, especially by Layne (1994), there is an additional observation about this case that seems strongly inconsistent with the normative argument. It is well known that France in this period was in the midst of serious domestic turmoil stemming from the Dreyfus Affair. Emile Zola's *J'accuse* was published in January 1898, and, at the end of August, a French colonel was arrested for forging a document that had been used to prove Dreyfus's guilt (Brown 1970, p. 8). The affair was thus thrust onto the political scene at the same time that the Fashoda incident was unfolding. The social and political unrest that accompanied this affair threatened not only the government but also the future of constitutional democracy. Throughout October, there were rumors that a *coup d'état* was in the making. Particularly frightening were the events of October 25, when the minister of war, General Jules Chanoine, announced his resignation and precipitated the fall of the cabinet (*ibid.*, pp. 109–11).

British decision makers were well aware of the danger and of their role in exacerbating the political situation. On October 14, the British ambassador in Paris, Edmund Monson, passed on a secret report suggesting that a group of dissident generals was planning a coup (Brown 1970, p. 111). Monson's warnings intensified after the events of October 25, when he wrote that Chanoine's resignation was "an act of treachery which looks like the first step to a military coup d'état." He further warned that the situation could lead to the "advent of a military government or of a nominally civilian government in the hands of the military party" (*ibid.*, pp. 110–11). Although the underlying cause of this instability was the Dreyfus affair, Britain's insistence that the French government accept either war or humiliation over Fashoda was not helping things. The British cabinet responded to these concerns, not by moderating its position, but by ordering the mobilization of the fleet, thereby turning the screws even tighter (*ibid.*, p. 112). This seems deeply problematic for an argument based on shared liberal norms. Liberal Britain was unwilling to make even the smallest concession to help ensure that a fellow liberal state did not succumb to military dictatorship.[13] Britain's intransigence – already problematic for the normative theory – seems damning in the light of this consideration.

Where the normative argument may be most useful is in providing some contextual factors that play an important role in this case. The crisis over Fashoda was a conflictual interlude in a relationship that was

[13] In a personal communication, Michael Doyle suggests that British concerns about a coup may have been mitigated by an expectation that an interruption of democratic rule in France would be temporary. This is a plausible argument, and I could find no evidence either to support or refute it.

otherwise becoming increasingly harmonious. Whether one attributes the growing closeness between Britain and France to balance of power considerations (e.g., Gowa 1999) or to shared liberal understandings (e.g., Russett 1993, pp. 7–8) – or both – it is clear that this period witnessed a growing affinity between the two countries, especially among liberal factions and moderate conservatives. This context likely contributed to France's assessment of its payoff from backing down.[14] Among French decision makers, there seems to have been a perception that, once the Fashoda matter was settled, the stage would be set for further cooperation between the countries, in both colonial and European affairs. Thus, while capitulation was not an attractive option, it was made more so by the perception that it would pave the way for more harmonious relations, rather than further predation. When responding to a threat, states must weigh both the credibility of the threat and the relative payoffs of war and capitulation. To the extent that the growing affinity in Anglo-French relations increased France's assessment of the latter, it was more likely to choose that course.

Turning to the institutional constraints argument, we again find much contradictory evidence in this case. Especially in Britain, accountability, competition, and diffusion of authority generated not caution and pacifism but belligerence and intransigence. As already noted, the British public was generally incensed that the French had challenged Britain's sphere of influence in Africa. Moreover, as we will see, Salisbury manipulated the popular mood in order to bolster his bargaining position. By taking advantage of and stoking the public's outrage, Salisbury was able to convince the French that he had no leeway to offer concessions. In this way, accountability and competition helped lead to a peaceful outcome, but they did so, not by increasing the political risks of war, but by highlighting the political risks of compromise.

The institutional constraints argument is particularly problematic given that Salisbury himself was inclined to be more flexible than he ultimately could be. The aging prime minister was trained in the old school of diplomacy, which emphasized polite negotiations and "graceful concessions" (Brown 1970, pp. 92–93). In addition, Salisbury doubted that British possessions in Northern Africa were particularly valuable, and he wanted to prevent entanglements there from adversely affecting Britain's position in Europe (Penson 1962, pp. 16–17; Peterson 1996, p. 104). Nevertheless, public opinion and cabinet politics ultimately forced

---

[14] I am grateful to Michael Doyle for raising this consideration.

Salisbury into an intransigent position. The public and the press were in no mood for diplomatic niceties. Salisbury noted as much in a letter to Queen Victoria on October 3, writing "No offer of territorial concession on our part would be endured by public opinion here" (Langer 1951, p. 556). The prime minister also had to contend with hard-liners in his cabinet, particularly Joseph Chamberlain, the colonial secretary (Peterson 1996, pp. 103–06). When the cabinet met on October 27, Salisbury passed on to his colleagues a compromise solution proposed by the French ambassador according to which the French would "spontaneously" recall Marchand from Fashoda and then the British would "spontaneously" offer negotiations that could lead to a French possession on the Nile. Salisbury was inclined to accept this formula; the cabinet, on the other hand, was in no mood for compromise and instead ordered the mobilization of the fleet (Sanderson 1965, p. 350; Brown 1970, pp. 112–13; Peterson 1996, p. 126). Thus, the prime minister was constrained, but not in the manner that the institutional constraints argument suggests. Had Salisbury enjoyed greater autonomy from domestic political pressures, he probably would have been more conciliatory and less willing to risk war.

Incomplete information and the onset of the crisis

The theory developed here offers an explanation for this case that avoids the gaps and inconsistencies of the other approaches. It suggests that the French decision to challenge Britain, in spite of the latter's obvious military superiority, stemmed from incomplete information about the British government's preferences and constraints going into the crisis. Moreover, it points to the role of democratic political institutions in bringing about a peaceful resolution of the crisis – not by inducing caution, pacifism, or mutual respect, but by allowing the British government to signal its resolve in a credible and unmistakable manner. The French ultimately backed down, not simply because Britain was militarily stronger, but because the British were able to convince the French that they were politically able and willing to risk war rather than make concessions.

The main source of the uncertainty at the outset of the affair surrounded the nature of British preferences and, particularly, the level of concessions the British government would make in exchange for Fashoda. Recall that the Marchand mission was primarily political in nature. His small band was sent not to hold Fashoda against an attacking force but rather to assert French rights in the region and to provoke a settlement of outstanding colonial issues. When Kitchener's much larger force confronted the French at Fashoda, there was little doubt that, if the British wanted to take the fortress, they could. The question for France was: what might they get in return for recalling Marchand? Though Britain would clearly win in the event of a war, it was not at all clear *ex ante* that Salisbury would insist on an unconditional withdrawal. After all, war is costly even to the winning side. The greater these costs, the more a government may be willing to compromise to avoid incurring them. In provoking the crisis, France was gambling that Britain would prefer making minor concessions to fighting a war.

The initial French plan – using a confrontation to spark an international conference – was abandoned before the meeting at Fashoda even took place, as other countries, especially Russia, expressed little interest in getting involved. Nevertheless, once the crisis had begun, Delcassé expressed optimism that France could get small, but strategic, gains in return for recalling Marchand. Delcassé hoped to acquire territory in the Bahr-el-Ghazal region and a French outlet on the Nile (Bates 1984, pp. 152–53; Brown 1970, p. 92; Sanderson 1965, p. 344).

In forming these expectations, the French had reason to believe that the British would not look kindly on their incursion. In 1895, Sir Edward Grey, the under-secretary for foreign affairs, had made his famous declaration that any French expedition to the Upper Nile would be considered "an unfriendly act" (Langer 1951, p. 265). Then, in December 1897, Salisbury sent an unusually blunt note to Hanotaux telling him that Britain would not recognize any claims to the Nile Valley by any other European power and that France should abandon its designs in the Bahr-el-Ghazal (Sanderson 1965, pp. 319–20). Such signals led Hanotaux, and later Delcassé, to expect modest gains at best.

Nevertheless, French decision makers did not predict the intransigence of the British response. As a well-connected French publicist later noted, "it was never foreseen that one could be made to leave the field of diplomacy" (quoted in Sanderson 1965, p. 361). While British claims to the region were well known, it was not believed at the outset that Britain would be willing to fight rather than make even the smallest concession. On March 17, 1897, a French agent in Cairo wrote to Hanotaux that a French force at Fashoda "would form a barrier that England could cross only at the cost of a war which is hardly to be feared, or of concessions which it will be up to us to assess" (quoted in Sanderson 1965, p. 361). In November 1898, following the French retreat, the same agent wrote to Hanotaux again to explain why that expectation, which was clearly wrong after the fact, had seemed reasonable at the time:

> Intelligent people never thought that we would go so far as to make war for the Nile, when we would not do it for the Rhine; but almost everyone accepted as proven truth that England would never open hostilities; that her warships were only designed to frighten, that her commercial interests would always prevent her from seeing her communications with the continent interrupted by a state of war.
>
> (Quoted in Sanderson 1965, p. 361)

In addition, the French knew that in Salisbury they faced a diplomat with a reputation for making "graceful concessions" (Brown 1970, pp. 92–93). In August 1898, a month before the crisis erupted, the French chargé d'affaires in London, M. Geoffray, referred to the prime minister as "the English statesmen with whom negotiations were most likely to bring good results, and with whom one was most likely to find a common ground to satisfy all interested parties" (quoted in Peterson 1996, p. 114). The initial reading from the French side was that Salisbury had incentives to smooth things over with France (e.g., France, MFA 1957, pp. 571–73).

Given these beliefs, Delcassé went into the affair with modest, but optimistic, expectations. That Marchand would have to be recalled was clear from early on. Delcassé paved the way for such a move even before the mission reached Fashoda. In July, the minister of colonies, Georges Trouillot, wrote to Delcassé to inform him that Marchand was nearing Fashoda and that Kitchener's army was likely to be close behind. Trouillot asked for advice on how to proceed. Delcassé responded in early September, after a two-month delay, that Marchand should not go as far as Fashoda. By this point, of course, it was too late to change Marchand's instructions. The letter's purpose was primarily political: it gave the French the ability to disavow the Marchand mission should things go badly (Bates 1984, pp. 143–44). Indeed, in conversations with Monson during September, when the meeting at Fashoda looked imminent, Delcassé insisted that "there is no Marchand mission" and that the French explorer was simply "an emissary of civilization" (Foreign Office 1927, pp. 163; 165; Langer 1951, pp. 555–56).

Still, Delcassé chose not to use this ploy to avoid the showdown altogether. The French foreign minister thought he could score a small diplomatic victory by wresting concessions from Britain. Rather than simply pulling Marchand out without a quarrel, he insisted to Monson that the French had never recognized Britain's claim to a sphere of influence in the Upper Nile and that France had as much right to be at Fashoda as Kitchener had to be at Khartoum (GB, Foreign Office 1927, pp. 165; 169–70; 171; Brown 1970, p. 89). In these initial discussions, Delcassé even went so far as to state that France would prefer war to outright submission (GB, Foreign Office 1927, p. 172). Thus, even though Delcassé had been dealt a questionable hand, he chose to play rather than fold. The intensifying domestic turmoil surrounding the Dreyfus Affair seems to have reinforced this motivation. Delcassé reasoned that any concessions won in exchange for Marchand's recall would allow the government to claim a major political achievement, thereby preventing its fall (Brown 1970, p. 92). Given the expectation that Salisbury did not want a war, this gamble seems not unreasonable *ex ante*.

Domestic politics and signaling in Great Britain

Over the course of the following month, the French learned that these initial expectations had been incorrect. The signals emanating from Britain during this period took many forms, but all contained the same message: the French would have to evacuate Fashoda unconditionally or face war. Actions taken by the government – and confirmed by the opposition – made it clear where the former's political incentives lay. Public opinion was such that the political risks of war were small while the political risks of compromise were potentially large. Moreover, these constraints were not simply fixed, but also manipulated. Rather than working against the jingoism of the public, Salisbury and his ministers cultivated the public's hostility in order to convince French decision makers that they could not grant concessions. Similarly, the stance of the opposition, rather than giving the government a way out, reinforced and reiterated these political constraints. The overall result was a clear message that France would have to withdraw unconditionally if it wished to avoid war.

As predicted by Fearon (1992, 1994a), signals from the government were sent in a way that entailed high and visible audience costs. They were made publicly, in full view of the British electorate, and they were designed to arouse public opinion so that it would be difficult for the government to later back down. The most prominent example of such signaling came on October 10, when Salisbury took the unusual step of publishing a blue book on the crisis, a collection of key dispatches between the two countries. Until this point, the negotiations had taken place in private. With the publication of the blue book, the positions taken and arguments made by both sides were out in the open. The British public could see for its own eyes the uncompromising position of the government, as well as the audacity of French claims. Salisbury's action was not only unusual but a breach of prevailing diplomatic norms: "as a matter of courtesy, records of diplomatic negotiations are not generally given to the public until the negotiations with which they are concerned are ended" (Grenville 1964, p. 228). At the same time, the move had tremendous signaling value. By publicizing Britain's stance in such an unusual manner, Salisbury effectively painted himself into a corner: retreat from this position would entail substantial political costs. The impact of the move was not lost on contemporaries. The day the blue book was published, *The Times* noted: "We cannot conceal from ourselves that Lord Salisbury and his colleagues have taken a position from which retreat is impossible. One side or the other will have to give way. That side cannot, after the publication of these papers, be Great Britain" (quoted in Riker 1929, p. 67).

In addition to the publication of the blue book, members of the governing Tory party made numerous public statements reaffirming their country's uncompromising stance in the crisis. Prominent among these were the remarks of Sir Michael Hicks-Beach, the chancellor of the exchequer, who declared on October 19 that "this country has put its foot down. If, unhappily, another view should be taken elsewhere, we, the Ministers of the Queen, know what our duty demands. It would be a great calamity. . . But there are greater evils than war" (quoted in Langer 1951, p. 553). In making such statements, Hicks-Beach and others put their political fortunes – and that of their party – on the line: backing down after making such unequivocal statements would have entailed substantial political risks. Such a move would call into question the credibility of the government. Thus, threats and statements of this kind were not costless, cheap talk. Instead, they exposed the government to substantial audience costs and, in doing so, sought to convey information to the French. And the message being sent was clear: Britain would fight rather than accept French demands.

Despite the clarity of this message, Riker (1929) argues that the success of these threats was due in large part to the approval they received from outside the governing party. Salisbury could be expected to toot his own horn, though the way in which he did it strongly suggested that he was not bluffing. Support from other elements of society – and especially those with different preferences from the government – was crucial: "for, if that support were meagre or half-hearted, the French cabinet would be able to temporize without incurring too great a risk" (Riker 1929, p. 67). As predicted by the theory developed here, the expectations that war would be successful, both militarily and politically, generated support from across the political spectrum, including the opposition Liberal Party. As Langer (1951, p. 553) notes, "Liberals vied with Unionists and Tories in putting themselves at the disposal of the government and in calling upon the cabinet to assume an unyielding attitude."

The most prominent example of this support came in a speech delivered by Liberal Party leader Lord Rosebery on October 12. In this speech Rosebery gave adamant, though uncharacteristic, approval to the stance taken by his political rival, Lord Salisbury, declaring that "Behind the policy of the government is the united strength of the nation. No Government that attempted to recede from or palter with that policy would last a week. The nation will make any sacrifice and go any length to sustain them" (quoted in Wright 1951, p. 41). Clearly, Rosebery's words conveyed the message that the government had the public support and political cover to take a hard line against France. In taking this stand, Rosebery sought to claim credit for what he had every reason to expect would be a foreign policy victory. The Liberal leader pointed out in his speech that the Grey Declaration of 1895, which was being used to justify Britain's negotiating position, had been issued under his administration. Indeed, Rosebery claimed, he was "personally and Ministerially responsible" for it (quoted in Sanderson 1965, p. 347). This tactic is entirely consistent with the argument made in Chapter 3 that opposition parties support the government when they expect a favorable outcome in order to share some of the credit and thereby blunt the political impact of the government's likely success.

Rosebery's lead was followed by every major Liberal politician. The *Annual Register* (1899, p. 166), a yearbook of British events, lists more than a half dozen prominent Liberals who publicly lined up behind Salisbury, concluding that "hardly a single politician of any note raised his voice in unfavorable criticism of the position taken by her Majesty's Government." Only the radical John Morely strayed from this line (Sanderson 1965, p. 359; Lebow 1981, p. 322).

It is important to note that the support of the Liberals came at a time when that party was split into imperialist and anti-imperialist wings. Because of this split, the Liberal party rarely spoke with one voice on colonial matters. In the Fashoda case, however, even the more strident skeptics of Britain's imperial policy lined up behind the government.

The anti-imperialist Harcourt, who had expressed displeasure with the Grey Declaration and would later become an outspoken critic of the Boer War, nevertheless gave his public backing to the government's policy in a speech on October 28 (Gardiner 1923, pp. 335–36, 470). The significance of this development should be clear from our discussion of policy preferences in Chapter 4. Although the support of pro-imperial Liberals is not entirely unexpected, the support of anti-imperial Liberals is noteworthy.

How were all these signals interpreted by French decision makers? At first, the French ambassador, Baron de Courcel, seems to have been unsure what effect the publication of the blue book would have. He initially greeted this action with the cautious hope that the British public would reflect soberly on the arguments made by both countries and that the mounting tide of anti-French feeling would subside (France, MFA 1957, pp. 647–48). On the other hand, he also realized that the move could have precisely the opposite effect. In a letter to Delcassé the day the blue book appeared, he noted, "It seems that, with this haughty language, the English government will cut itself off from all retreat, and that it will be impossible for it to back down from demands made in such a manner" (*ibid.*, p. 651). As it turns out, the latter warning was more accurate.

It did not take long for French diplomats to notice this development and to realize the implications it had for France. In a letter to Delcassé dated October 20, Geoffray, the French chargé d'affaires in London, observed the aggressive mood of the British public: "The possibility of an armed conflict with France . . . is seen as almost the only way out of the present difficulties." Geoffray was somewhat dismissive of the speech made by Hicks-Beach, since he saw the chancellor of the exchequer as a man who was prone to belligerent talk (France, MFA 1957, pp. 679–80). Courcel, however, observed these events with less optimism. He had hoped that the British public would calm down with the passage of time, but this was not turning out to be the case. In a letter to Geoffray on October 21, he wrote, "The tone of the English newspapers, which have again become so acrimonious for some days, the same tone that members of the cabinet have adopted in their public discourse, disturbs me and frightens me" (*ibid.*, p. 693). A few days later, the ambassador conveyed these fears to Delcassé, noting that "British opinion [is] very much aroused over the Fashoda affair. In every class of the population, the idea has spread that war is the only possible way out of the current difficulties." Courcel observed that the war-like mood of the public would make it quite difficult for Salisbury to show any signs of weakness (*ibid.*, pp. 708–09).

The French ambassador clearly appreciated the audience costs that Salisbury and his government had generated and feared that war would be inevitable unless France backed down. Although he believed that Salisbury desired peace, Courcel also understood that the British leader's hands were tied by the uncompromising stance he had so publicly taken. Writing to Delcassé on October 29, he reported that the "suspicious state of English public opinion does not allow the Prime Minister to seem at all lenient toward any rapprochement with France" (France, MFA 1957, p. 730). Moreover, Courcel suspected, correctly, that Salisbury was using the public's war-like mood to tie his hands and improve Britain's bargaining position. In a letter of October 28, he told Delcassé that "Lord Salisbury has entrenched himself in English public opinion thereby preventing his government from negotiating as long as French forces occupied Fashoda" (*ibid.*, p. 720).

Like the costly signals coming from the government, the support of British opposition groups was not lost on French diplomats. Geoffray's letter of October 20 noted that "the Liberals have come out as much if not more intransigent than the partisans in the government" (France, MFA 1957, p. 679). As before, Geoffray was somewhat dismissive of this at first, because he considered such "bluff" to be common among the English, and he held out the hope that cooler heads would eventually prevail. The sustained support and belligerence of the opposition, however, convinced Courcel otherwise. In his letter of October 26, the French ambassador noted that the Liberals' willingness to capitalize on the public's pro-war sentiment had placed Salisbury in a political bind: "It is certain that this state of mind has made much more difficult the job of the government, which seems attached to the cause of peace, but which fears being accused of weakness, all the more so because its political adversaries are expressing even more intransigent patriotism" (*ibid.*, p. 709). He added that the unanimity of opinion in England resembled the situation in the United States prior to its declaration of war against Spain – implying that France should not make the same mistake Spain did under those conditions (*ibid.*, p. 709).

On October 29, after the British cabinet publicly reiterated its uncompromising position and set naval preparations in motion, Courcel concluded that the only remaining choice was between war and withdrawal. In his letter to Delcassé, Courcel wrote, "There is simply no alternative. Procrastination and delays will only heighten tensions. It is, therefore, up to us, if we want peace, to find a way of leaving Fashoda with honor and our head held high" (France, MFA 1957, p. 727). Courcel was convinced that Britain would not, and could not, back down at this point. Delcassé came to the same conclusion. On the same day that Courcel wrote this letter, Delcassé wrote to Courcel instructing him to propose yet another compromise. The next day, he reversed himself, declaring that it was "useless" to try making such an offer (Brown 1970, p. 115). Given all the signals coming out of Britain, there could be little doubt at this point that any offer other than unconditional withdrawal would be rejected, quite possibly leading to war. The actual order to evacuate Fashoda awaited the formation of a new government, since the previous cabinet had fallen several days before. On November 1, a new cabinet was formed, and two days later, at Delcassé's urging, it voted to recall Marchand.

Domestic politics and signaling in France

Although the story of the Fashoda crisis is primarily a story of credible signals sent by the British side, it is also worth discussing the signals emanating from the political scene in France. The behavior of government and opposition figures foreshadows the patterns we will see in Chapter 7 – which examines additional cases of domestic dissent – rather than the pattern we saw above. Whereas the British government made forceful signals that were intended to commit it to an intransigent position, the French government was much more cautious about making public commitments. Whereas Salisbury enjoyed support from across the political spectrum, Delcassé found himself in the cross-fire between the anti-imperialist left and the pro-imperialist right. In short, whereas Britain signaled unanimity and resolve, France could not hide obvious indicators of division and weakness.

The French government's expectations about war were driven both by the country's military inferiority and by the ambivalence of the electorate. The military balance has already been addressed, and there is no doubt that the prospect of likely defeat contributed to the French government's low expectations. But, of course, weak states can and do challenge stronger states, if they are sufficiently interested in the matters under dispute. Here, too, though, conditions militated against a forceful response on France's part. Unlike in Britain, public opinion in France was apathetic and divided over the Fashoda issue (Carroll 1931, pp. 172–75; Sanderson 1965, pp. 359–61; Brown 1970, pp. 107–08; Lebow 1981, p. 325). Although there was a strong nationalist faction that openly called for war, those in the middle and on the left felt that such war would be for the wrong reason – since a symbolic possession in the Sudan was not worth very much – and against the wrong foe – since, after all, Germany was still public enemy number one. The divisions of opinions on foreign policy were reinforced by the divisions which the Dreyfus Affair had uncovered. Many anti-Dreyfusards were pro-military and pro-colonial, while many Dreyfusards were anti-imperialist and pacifist.

War was thus a bad bet, both militarily and politically. In response to these constraints, Delcassé adopted a tone much less strident than that of his British counterparts, and when he did choose to makes threats, he generally refrained from doing so in a public manner that would expose the government to audience costs. At the same time, the split within public opinion manifested itself as a split among political parties. Whereas British parties across the political spectrum lined up in support of an intransigent position, French parties were deeply divided.

The most forceful declaration from Delcassé came in a meeting with Monson, the British ambassador, on September 30, when Delcassé declared that France "would accept war rather than submit" to England's demand of unconditional withdrawal (GB, Foreign Office 1927, p. 172). He continued: "It is not from the minister before you that you can expect a capitulation" (Brown 1970, p. 99). Notice that although this statement is similar in content to the one from Hicks-Beach quoted above, the form of its delivery was quite different. Whereas Hicks-Beach made his threat in a public speech, Delcassé made his in a private meeting that was explicitly "unofficial" (*ibid.*, p. 172). The former exposed the deliverer to audience costs and thus conveyed some information; the latter could be considered meaningless cheap talk.

Delcassé's relative silence in public exposed him to a great deal of criticism from the nationalists, who accused him of abandoning French interests and honor. The foreign minister made some modest public efforts to mollify the right, but he was generally averse to conducting negotiations in the public view (Bates 1984, p. 154). One of the few public gestures he made was an article which appeared on October 5 in *Le Matin*, a paper which was generally considered a mouthpiece of the Foreign Ministry. The headline of that article read "No! The only response worthy of France," and it went on to argue that the government was fully responsible for the Marchand mission and had no intention of backing down in the face of threats (GB, Foreign Office 1927, p. 175; Brown 1970, p. 100). Delcassé's early threats and the article in *Le*

Matin seem to have shaken Monson, whose telegrams to Salisbury in late September and early October warn of the possibility that France might not back down. Monson seems to have been particularly worried that, in the midst of the Dreyfus Affair, the French government could not give in to British demands without risking an internal explosion (Brown 1970, pp. 99–100; Bates 1984, p. 154).

This effort to publicly commit the French government to a firm stance, however, was quickly undermined only a few days later. On October 7 and 8, *Le Matin* ran articles arguing, in the words of Monson, that the "abandonment of Fashoda is perfectly compatible with the preservation of the national honour" (GB, Foreign Office 1927, p. 178; see also Sanderson 1965, p. 346). Moreover, Delcassé's tone moderated considerably over the following weeks. Though he continued to demand that Britain abandon its intransigence, his statements sound more like pleas than threats. At one point, Monson noted that Delcassé "seemed very despondent" (*ibid.*, p. 179).

The French did respond to Salisbury's publication of the blue book by publishing a yellow book a little over a week later. However, Delcassé assured Monson that the published documents were chosen to be "as conciliatory as possible," a characterization with which Monson agreed (GB, Foreign Office 1927, p. 185). The French yellow book even omitted a telegram that might have been construed, inaccurately, as a promise from Russia that it would come to France's aid in the event of war (Sanderson 1965, pp. 356–57). Though Delcassé showed this telegram to Monson in private, he told the British ambassador that he did not want to make it public for fear of arousing "excitement" in Paris (GB, Foreign Office 1927, p. 185). Indeed, French President Félix Faure had insisted that the telegram be withheld from the yellow book for precisely this reason, noting "these dispatches were likely to overexcite the national sentiment of people who were counting on Russia's promises to make trouble" (quoted in Sanderson 1965, p. 359). Given that no aid from Russia was promised or forthcoming, the government wanted to avoid making its bluff to this effect in public. Thus, while Salisbury's blue book was intended to inflame his domestic audience, France's response had the opposite intention.

The weak signals coming from the French government were reinforced by the appearance of domestic opposition. The image of unity conveyed by British political parties stands in stark contrast to the divisions clearly evident in French politics. Domestic debate over the Fashoda crisis intertwined with debate over the Dreyfus Affair, reinforcing and emphasizing the discord between opposing parties. The situation in France was more complicated than the rather simple model presented in Chapter 4 portrays, yet the basic intuition of the model still applies: the weakness of the government's position was underscored by dissent from some opposition parties.

The main complication of the French case is that the party system was not very stable during this period, so it is harder to identify lasting parties that can be divided into government and opposition. Instead, there were a number of factions across the political spectrum. From the perspective of the Brisson cabinet, two opposition factions were particularly salient as the Dreyfus Affair heated up: the Dreyfusard left and the anti-Dreyfusard right. The former were generally anti-imperialist and anti-militarist, while the latter were strongly nationalist and imperialist (Brown 1970, p. 107). Reactions to the Fashoda crisis generally accorded with these biases. The far right demanded a strong stance against Britain and decried any sign of compromise. Interestingly, some declarations from the right conceded that France would probably lose a war with Britain, but demanded that one be fought anyway, for the sake of national honor (Langer 1951, p. 561). Such statements can hardly be considered a signal of strength, though they do reflect political pressures on the government to stand firm.

The left, on the other hand, denounced the Marchand mission and demanded that France withdraw. Dreyfusards of both socialist and non-socialist bent considered the crisis "senseless" and called a prospective war with Britain "the most criminal of adventures" (quoted in Brown 1970, p. 107; see also Sanderson 1965, pp. 359–60; Carroll 1931, pp. 172–75). The opposition of the French left stands in sharp contrast to the support Salisbury received from the British left, from anti-imperialist Liberals to a socialist worker's group (Riker 1929, p. 67). Thus, while nationalists and colonialists in both countries advocated firm stances, only in Britain did the government get support from *anti*-imperialist factions.

In sum, Britain saw in France a divided enemy that was unfit for war. The greatest fear among British policy makers was that the French government would fall to a military coup, which would install a much more militarist and reckless regime. "Seen from London, France appeared to be on the eve of civil war – weak, but potentially warlike and aggressive" (Brown 1970, p. 112). Given all the signals of France's weakness, though, the British government decided it was better off standing firm and risking war, than backing down and risking the wrath of its own people (*ibid.*, pp. 112–13). The probability that France would fight was sufficiently low that this course was judged to be optimal.

Conclusion

Ultimately, then, this story is consistent with the contemporaneous explanation offered by Joseph Chamberlain, who boasted that the British victory was due "as much to the spectacle . . . of an absolutely united people as it was to those military and naval armaments about which the foreign Press talks so much and knows so little."[15] Although the balance of military power was important, the decisive factor was Britain's ability to convince France that it was willing to use that power rather than make the slightest concession. In this, the government was greatly aided both by its ability to generate large audience costs and by the confirmatory signals that emerged from opposition figures of all stripes. French leaders, by contrast, generally avoided actions which would tie their hands and saw their position undercut by vocal opposition to the use of force among large segments of the body politic. By the end of the crisis, France knew that Britain was ready to fight, and Britain knew that France was not.

One feature of this crisis which deserves additional comment is the relationship between the confirmatory effect and the rally-around-the-flag effect. The argument that domestic support helps to confirm the signal sent by the government relies on the assumption that such support is freely given and motivated by the opposition's expectations about the political ramifications of war. The opposition's support is meaningful because it is not given automatically but only when the opposition expects war to be politically successful. If such support were automatic – as is implied by the rally-around-the-flag story – then there would be no confirmatory effect. An opposition that always backs the government's threats regardless of the state's type conveys no useful information. Rival states could dismiss such support as a patriotic reflex. Hence, there is a fundamental tension between the rally effect and the confirmatory effect.

The analysis of the Fashoda case suggests how this tension might play itself out. Early in the crisis, French envoys in London seem to have discounted the public's war-like mood and the belligerence of the Liberals

---

[15] Chamberlain's speech was reported in *The Times* of 16 November 1898.

precisely because they thought these reactions were nothing more than an emotional outburst that would soon subside. Hence, Courcel's initial reaction to the release of the blue book was that it would cause the British public to sober up and think more rationally about the issues under contention. The letters from Courcel and Geoffray express the hope that the passions stirred by the French challenge were temporary and that the public's distaste for war would soon reassert itself. Partly for this reason, the French tried to drag the affair out. Delcassé insisted that he would not recall Marchand until he had a chance to get the latter's report about conditions at Fashoda. Given the difficulties of communicating with an isolated outpost in Northern Sudan, this request gave the French several weeks to delay: Marchand's report did not arrive in Paris until October 22. Unfortunately for the French, however, the belligerent mood among British politicians and public did not subside. Thus, Courcel's later dispatches are quite pessimistic. By this point, it was clear that support for the government's position would persist beyond France's ability to temporize. What could initially be discounted as patriotic reflex had to be taken seriously as a signal of the British government's ability to risk – and, if necessary, to wage – war over Fashoda.

This suggests that the rally effect and the confirmatory effect can both coexist, if the former is seen as temporary. Indeed, Brody and Shapiro (1989) observe that the period in a crisis in which the government can count on support from opposition elites is rather short – often, only a matter of days. Once this initial period has passed, dissent sometimes emerges, and sometimes does not. Thus, while the first, reflexive response of oppositions and publics might be legitimately discounted, persistent support is informative. As the historical analysis of the Fashoda case and the statistical analysis of extended-immediate deterrence crises suggest, when both the government and its political adversaries publicly agree on the desirability of using force, the result is a highly credible – and hence effective – signal of resolve.

7 Credibility undermined: the implications of domestic dissent

"The representatives of a democracy cannot run contrary to the basic wishes of the people in any game of bluff."

John F. Kennedy[1]

Chapter 6 showed how public signals of domestic support can increase the credibility, and hence the effectiveness, of threats made by democratic governments. In this chapter, we consider the other side of the coin: how actual or anticipated dissent can constrain democratic governments from making threats in a crisis and undermine the credibility of the threats they choose to make. In particular, this chapter presents evidence to support two final hypotheses:

> **Hypothesis 9:** Expected dissent from the opposition party reduces the likelihood that the government will bluff.

> **Hypothesis 10:** When a democratic government makes a threat, foreign decision makers will interpret domestic opposition as an indication that the government has political incentives to avoid using force.

Together, these hypotheses articulate the causal mechanism underlying the restraining effect and the statistical evidence presented in Chapter 5. There, we saw that governments in competitive polities are less likely to initiate crises. Here, we show that the anticipation of domestic opposition can generate precisely such an effect: by encouraging foreign states to resist opposed threats and thereby inducing restraint on democratic governments.

For reasons that were partly evident in Chapter 6, these hypotheses are best examined through detailed case studies rather than statistical

[1] Kennedy (1940, pp. 227–28).

197

tests. The very nature of the hypothesized effect suggests that cases in which the government makes opposed threats may be quite rare. As we saw in Chapter 6, the small number of such observations can hamper statistical analysis. Moreover, the restraining effect, by its nature, tends to generate nonevents: threats not made because of the anticipated domestic and foreign reaction. The problem with this kind of nonevent is that it is overdetermined. Recall from the game that a nondemocratic government refrains from making a threat if its value for war is less than some cutpoint which we can label b_N; a democratic government refrains if its value for war is less than b_D. We saw from Chapter 4 that $b_N < b_D$, meaning that, all other things equal, a democratic challenger is more likely to choose the status quo. Of course, when the state's value for war is less than b_N, both kinds of challengers choose the status quo. The absence of a threat in this case is not a product of regime type. Where the restraining effect bites is for those types that fall between b_N and b_D – that is, types which would bluff if they were nondemocratic but not if they were democratic. To observe the restraining effect in action, therefore, we need not only to find cases in which the government chose not to make a threat but also to establish that the absence of a threat was plausibly related to domestic political considerations. This kind of evidence is best unearthed through careful case analysis.

That said, testing formal theories through case studies raises important difficulties. The virtue of formal models is that they abstract away from reality, distilling the essential strategic dynamic that lurks underneath complex interactions. A thorough case analysis, on the other hand, reveals the very richness of detail that these models intentionally strip away. Simple, dichotomous choices that appear in stylized models of crisis bargaining – e.g., stand firm versus back down – are only crude approximations of actual negotiating strategies, which can evolve in subtle ways over time. Parties that enter the model as unitary actors can in reality be groups of individuals with diverse motivations and beliefs. Moreover, the predictions of formal models usually come in the form of comparative statics: holding everything else constant, what happens when we change the value of one variable? Large sample, statistical analyses are well suited to dealing with such predictions, since they permit a wide range of controls and take into account the "error" induced by the idiosyncratic features of each observation. It is generally harder to introduce such controls in case analysis.

These considerations shape the following discussion in several ways. First, we need to be clear about the purpose of this exercise. Entire books can and have been written about each of the cases discussed in this chapter. The goal is not to rewrite the histories of these events but rather to demonstrate patterns that are not otherwise apparent when they are considered in isolation. A second way we can mitigate the difficulties mentioned above is through careful case selection. All of the cases considered here come from the historical experience of Great Britain, a country which has several useful features from the perspective of this analysis. It is a country that has enjoyed institutionalized competition for much of the last two centuries and has been sufficiently active in international affairs during this period to offer both a large number of dispute cases as well as measurable variation over time. Furthermore, the British political system mirrors the stylized model employed here in several important ways. The Westminster system features parliamentary government, a preference for one-party cabinets, and, despite occasional third-party activity, competition between two major parties (Lijphart 1984, pp. 4–9). Since divided government is impossible and coalition government rare, the model's basic assumption of two parties – one governing, one in opposition – is no stretch. In addition, the high level of party loyalty in this system means that treating parties as unitary actors is not a bad approximation of reality. The experience of Great Britain thus offers a relatively clean test of the ideas developed here.

The cases considered in this chapter were selected because they represent historically important disputes in which Britain's main opposition party decided to oppose threats to use force. Two of them, the Boer War and the Suez crisis, are traditional militarized crises since, in both instances, the government threatened and used military force. The disputes over Germany's remilitarization of the Rhineland and Rhodesia's unilateral declaration of independence were cases in which the British government did not resort to explicit threats; however, it is clear from the statements of opposition leaders that such threats would have been opposed in both instances. While the population of such non-events is potentially very large, the two cases considered here stand out because both required the government to respond to a challenge from another state, so the decisions not to threaten force can actually be observed. More importantly, these cases provide strong evidence that the absence of a threat was a product of the restraining effect, rather than simply a response to a low expected value for war. In each case, important members of the government argued in favor of making a threat, even though they knew it to be a bluff, but ultimately chose not to or were overruled. Moreover, the decision to refrain from threats can be traced to concerns about the domestic political reaction and the likelihood that the bluff would be called. Hence, in every case, the absence of a threat is not a trivial nonevent but rather a choice that can be plausibly attributed to the causal mechanisms discussed here.

This chapter proceeds by considering the cases in chronological order. The concluding section then draws out the essential similarities.

The Boer War, 1899

Conflict between Great Britain and the Boers in South Africa can be traced at least as far back as 1877, when Britain annexed the Transvaal, an independent Boer state, touching off a revolt in 1880. This first Boer War (1880–81) led to the creation of the South African Republic, a nominally independent state over which Britain exercised an ambiguous "suzerainty." Relations between the two countries were set on a collision course in 1886, when the discovery of large gold deposits in the region led to massive immigration by British citizens. The second, or Great, Boer War (1899–1902) stemmed from a conflict over South Africa's treatment of these immigrants, who came to be known as Uitlanders (Outlanders). Rather than considering the two decades of conflict that led up to this war, this section looks at the crisis that developed over the spring and summer of 1899 and ultimately escalated to war in October of that year.

The 1899 crisis grew from British demands that the South African government relax franchise restrictions that denied most Uitlanders the right to vote. South African law dictated that a person could become eligible to vote only after living in the Transvaal for twelve years. This restriction was considered necessary to prevent a loss of political independence, since Uitlanders outnumbered Boers in the region (Fisher 1974, pp. 215–16). The British government – primarily Colonial Secretary Joseph Chamberlain and the high commissioner in South Africa, Alfred Milner – became convinced that extension of the franchise to the Uitlanders would greatly improve their lot and, not incidentally, extend British influence in the region. Accordingly, the government demanded that the length of residence be shortened to five years, that this criterion be applied retroactively, and that the number of seats in the legislature devoted to mining areas be increased. The crisis started in earnest when South African President Paul Kruger rejected these demands at a conference with Milner in early June.

The evolution of this crisis over the next several months illustrates how the government's willingness to threaten force and the foreign state's estimate of the government's intentions are influenced by the public position taken by the opposition party. Though divided at times and not unsympathetic to the Uitlander's grievances, the opposition Liberal Party consistently opposed the use or threat of force to get Kruger to concede on the franchise issue. This position was in part ideological, in part political. Many Liberals sympathized with and admired the Boers, and a substantial faction of the party was opposed to an extension of Britain's imperial claims (Davey 1978; Butler 1968, ch. 2). Moreover, through much of spring and summer of 1899, Liberal opposition to the use of force catered to a public that was largely unconcerned about events in South Africa and unwilling to wage war on behalf of the Uitlanders (Pakenham 1979, pp. 52–54; Langer 1951, p. 608). Even Chamberlain had to admit, as he did in a letter to Milner in July, that "opinion here is strongly opposed to war although the necessity of resorting to war in the last resort is gradually making its way among all classes" (Garvin 1934, p. 410).

The government's stance during this period was highly constrained not only by the views of the public, but also by the open opposition of the Liberal Party. Reports from South Africa led Chamberlain to believe that Kruger would quickly back down if faced with the prospect of a fight. Even though opinion in Britain was opposed to war at this time, it was felt that a costless show of force would be sufficient to close the deal (Langer 1951, p. 612). To that end, Chamberlain devised a plan to deploy 10,000 troops to the area, and he arranged a meeting with Liberal Party leader Henry Campbell-Bannerman to seek the latter's support. Campbell-Bannerman had already made public his opposition to such a move. In a debate in the House of Commons on April 21, he had criticized a proposal to build barracks in South Africa to house potential reinforcements, and in a speech on June 17, he reiterated that he "could discern nothing in what had occurred to justify either warlike action or even military preparations" (Spender 1923, p. 231). Chamberlain arranged the meeting three days after this speech in order to convince the Liberal leader to change his tune. According to Campbell-Bannerman's record of the meeting:

> [Chamberlain] said that . . . he was striving, and always had been, for a peaceful settlement. But he was afraid that a demonstration of the kind indicated would be necessary. It would, however, be a game of bluff, and it was impossible to play that game if the Opposition did not support the government. (Spender 1923, p. 234)

Chamberlain clearly realized that the opposition could undermine the bluff and sought to enlist the Liberal Party in his game. Campbell-Bannerman was unsupportive, however, and two days later he officially notified Chamberlain that he could not endorse any "open military demonstration" against the Boers (*ibid.*, p. 235).

The effect of this interchange is clearly visible in the government's subsequent actions – or, more accurately, inaction. The cabinet met the same day and decided not to go forward with the deployment. In a letter to Milner the next day, Chamberlain made explicit his belief that domestic opposition to the ploy would have rendered it ineffective: "To provoke a Parliamentary division by premature action and thus show Kruger that the country is divided would be mischievous and tend to confirm his obstinacy" (quoted in Porter 1980, p. 221). Chamberlain was influenced by the memory of the previous year's crisis over Fashoda, in which bipartisan support made it possible for the government to prevail without recourse to war (Pakenham 1979, p. 79). His inability to engineer the same show of unity over the Transvaal conflict led him to proceed cautiously and to look for a diplomatic settlement without recourse to threats. The bluff could not be made because the resultant display of disunity would make it likely that the bluff would be called, leading either to a humiliating retreat or to a war that the British public was not yet willing to accept.

And indeed, South African decision makers do seem to have believed, at least in this early stage of the crisis, that Chamberlain could not back up his demands through force. Kruger's consul-general in London, Montagu White, was in close contact with Liberal politicians, whom he referred to in dispatches as "our friends" (Davey 1978, pp. 36–43). From his talks with these people, White learned that there was widespread sympathy for the Uitlander cause and that modest internal reforms would be desirable; however, they also confirmed that the British government could not go to war without provoking opposition from considerable segments of the public. In early August, for example, White reported to his secretary of state information passed along by several prominent Liberals. The gist of their advice was that the Cabinet was not firmly behind Chamberlain and that public opinion, though temporarily roused due to Chamberlain's activities, would cool in due course (Thorold 1913, pp. 404–06). Direct evidence about Kruger's beliefs at this stage is generally lacking. Nevertheless, one of his biographers concludes that Kruger believed early on that British demands were a bluff and that the Liberal Party would "fight his battles with Chamberlain" (Fisher 1974, p. 218).

Throughout the summer, Liberal opposition to the use of force continued unabated. In a House of Commons debate on July 28, Campbell-Bannerman declared that a war in South Africa "would be one of the direst calamities that could occur" and urged that the matter be resolved "not by force nor by threats." Though Campbell-Bannerman expressed sympathy for the Uitlander cause, and even endorsed the government's efforts to promote franchise reform, he insisted that the stakes were not worth fighting over. This was especially true given that Kruger had already agreed to shorten the residency requirement to seven years. While Chamberlain was insisting that the requirement be reduced to five years, the opposition leader ridiculed the idea that a difference of two years was grounds "even for the threat of war" (GB, *Parl. Deb.* 4s, 75: 686–97). Similar remarks came from other prominent Liberals through the month of September (Spender 1923, pp. 240–41).

Understanding that Liberal opposition made it difficult to convince Kruger of his seriousness, Chamberlain and Milner undertook an extensive effort to mobilize public opinion behind a more forceful stance. From July to September, the colonial secretary stepped up the propaganda campaign intended to dramatize the plight of the Uitlanders and to demonize Kruger (Porter 1980, pp. 239–46). The purpose behind this campaign was two-fold. First, Chamberlain hoped to convince an otherwise inattentive public that Britain had a strong stake in getting its way – if necessary, by force. In this respect, he seems to have had reasonable success. In a letter to Milner on September 2, Chamberlain wrote: "Three months ago we could not – that is, we should not have been allowed to – go to war on this issue. Now – although most unwillingly and with a large minority against us – we shall be sufficiently supported" (Garvin 1934, p. 458; also Langer 1951, p. 615). Hence, the propaganda campaign moved public sentiment to a point at which war was no longer politically unthinkable.

The second effect of this effort was to create a political climate in which the cabinet would find it difficult to back down. By increasing the government's stated commitment to wringing reforms out of Kruger, Chamberlain hoped to tie the cabinet's hands so that, if faced with a choice between backing down and using force, his colleagues would be compelled to choose the latter. Thus, consistent with Fearon's (1994a) argument, Chamberlain and Milner sought to add credibility to their position by exposing the government to audience costs. In this respect, they were also successful. By August 30, Prime Minister Salisbury expressed frustration that his freedom of action was increasingly constrained: Milner's "view is too heated, if you consider the intrinsic significance and importance of the things which are in controversy. But it recks little to think of that now. What he has done cannot be effaced. We have to act upon a moral field prepared for us by him and his jingo supporters" (Newton 1929, p. 157). Nor was the tactic lost on outside observers. Count Hatzfeld, the German ambassador in London, noted in July that, "though the majority of the British Ministry is against war, it is tied by Mr. Chamberlain's public action which the Government permitted" (Germany, *GDD* 1930, p. 88). By late August, Hatzfeld concluded that the risk of war was quite high, since Chamberlain's public campaign against the Boers made it unlikely that the cabinet could consider backing down (*ibid.*, pp. 93, 96). Thus, unable to muster a show of unity between government and opposition, Chamberlain instead sought credibility in efforts to increase the cabinet's exposure to audience costs.

At this point, all that remained was to issue an ultimatum backed by an explicit threat of force. The main stumbling block to such a move was the state of military readiness. The reinforcements that had not been sent in June were now needed before any threat could be effective. Continued negotiations at this point served mainly as a play for time, and the British bargaining position became more intransigent (Langer 1951, 614–15). Chamberlain upped his demands and worked on convincing the cabinet first to send 10,000 reinforcements to the region and, later, to secretly mobilize 70,000 troops for the coming action. Even these moves were colored by the domestic political situation and a desire to minimize the effect of Liberal dissent on the credibility of his threat. Moving army units from England was problematic since doing so would have required the government to recall parliament in order to appropriate the necessary funds. Chamberlain disliked this option, since going to parliament risked an open division over the matter (Garvin 1934, pp. 454, 459). The solution was to shift troops from India, a move that could be made without parliamentary approval. Interestingly, a number of people in the War Office, including the commander-in-chief, opposed the use of Indian troops on the grounds that they were not best suited for the military operation (Pakenham 1979, p. 94). Nevertheless, the political necessity won out, and the first batch of reinforcements were drawn primarily from India.

That the government had a low expected value for war is indicated by the reluctance and gloom with which cabinet members responded to these moves. The cabinet was clearly willing to fight, but several prominent ministers were unconvinced that the gains exceeded the likely cost. Salisbury wrote that war seemed likely even though it would be "all for people whom we despise and for territory which will bring no profit and no power to England" (Newton 1929, p. 157). Similar views were held by the secretary of war, the chancellor of the exchequer, and the first lord of the treasury, Alfred Balfour, who wrote that military action was not the best course, but perhaps the "least bad" (Porter 1980, pp. 253–54). These ministers went along in large part because they held out hope that the Boers would back down when faced with war. Milner, after all, had repeatedly assured them that Kruger would "bluff up to the cannon's mouth" (Langer 1951, p. 616; Pakenham 1979, pp. 91–93).

This hope, of course, was not borne out. As British troops rushed to the region, military logic overcame political logic. The Boer commander, Jan Smuts, had declared that the republic's only chance of prevailing in a war would be to strike quickly, while it still enjoyed a numerical advantage on the ground and before Britain had a chance to bring its full power to bear (Pakenham 1979, pp. 102–03). It was hoped that early setbacks would weaken the British government both domestically and internationally. Thus, with British strength increasing daily, the Boers could not afford to wait, so Kruger decided to preempt the inevitable British ultimatum with one of his own. On October 9, he demanded that the troops be withdrawn and that British ships in the area not land. The British government saw this ultimatum as sufficient justification for war, and the Boer War was on. These events took place while parliament was out of session, so, by the time Liberal MPs had a chance to vote on this matter, the war had already started. At that point, the Liberals had little choice but to support the government in voting for military supplies, but a large faction of the party qualified its support by voting for an amendment critical of the government's conduct during the crisis (Spender 1923, pp. 248–49).

This case demonstrates the effect of the opposition on both the government's policy and the foreign state's beliefs during crisis bargaining. The Liberal Party's stance revealed potential weaknesses in the government's political support. During the spring and summer of 1899, when public opinion was such that the government could not contemplate war, this opposition stayed the hand of those, like Chamberlain, who wished to cow Kruger into submission through a show of force. Chamberlain responded with a public campaign aimed at increasing public support and tying the hands of the cabinet by exposing the government to audience costs. At this point, Kruger's continued defiance made war the inevitable outcome.

It should be emphasized that, in opposing the government, Liberal politicians were not hoping that war would result. Most earnestly believed that war would be a tragedy for both countries. Nevertheless, a policy of opposition seemed the best response given their estimate of the likely ramifications of war. In his letter to Chamberlain, Campbell-Bannerman wrote that he was unwilling to support the government since "the hands of the Opposition should be entirely free" in this matter (Spender 1923, p. 235). Campbell-Bannerman clearly wanted to retain the freedom to criticize the government's actions in this affair. This suggests that he was sufficiently concerned about the consequences of war that he did not wish to tie his party's fate to that of the government. The ambivalence with which the cabinet ultimately approved of war attests to the fact that these concerns were not his alone. Such ambivalence is consistent with the model's prediction that wars opposed by the opposition are associated with an expected payoff less than or perhaps marginally greater than zero.

The Rhineland crisis, 1936

The Rhineland crisis of 1936 stemmed from German attempts to revise the post-war settlement embodied in the Versailles Treaty. That agreement had proscribed Germany from building fortifications or placing troops west of the Rhine River and within 50 kilometers of the east bank. To ensure compliance, the allies insisted on a fifteen-year occupation of the west bank, including the Rhine bridgeheads. The terms of this agreement were modified slightly by the Locarno Treaties of 1925, which reaffirmed the demilitarization of the region and called on the treaty signatories to enforce this provision. These agreements paved the way for an early end to the allied occupation, which terminated in 1930.

Though there had been minor violations of the Rhineland provisions even before Hitler came into power, tensions came to the fore in 1935, when France and the Soviet Union signed their Mutual Assistance Pact. Shortly after the signing of this treaty in May of that year, Hitler ordered his generals to plan for a remilitarization of the region. At the same time, Hitler started making his displeasure known to allied diplomats, warning that he did not consider the matter of the Rhineland to be permanently settled (Haraszti 1983, p. 39). Through the remainder of 1935 and into the following year, there were growing indications that

Germany was planning to renounce the Locarno Treaty and remilitarize the region (Emmerson 1977, p. 39).

The prospect of such a move was troubling primarily to the French. Not only would remilitarization put German troops on their borders, but it would hamper France's ability to defend its allies in Eastern Europe, should the need arise. Moreover, the French public had long been told that a demilitarized Rhineland was central to their security, meaning that complete inaction in the face of a German coup would be difficult. For these reasons, the cabinet publicly announced on February 12, 1936, that maintenance of the zone was not negotiable (Emmerson 1977, p. 44). Despite these tough words, however, the French government knew that it was not in a position to make explicit threats. The primary impediment was the General Staff's reluctance to confront Germany without a general mobilization and strong allied support. As has been well documented elsewhere (e.g., Posen 1984), the French military was not designed to carry out offensive actions on short notice. The regular army was a skeleton force which needed substantial contributions from reservists to make it fully operational. Hence, for any threat to be backed by credible military force, a general mobilization of the reserves would be needed. Moreover, the General Staff was convinced that moving against Germany in the Rhineland threatened all-out war – a risk that was unthinkable unless France was assured of allied support, primarily from Great Britain. Thus, in a February 17 memo to Foreign Minister Flandin, the minster of war declared that a military operation could not be contemplated without the "full support of the British government" (France, *DDF* 1963, p. 291).

Military weakness was exacerbated by the instability of the French government in the lead-up to the crisis. The cabinet of Pierre Laval collapsed on January 24, 1936, and new elections were set for the end of April, when it was widely expected that the Popular Front of Socialists and Communists would sweep to victory. This left a stop-gap government led by Albert Sarraut to deal with the German threat. Lacking any popular mandate, Sarraut was reluctant to commit France to a course that might require a general mobilization on the eve of the elections. Thus, in response to Hitler's rumblings, the government decided against issuing an explicit deterrent threat and instead spent much of its effort trying to get assurances of help from Great Britain (Emmerson 1977, pp. 51–52).

Unfortunately for the French, they would find little support from their allies across the Channel. Throughout the affair, the British government was constrained by two stubborn facts. First, military preparations were at too early a stage for the government to contemplate a forceful response to any German coup. Rearmament did not begin in earnest until 1936, leaving Britain with an undersized army, insufficient air-power, and an overstretched navy (Emmerson 1977, pp. 136–38). The second constraint came from domestic politics. While claims about the pacifism of the British public during this period can be overstated – over 11 million voters in the "Peace Ballot" of 1935 said they were willing to support military sanctions to stop aggressors – the prospect of a German move into the Rhineland was seen more as an act of perfidy than one of aggression. The prevailing mood both before and after the reoccupation was summed up by Lord Lothian's famous comment that "After all, they are only going into their own back-garden" (quoted in Churchill 1948, pp. 196–97).

Given these considerations, the British government decided early on that it would be unwise to make threats over the Rhineland. In February 1935, Robert Vansittart and Ralph Wigram, both of the Foreign Office, recommended that Hitler be warned about British concerns on this matter. "We may not be going to *do* anything about it," Vansittart wrote in a memo to his colleagues, "but surely we cannot contemplate *saying* nothing about it either" (Emmerson 1977, p. 58). Wigram agreed that silence on this matter would only encourage Germany to believe that Britain was walking away from its Locarno commitments. The cabinet rejected this recommendation, however. Making such a threat would leave the government in an awkward position should Hitler move into the Rhineland anyway. It would then face an undesirable choice between carrying out the threat – in the face of military and political weakness – or backing down. Rather than expose itself to that risk, the cabinet decided to remain silent (Emmerson 1977, p. 58).

Given their inability to muster a deterrent threat, the British decided instead to seek a comprehensive settlement in which the Rhineland would be traded as a bargaining chip (Emmerson 1977, pp. 62–67; GB, *DBFP* 1976, pp. 641–43). Consequently, as German rumblings over the zone increased in early 1936, Foreign Secretary Anthony Eden offered to start negotiations on an air-power pact. At the same time, Eden counseled the cabinet against making threats. In a memo dated February 14, 1936, the foreign secretary warned that it would be "undesirable to adopt an attitude where we would either have to fight for the Zone or abandon it in the face of a German reoccupation" (*ibid.*, p. 659). Eden realized that, because of the likely domestic opposition, threatening

Germany would have been useless: "No declaration warning the Nazis off was possible, neither the British Government nor the people would have been willing to carry it through, and it would have been useless to threaten when we were not prepared to act" (Eden 1962, p. 379). This quotation suggests not only that Eden thought making an empty threat was worse than doing nothing, but also that he expected the threat would fail to achieve its purpose.

He was likely correct in this expectation, for, as Hitler surveyed the political situation in France and Britain, he saw clearly that both governments would face strong opposition if they attempted to meet him with force. From France, Hitler received regular reports that, while the French would no doubt react angrily to a *fait accompli*, the government was in a weak position to respond with force. The French cabinet's warning of February 12 was noted, but the conclusion in Berlin was that France would not react militarily if the operation was confined to German territory and was not seen as preparatory to an attack on France (Germany, *DGFP* 1962, pp. 1142–43; Emmerson 1977, pp. 77–79). Numerous reports came in describing the pacific mood of the French people, whom the German ambassador in Paris characterized as being "opposed, under all circumstances, to military action beyond their frontiers" (Germany, *DGFP* 1962, p. 916; see also 851, 926, 1034). The political weakness of the Sarraut cabinet was also well known. In a meeting on February 12, the chargé d'affaires in Paris, Dirk Forster, told Hitler that the current government was "widely regarded as a stop gap expedient." When pressed, Forster would not "guarantee" that France would refrain from military action, but he also doubted the government's ability to stand firm (Forster 1956, p. 48). Hitler could also take comfort as he watched the debate in the Chamber of Deputies over ratification of the Franco-Soviet treaty. The agreement was ultimately approved, but the debate revealed deep political and ideological divisions in the country. Rightist deputies argued against the treaty and openly predicted that Germany would respond by moving into the Rhineland and that France would be powerless to stop it (Emmerson 1977, pp. 78–79). In discussions with his ambassador in Rome, Hitler noted the opposition to the treaty in France and Britain and suggested that this would work to his advantage, because the contemplated action would be publicly justified as a reaction to that pact (Germany, *DGFP* 1962, p. 1142).

The signals emerging from Britain were equally encouraging. Both the political consensus against using force and the poor state of the country's military preparations were readily apparent to German observers. Indeed, for the past year the government had been actively publicizing Britain's military weakness as a way to win support for its rearmament program. The defense White Paper of March 1935 warned that "serious deficiencies were accumulating in all the Defence services" and pointed out that the deterrent value of the Locarno Treaty was jeopardized by the fact that Britain's potential contribution in a crisis "could have little decisive effect" (GB, Parliament 1935, pp. 4–5). The release of this paper kicked off extensive parliamentary debate about the country's military needs and plans (Shay 1977, ch. 2). A second white paper, released just days before Hitler's move into the Rhineland, suggested that the "relative decline in the effective strength of [British] armaments by sea, land and air" had not yet been halted (GB, Parliament 1936, p. 6). Thus, the normal democratic process and the need to build public support for government policies brought out a good deal of information about the country's military capabilities. The absence of any political will or public pressure to maintain the demilitarized zone was similarly evident in a number of signals, both public and private (see Germany, *DGFP* 1962, pp. 1071, 1139–41, 1147–49). In the month before the coup, for example, prominent newspaper editorials – widely circulated in Berlin – argued against taking strong action to prevent reoccupation. The *Manchester Guardian* predicted that Hitler would soon act unilaterally, daring the West to do its worst, "which, whatever it may be, will not be war" (Emmerson 1977, pp. 81–82).

Based on these signals, German decision makers concluded that France would not march without support from Britain, and Britain would not lend that support. Hence, when Hitler confided his plan to his ambassador in Italy on February 14, the latter recorded Hitler's optimistic expectations: "England was in a bad state militarily, and much hampered by other problems; France was distracted by internal politics . . . He did not think that such a step on Germany's part would be answered by military action. . ." (Germany, *DGFP* 1962, p. 1142). In discussions in Berlin a few days later, Foreign Minister Neurath echoed these sentiments. The record of the meeting notes that, despite the foreign minister's reservations about the proposed action, he "did not, however, really think that the other fellows would march against us" (*ibid.*, p. 1164). The move into the Rhineland took place a few weeks later, on March 7.

German expectations turned out to be accurate. Once Hitler presented the West with his *fait accompli*, the obvious constraints operating on the French and British governments continued to work in his favor.

In France, the decision against taking unilateral military action was quickly reaffirmed. At a cabinet meeting the day after occupation, a proposal to respond quickly and independently was strongly rebuffed for both military and political reasons (Emmerson 1977, pp. 104–12). The General Staff continued to insist that any military action would require a general mobilization of over 1 million men. This advice was partly a result of exaggerated estimates of German strength in the Rhineland. Though Hitler had sent in 10,000 regular army units and another 22,000 armed police units, French military intelligence came up with a figure of 295,000 German troops (*ibid.*, p. 106). The misestimate was partly a result of worst-case analysis, but it also stemmed from a conscious decision on Hitler's part to conceal the size of the troop movement (Germany, *DGFP* 1966, pp. 142–43). In any event, military leaders were convinced that, in the event that they moved against German troops in the Rhineland, an all-out war would likely follow – a war that France was not prepared to fight, and certainly not if it had to do so alone.

Cabinet members also rejected the idea of mobilizing units simply as a show of force – that is, rushing them to the border, without actually crossing it, in the hope of bluffing Hitler into withdrawing. Domestic political constraints argued against such a move. Ordering a general mobilization on the eve of the election was seen as politically dangerous. Naval Minister Marcel Déat summarized the views of many when he warned that the government would be "swept out of parliament tomorrow" if it issued a mobilization order within six weeks of the election (Emmerson 1977, p. 111). Defense Minister Louis Maurin raised the specter of audience costs, pointing out that the government risked public ridicule if it were to mobilize a million men, only to march them back home if Hitler did not cave in (*ibid.*, p. 112).

Unwilling to take forceful action without support from Great Britain, the French resorted to little more than brave words and minor military maneuvers. On the evening of March 8, Sarraut read a speech over the radio in which he declared that France would not negotiate until German troops had withdrawn, but he stopped short of explicitly threatening military action. In his speech, the prime minister attributed Hitler's move to partisan discord that had accompanied the ratification of the Franco-Soviet pact and the onset of the electoral campaign, and he implored the French people to pull together behind the government's position (Wheeler-Bennett 1937, pp. 46–51). The public response, however, was one of resignation rather than defiance. In the days following the coup, newspapers on both the left and the right argued against issuing any kind of ultimatum backed by force. Sarraut's speech was greeted by anxiety, as people feared that the government's intransigence could lead to war. Candidates from all parties steered clear of comments that could lead to their being branded pro-war (Emmerson 1977, pp. 116–18). Similarly, when Sarraut raised the possibility of unilateral action in a speech to the Chamber of Deputies on March 10, the suggestion received a chilly reception (Adamthwaite 1977, p. 38). By March 11, the German chargés d'affaires in Paris could tell his superiors that the French government realized the "impracticability" of demanding immediate evacuation as a precondition for negotiations (Germany, *DGFP* 1966, p. 101).

With isolated action by France having been ruled out, the prospects for a military response depended entirely on whether London could be persuaded to go along. Flandin pressed the British government for assurances of support, pointing out that Britain was bound by its obligations under the Locarno Treaty to help preserve the demilitarized zone. No such assurances were forthcoming, however. In Eden's initial public statement on the crisis, he argued that Britain was bound to support France and Belgium in the event of an attack on their territory – but no more (Emmerson 1977, p. 115).

Though many in the British cabinet were reluctant to act militarily, some hard-liners, like Winston Churchill and Austen Chamberlain, preferred a forceful response. Moreover, both British hard-liners and the French foreign minister were convinced that the German move was a bluff and that a firm show of resolve by the Locarno powers would force Hitler to back down. There were some reports that German troops in the Rhineland had orders to back down if confronted and that Hitler faced opposition to the move within his own government (Churchill 1948, pp. 196–97; Nicolson 1966, pp. 249–51).

In spite of this belief, however, the British were unable and unwilling to muster a show of force. This reluctance was based on two related considerations – one explicit, the other implicit. The explicit concern was that, given the state of British military preparations and the generally pacifist mood of the public, the government would be unable to follow through on a threat to use force (Emmerson 1977, pp. 135–46). A cabinet meeting on March 11 noted both of these facts. A report from the military service ministers cast doubt on readiness of the army, navy, and air force. The cabinet also observed that "public opinion was strongly opposed to any military action against the Germans in the demilitarised zone" (Haraszti 1983, p. 159). Prime Minister Baldwin and the majority of the cabinet concluded that Britain could not risk a war and should instead pursue a conciliatory stance. When Flandin later assured Baldwin that any show of force would be a simple police action since Hitler would back down, Baldwin replied: "You may be right, but if there is *even one chance in a hundred* that war would follow from your police operation, I have not the right to commit England" (Churchill 1948, p. 197 [italics in original]). This statement was likely an exaggeration intended to overstate Britain's inability to aid France; nevertheless, it reflects the government's low estimation of its likely payoff from war. Under these conditions, any threat to evict the Germans through force would have been a bluff.

The implicit consideration underlying British inaction was that, given the opposition to the use of force among the public and the other parties, the chances that a bluff would be called were too high to risk. Harold Nicolson noted this dilemma in a letter to his wife on March 12. After first observing that Hitler was probably bluffing and that "if we send an ultimatum to Germany, she ought in all reason to climb down," Nicolson lamented that such a strategy was impossible: "the people of this country absolutely refuse to have a war. We should be faced with a general strike if we even suggested such a thing. We shall therefore have to climb down ignominiously and Hitler will have scored" (Nicolson 1966, pp. 249–50). This fear that a threat of force would lead to widespread domestic criticism was underscored by the public positions taken by the opposition Labour and Liberal Parties.[2] In a debate in the House of Commons on March 26, Labour's spokesman on foreign affairs, Hugh Dalton, confirmed that his party stood willing and able to go on the attack if the government considered using force (GB, *Parl. Deb.* 5s, 310: 1449–61). Dalton was joined in this stance by Liberal Party icon Lloyd George, as well as by the leader of the Liberal Party, Archibald Sinclair (*ibid.*, 1461–68, 1472–82).

Recognizing that any attempt to threaten Germany would generate widespread domestic opposition, the cabinet took care to avoid any harsh words or actions that might be taken as a threat. In the place of military action, the government proposed military conversations between the Locarno powers: staff talks designed to facilitate coordination in military planning. Even this modest plan, however, needed

---

[2] The British government at this time was made up of a National coalition dominated by the Conservatives, but also containing members of the National Labour and National Liberal parties. The main opposition came from members of the Liberal and Labour parties who had refused to join the coalition.

213

careful packaging given the danger of a negative public reaction. The minutes of the March 18 cabinet meeting suggest how constrained the ministers felt in this regard:

> It was suggested that the best plan would be to offer military conversations limited to action to be taken to resist a German aggression. Even this was criticised on the ground that public opinion would not appreciate how limited the scope of the conversations was to be and would jump to the conclusion . . . that the conversations were bound to cover action against Germany.[3]

On the eve of the March 26 parliamentary debate over the proposed staff talks, the cabinet revisited these concerns, noting that "both in Parliament and outside there was a good deal of anxiety" over how Britain would respond. The cabinet consequently decided that Eden's speech should first emphasize the strength of Britain commitments under Versailles and Locarno, so that the proposed plan would seem minor by comparison.[4] In short, the political climate ruled out the use of threats or any action that might be remotely interpreted as a threat. Even Churchill had to admit that Britain lacked the "solidarity of conviction" to "take a line of undue prominence or to seek to dominate this issue" (GB, *Parl. Deb.* 5s, 310: 2488).

The German government reached a similar conclusion. Numerous reports from the German ambassador in London, Leopold von Hoesch, tell of the pro-German stance of the British public and report the numerous declarations in support of a peaceful settlement. In an analysis written shortly after the reoccupation, Hoesch noted that although the government might feel pressure to uphold its Locarno commitments, the public and parliament would serve as a counterweight (Germany, *DGFP* 1966, pp. 92–95). Hoesch observed that the "'man on the street' . . . does not care a damn if the Germans occupy their own territory with military forces" and that discussions in the House of Commons made it plain that most MPs hoped to "eliminate as far as possible the risk of war." While this sympathetic attitude could change, the ambassador concluded that "it does constitute a valuable basis upon which a Government, determined to be moderate and reasonable, could pursue and implement a policy of reconciliation, unhampered by internal difficulties" (*ibid.*, p. 94). Similar reports were sent during the month of

---

[3] Public Record Office, London (hereafter PRO), CAB 23/83, CC 21(36).
[4] PRO, CAB 23/83, CC 24(36).

March, as negotiations over the matter proceeded (see *ibid.*, pp. 102–3, 233–40, 293–95).

Hoesch also reported on the March 26 Commons debate and observed that, despite anti-German sentiment due to Hitler's unilateral violation of the Locarno Treaty, the government faced opposition even to its modest plan of arranging military staff talks between London, Paris, and Brussels (*ibid.*, pp. 315–18; see also pp. 293–95). Awareness of this opposition encouraged Hitler to voice strong objections to the plan, and Eden was forced to water down the talks by depriving them of any real content (Emmerson 1977, pp. 215–17). The British government's political incentives and constraints were quite transparent to German decision makers, and they took full advantage by refusing to offer anything but the most superficial concessions.

The Rhineland crisis is also interesting since it demonstrates the superior ability that nondemocratic states enjoy in concealing information about their resolve. Faced with the German challenge, British and French decision makers tried hard to uncover information about Hitler's preferences. Whereas the Western governments' political constraints were plainly evident in press reports and parliamentary proceedings, Hitler's were less obvious. There was some evidence of dissension within the German government, particularly the fact that Hitler's military advisers had counseled him against the move (Nicolson 1966, p. 249). Ultimately, though, it was understood that Hitler's preferences could not be readily gleaned from observations of German public opinion or rumors of dissent among his advisors. The political constraints that operate on a dictatorial leader are generally difficult to perceive. This uncertainty is evident in Neville Chamberlain's response to French assurances that Hitler would back down if challenged: "We cannot accept this as a reliable indicator of a mad Dictator's reaction" (quoted in Churchill 1948, p. 196).

This inability to reliably assess Hitler's intentions is all the more interesting given that the move into the Rhineland may have been a bluff. Though there is some controversy on this point, there is evidence that German troops were under orders to retreat if confronted (Emmerson 1977, pp. 98–100). If indeed Hitler was bluffing, the bluff was made possible by his lack of visible political constraints. Germany's closed, uncompetitive system facilitated strategic misrepresentation on a major scale. By contrast, the Western governments' inability even to consider a threat of force was driven by their obvious and undeniable constraints. Their transparent, competitive systems effectively ruled out using a bluff to call a bluff.

The Suez crisis, 1956

The 1956 Suez crisis stemmed from Egyptian President Gamel Abdal Nasser's decision on July 26 to nationalize the Suez Canal Company, which had been controlled by British and French interests. The move threatened not only international access to the economically vital waterway but also the two countries' claims to great power status. Consequently, from the very start of the crisis, the Conservative-run British government contemplated using force to retake the canal and to depose Nasser, who was seen as a constant irritant in the region. When the British cabinet met on July 27, it was decided that, if necessary, military action would be taken to restore international control over the canal. However, Prime Minister Anthony Eden's desire for a rapid military response was squelched by a report from the chiefs of staff that preparations for such a move would take several weeks (Carlton 1988, pp. 35–37). Still, the government ordered that military plans be prepared and that reservists be called up.

What followed were three months of inconclusive diplomacy in which Britain and France pushed for a reversal of the nationalization, Egypt stood firm, and the United States sought to assure international access to the canal through a peaceful compromise. Here is not the place to recount the details of these negotiations. It is sufficient to note that Nasser steadfastly refused to accept the offers of the Western powers and that the United States clearly voiced its opposition to the use of force. In response, the British and French hatched a plan according to which Israel would attack Egypt, after which the two governments would demand a cessation of hostilities and insert troops with the ostensible purpose of protecting the canal. An Israeli attack on October 29 was followed by an Anglo-French ultimatum the following day. When Egypt refused the ultimatum, aerial attacks began on October 31, and British and French paratroopers landed on November 5. Under intense US pressure, the combatants agreed to a cease-fire the following day, and Anglo-French troops were withdrawn in December.

What is interesting for our purposes is to understand how the constraints of political competition affected the British government's decision making and how signals that emerged from the political process influenced other states' behavior in the crisis. Throughout the crisis, the opposition Labour Party consistently voiced opposition to military action to retake the canal unless that action took place with a mandate from the United Nations Security Council.[5] This position stemmed from a mixture of ideological and political considerations. An aversion to the use of force and a desire to channel such activities through the United Nations were consistent with the labor movement's internationalism and anti-imperialism. At the same time, the party's stance had potential appeal to the broader public. After a brief surge of indignation in response to the nationalization, British public opinion quickly cooled to the idea of retaking the canal through force (Kyle 1991, p. 188). Opinion polls conducted in August, September, and November revealed that a plurality of respondents disapproved of military action (Epstein 1964, pp. 141–42).

Labour's opposition to the use of force was voiced early in the crisis and continued even after military operations began. When the House of Commons met on August 2 to discuss the Suez issue, party leader Hugh Gaitskell condemned Nasser's move in strong terms, even comparing the Egyptian leader to Mussolini and Hitler. Still, Gaitskell insisted that any military action against Egypt take place under a UN mandate and only as a last resort (Gorst and Johnman 1997, pp. 64–65). Shortly thereafter, when Gaitskell realized that press reports had emphasized the comparison to Hitler and underplayed his statements about the UN, he took pains to clarify his party's opposition to the use of force, both in public pronouncements and in private letters to Eden (Kyle 1991, p. 189).

By mid-September, as rumors of Anglo-French military preparations grew, the partisan divide over Suez had sharpened further. In a vigorous debate on September 12–13, the Labour Party staked out an unmistakable opposition to any use of force outside the purview of the United Nations. While reiterating his condemnation of Nasser's action, Gaitskell warned that any military action not provoked by the Egyptian leader and not carried out by the United Nations would have "disastrous" consequences (GB, *Parl. Deb* 5s 558: 15–32). The government, and any outside observers who cared to look, were put on notice that military action by Great Britain would be undertaken with substantial internal dissent from the Labour Party and, by implication, a sizable portion of the British electorate.

After Britain and France issued their ultimatum on October 30, the Labour Party carried through on this threat. Though Eden asked the

---

[5] As Epstein (1964, p. 67) points out, the requirement for a Security Council mandate in effect ruled out the use of force, since the Soviet Union could be expected to veto any resolution approving military action against Egypt.

House of Commons to defer judgment on the ultimatum, Gaitskell condemned the government's decision to act without a Security Council mandate and forced a division of the House. The government won, but the close vote (270 to 218) revealed that the government would be waging war without robust support in parliament (Epstein 1964, p. 69; Kyle 1991, pp. 361–32). When the bombing campaign began the next day, Labour went on an all-out attack, despite the obvious risk of being labeled unpatriotic. What followed, in the words of one writer, was "the most intense parliamentary attack in recent political history" (Epstein 1964, p. 75). Labour's assault on the government's actions got so intense that, at one point, the speaker of parliament had to suspend the sitting for half an hour so that tempers could cool (Kyle 1991, pp. 387–90).

Consistent with the theory developed here, there is good evidence that the Labour Party's position affected the government's assessment of its ability to make credible threats. The minutes of the Egypt Committee, a cabinet subcommittee charged with coordinating the government's response to the crisis, include confidential annexes that record conversations relating to the military operation. What is remarkable about these annexes, especially from the August meetings, is how discussions about when to call parliament into session are intermixed with discussions about the timing of troop and naval deployments. Committee members clearly felt that prevailing in this matter would require not only displays and threats of military force, but also careful management of the domestic political front.[6]

This effect was particularly pronounced in the early meetings of the committee, as military preparations were getting underway and the United States was pushing for an international conference. In a meeting on August 9, the committee decided that political conditions were not ripe for an ultimatum backed by a threat of force and, in particular, that Labour's opposition would make it quite difficult for the government to go forward in the face of US resistance:

> It would be highly embarrassing, to say the least, to have to invite Parliament to approve a proposal to launch a military operation against Egypt. If the issue were put to Parliament at that stage, such division of opinion as there was in the country would tend to be accentuated. It would not be easy for the Government to proceed with their

[6] See, in particular, PRO, CAB 134/1216, EC 13 (56) 3 of 9 Aug. Confidential Annex; CAB 134/1216, EC 15 (56) 1 of 14 Aug. Confidential Annex; CAB 134/1216, EC 21 (56) 2 of 24 Aug.; and CAB 134/1216, EC 24 (56) 2 of 4 Sept.

intentions on the basis of a relatively narrow majority in a division in the House of Commons.[7]

As a result, the government decided at the time that military action could not be considered unless Egypt engaged in further provocation. The hope was that Nasser would overreach and provide some pretext for a forceful response, at which point parliament could be called in to ratify an action that had already been taken. Indeed, the committee's first preference was to keep parliament out of session until the military operation was well underway, when there would be tremendous pressure to rally behind British troops in combat.

In the end, neither part of this plan worked. Opposition attacks in the press prompted the government to recall parliament early, in mid-September, so that it could directly confront Labour's criticism.[8] More importantly, Nasser neither gave in to demands to accept international control of the canal, nor did he engage in the kind of provocative action that might have justified a military response. Feeling that Britain's great power status was in jeopardy, the government sought some other pretext for military action – and found it in the Anglo-French-Israeli plot.

The extent to which Nasser's refusal to compromise was influenced by domestic opposition within Britain is difficult to document given the paucity of reliable accounts from the Egyptian side (Lucas 1996, pp. 121, 130). Nevertheless, there is some partial evidence suggesting that Nasser observed the divisions within Britain and understood that domestic opposition could undermine the government's ability to wage a protracted war. On November 1, with military action underway, the United Nations General Assembly met in emergency session to discuss the Suez matter. In the course of these debates, the Egyptian delegate made explicit references to the domestic political situation in Britain and even quoted excerpts from the Commons debate. The delegate continued, "The conclusion to be drawn from these quotations is that, even in the United Kingdom, public opinion by no means approves of the policy of Sir Anthony Eden's Government" (UN General Assembly 1956, p. 4). The second piece of suggestive evidence comes from the account of Mohamed Heikal, a self-described adviser to Nasser. According to Heikal, the Egyptian president was well aware of the Labour Party's position. On November 4, the day before the Anglo-French forces

---

[7] PRO, CAB 134/1216, EC 13 (56) 3 Confidential Annex.
[8] PRO, CAB 134/1216, EC 24 (56) 2.

arrived, there was a mass rally in Trafalgar Square at which 30,000 heard Labour's shadow foreign secretary, Aneurin Bevan, denounce the government's actions. Heikal notes,

> Nasser watched with fascination films of the Trafalgar Square meeting with the speech of his friend Bevan, and the visible evidence of the strength of opposition to Eden. So by Monday, when the landings actually took place, Nasser could see that their failure was inevitable. All plans for the Egyptian leadership to go underground and preparations for a guerrilla war were canceled. (Heikal 1986, p. 195)

Nasser seems to have predicted correctly that Britain could not sustain an extended military campaign in the face of domestic and international criticism.

Still, we are left to speculate as to how large an impact Labour's opposition had on Nasser's bargaining position. Eden, of course, would later claim that Labour's opposition amounted to a "stab in the back" that encouraged Nasser to resist British and French demands (Epstein 1964, pp. 74–87). Since these claims are obviously self-serving, they have to be discounted appropriately. Nevertheless, a similar conclusion was reached by decision makers in the United States, who had less obvious biases on this point. On August 19, shortly after the Labour Party clarified its opposition to the use of force, Secretary of State John Foster Dulles wrote a memo to President Eisenhower in which he noted that

> The attitude of the Labor Party is a hard blow for the government at this juncture when bi-partisan unity would give Britain the best chance of retrieving its position without actually having to use force. I have no doubt that Nasser is fully aware of the situation and may calculate that if he stands firm the result will not be solid strength against him but perhaps a Labor government which would be softer.
> (US, Dept. of State 1990, pp. 231–32)

Dulles echoed these sentiments on several other occasions (US, Dept. of State 1990, p. 314; Williams 1983, p. 589). He also noted that Soviet Foreign Minister Dimitri Shepilov, who must have been in close contact with Nasser, had expressed the belief that British public opinion would not support the use of force (US, Dept. of State 1990, p. 234). Thus, US decision makers seem to have been convinced that Nasser's intransigence was partly due to the domestic opposition he could readily observe in Britain.[9]

---

[9] I consider these statements to be credible since they were made early in the crisis, before the recriminations between Britain and the United States over the latter's "abandon-

It is important not to overstate this point, however. Nasser was also encouraged in his stance by the clear signals coming from Eisenhower and Dulles that the United States was unlikely to support its allies if they resorted to force (Kyle 1991, pp. 220–21). A better interpretation is that, because any military action by Britain and France would take place in the face of US resistance, the political divisions within Britain cast doubt on whether such action could be sustained for long (Epstein 1964, p. 86).

Moreover, it is likely that the US position was itself influenced by the discord in Britain. US decision makers paid close attention to British political developments and the growing opposition to the use of force. Numerous dispatches and memoranda make reference to the stance of the Labour Party as well as to the general state of public opinion there.[10] Dulles even met with Gaitskell on August 24 and reported the latter's opinion that, in the event of an armed action outside the auspices of the United Nations "not only would the Labor Party be strongly opposed, but at least half the nation" (Williams 1983, p. 589).

In the face of such signals, Eden tried hard to convince the Americans otherwise. At an August 19 meeting in the US ambassador's residence, Eden contradicted Dulles' assertion that public opinion would not support a use of force to settle the matter. The prime minister told his hosts that, if the public was hesitant now, it was only because he had so far refrained from making the case for military action. According to the memorandum reporting the conversation, Eden said "he was absolutely confident that when the chips were down, the Government would have the full backing of the public in any military operation." Later that evening, Eden pulled the US ambassador aside and asked him to assure Dulles that even Gaitskell would "stand with the government" if the use of force became necessary (US, Dept. of State 1990, pp. 234–35).

Despite these efforts, however, US decision makers seem to have been more convinced by Gaitskell's assessment of the situation than by Eden's. Indeed, Eden later expressed frustration over Dulles' refusal to

---

ment" of the former. After the crisis, US officials were sensitive to British charges that Eisenhower's repeated pronouncements against the use of force had encouraged Nasser to stand firm. Given this, Dulles might have had an incentive to project blame onto the Labour Party. However, the early timing of these statements suggests that they were not tainted by such considerations.
[10] In addition to those references noted above, see US, Dept. of State (1990, pp. 328, 331, 346, 521, 543, 671, 910, 951, 1051).

believe his repeated assertions about British public opinion (Finer 1964, p. 177). It is interesting, and consistent with the argument of this study, that US decision makers discounted statements by the British leader that conflicted with the signals sent by the opposition party. Eden had an incentive to overstate his domestic support; the Labour Party, on the other hand, had little reason to publicly oppose the use of force – and thereby expose itself to charges of being unpatriotic – unless that stance enjoyed significant political appeal.

Though it is difficult to say so conclusively, the information revealed by Labour's opposition may have played a role in the US decision to pressure Britain into backing down. The Suez affair put Washington in the difficult position of siding with an ally of the Soviet Union and against two of its closest allies. While the decision to oppose the Anglo-French plan was driven by a number of factors, the realization that military action was not supported by a significant segment, and perhaps a majority, of the British public influenced the strategic calculus (Risse-Kappen 1995, p. 92). Because the British government's position rested on tenuous political support, US decision makers understood that the task of pressuring Britain would be relatively easy. The level of coercion required was sufficiently low that the United States would incur few costs and any damage to NATO and the "special relationship" would be minimal. As a result, this course of action became more palatable.

Indeed, there is evidence suggesting that US decision makers hoped to take advantage of growing dissent in Britain to defuse the crisis quickly. In a meeting on November 3, Deputy Under Secretary of State Loy Henderson told Arab ambassadors that opposition to the use of force in Britain would help bring a halt to the hostilities and that the United States was tabling new resolutions in the United Nations which he thought would strengthen that opposition (US, Dept. of State 1990, p. 951). Then, on November 7, Eisenhower refused a request from Eden to visit Washington. Eden had hoped that a summit with the American president would varnish his image in the wake of the humiliating cease-fire and on the eve of a vote of confidence in the Commons (Carlton 1988, pp. 82–83). Eisenhower understood this at the time of his decision, having just been told of a British opinion poll showing strong disapproval for the military action (US, Dept. of State 1990, p. 1051). Thus, one effect of the refusal was to deprive Eden of an opportunity to silence some of his critics. Though Eisenhower had sympathy for his British counterpart, he was able to exploit the latter's obvious domestic difficulties to increase his leverage. Finer (1964, p. 177) comes to a similar conclusion about Dulles, noting that "His speeches were calculated to encourage, even as he drew comfort from, the Opposition."

Hence, the Labour Party's behavior helped reveal the government's political incentives – and particularly the lack of support for military action – to decision makers in Egypt and the United States. The response of both foreign powers is consistent with the predictions of the model. Both sought to exploit the underlying weakness of the government's position by standing firm in the face of threats and actions which they knew could not be sustained.

The crisis over Rhodesian independence, 1965

The issue of Rhodesian independence was a thorn in the side of successive British governments from the late 1950s, when rumblings for independence began in earnest, until 1980, when the newly christened Zimbabwe achieved full international recognition. At the center of the crisis was a dispute over the constitutional make-up of the new regime. The drive for independence came from Rhodesia's white minority government, which sought to cast off colonial status while preserving its political privileges over the African majority. The British, on the other hand, had no strong objections to granting independence, but governments of both parties insisted that greater African representation had to come first. This section deals with the first stage of the crisis, which ended in November 1965 with Rhodesia's unilateral declaration of independence (UDI). This was the only stage of the crisis in which a threat to use force was even contemplated – and ultimately rejected in favor of economic sanctions.

The crisis was precipitated in the early 1960s when Britain decided to dissolve the Central African Federation, which consisted of Southern Rhodesia (later Zimbabwe), Northern Rhodesia (later Zambia), and Nyasaland (later Malawi). When the latter two regions were granted independence under African majority rule, whites in Southern Rhodesia began their own drive for independence. In Britain, the Conservative governments of Harold Macmillan and Alec Douglas-Home were sympathetic to the Rhodesian cause but were unwilling to grant independence until steps were taken to ensure greater African representation. Though several rounds of negotiations took place, the only agreement came at a constitutional conference in 1961. At that conference, Britain agreed to relinquish its right to intervene in Rhodesian affairs on behalf of African interests in exchange for some modest constitutional revisions intended to protect African rights. Neither side was fully content with this settlement, however, since formal sovereignty over Rhodesia still resided in London and the constitutional safeguards were generally recognized as inadequate (Windrich 1978, pp. 11–12).

The crisis intensified in 1964 due to domestic political developments in both countries. In April, hard-liner Ian Smith took over as head of the Rhodesian Front, the party that dominated Rhodesia's white minority government. Then, the October general elections in Great Britain brought to power a Labour government led by Harold Wilson. The Labour Party was stridently opposed to Rhodesian independence and even spoke of amending the 1961 constitution to ensure greater African representation. With the positions of the two governments increasingly intransigent, what followed was a year of on-again, off-again negotiations that produced no substantial movement. This stalemate culminated with the unilateral declaration of independence on November 11, 1965.

From our perspective, what is interesting about this period is that Wilson, in spite of his disdain for the Rhodesian regime, repeatedly and publicly disavowed the threat of force to deter a UDI. Shortly after he came into office, alarmed by rumors that a UDI was imminent, Wilson published a statement in which he detailed what the consequences of such a move would be. No threat to use force or even apply economic sanctions was mentioned; rather, the only actions threatened were a severing of diplomatic relations and the disruption of financial and trade relations that would naturally follow Rhodesia's expulsion from the Commonwealth (Windrich 1975, pp. 208–09). As the impasse intensified over the ensuing months, the cabinet and the Overseas Policy Committee occasionally revisited the question of how to deal with a possible UDI, but the use or threat of force was consistently ruled out as impractical and undesirable.[11]

The government made no secret of this fact. When *The Times* published an article about British military preparations under the title "Police Action Plan for Rhodesia Considered," the minister of defense and the head of the RAF quickly moved to denounce the story as inaccurate and purely speculative (Good 1973, p. 63). At a meeting between Wilson and Smith in October 1965, the strongest threat the former could

---

[11] For cabinet meetings at which force was ruled out, see PRO, CAB 128/39, CC 34 (65) 2 of 24 June; CAB 128/39, CC 47 (65) 2 of 12 Sept.; CAB 128/39, CC 50 (65) 4 of 7 Oct. For meetings of the Overseas Planning Committee at which the same determination was discussed, see CAB 148/18, OPD 40 (65) of 22 Sept.; CAB 148/18, OPD 43 (65) of 7 Oct.

muster was that, despite what Britain thought about the matter, the United Nations or other African states might react to a UDI with armed intervention (Young 1969, p. 235). Shortly after, the British delegation at the United Nations refused to participate in a General Assembly resolution calling for "all possible measures" to prevent a UDI (Windrich 1978, pp. 44–45). Then, as the final round of talks came to an end, Wilson explicitly rejected the use of force three times in less than week. On October 30, at a press conference in the Rhodesian capital of Salisbury, Wilson warned African nationalists against wishful thinking: "If there are those who are thinking in terms of a thunderbolt hurtling from the sky and destroying their enemies, a thunderbolt in the shape of the RAF, let me say that thunderbolt will not be coming . . ." (quoted in Windrich 1978, p. 49). Two days later in the House of Commons, Wilson reiterated these remarks (GB, *Parl. Deb.* 5s, 718: 633–34), and three days after that, he again told the Commons, "I have made it clear that Her Majesty's Government do not believe that this constitutional problem can be settled by the use of force" (GB, *Parl. Deb.* 5s, 718: 1232). The Rhodesian UDI came exactly a week later, and the only British military response was the deployment of some aircraft to neighboring Zambia.

In opting for economic sanctions over military force, Wilson was bowing to a number of factors that made the latter unattractive (Good 1973, pp. 55–65; Verrier 1986, pp. 152–56). The defense chiefs were strongly opposed to military action given the logistical difficulties and the fact that Rhodesia had a well-financed and organized security force, including an air force. There were also worries about what would happen when British soldiers were asked to shoot their "kith and kin," the white Europeans who ran the rebellious government. Moreover, even if the intervention succeeded, Britain would somehow have to create a new order with the cooperation of rival African nationalist groups. The domestic political risks of a military response also weighed against this option. The Labour government had been elected with an absolute majority of only five seats in parliament, a margin that had dwindled to three by the time of the UDI. Given its precarious existence, the government could not readily ignore public opinion polls showing a strong aversion to the use of force in this matter (Good 1973, p. 62; Young 1969, p. 253). These considerations suggest that the government's expected payoff from using force was quite low; any threat to respond to a UDI with military action would have been a bluff.

Still, a number of observers at the time wondered why Wilson not only refused to make the bluff but even went so far as to explicitly rule out the use of force. The President of Zambia referred to this move as "one of the greatest blunders any government could make" (Good 1973, p. 63). Minister of Defense Denis Healey had a similarly harsh assessment: "I think it was insane . . . I simply cannot understand the Prime Minister letting Ian Smith know that we wouldn't intervene by force, because in the situation where you've so few cards in your hand, you mustn't tell the other side that you have no cards" (quoted in Flower 1987, p. 51; see also Healey 1989, p. 332). By renouncing a military response, Wilson substantially weakened his bargaining position and paved the way for the very outcome he hoped to avoid. According to Smith's chief of intelligence, Kenneth Flower, the Rhodesian government was in a precarious position because of its relative military weakness: "Smith was holding fewer cards [than Wilson] . . . knowing that neither his Army nor his Air Force would oppose force with force" (Flower 1987, p. 51). Indeed, Flower had advised against UDI precisely because he was concerned about the outcome should Britain call Smith's bluff. The effect of Wilson's statement on October 30, however, was to "throw away what little advantage he had": "By making this statement Wilson had removed any immediate prospect for a negotiated settlement and had cleared the way for the [Rhodesian Front] government to take matters into its own hand" (*ibid.*, p. 51). The threat that remained – economic sanctions – was much less worrisome to Smith. Sanctions would have to be sustained for a long period and at great cost to Britain over time; in addition, Smith knew that he could count on support from Portugal and neighboring South Africa (Young 1969, p. 170). Despite optimistic pronouncements to the contrary, even the British government's own analysis cast doubt on the deterrent value of the economic threat.[12]

Why, then, did Wilson "renounce in advance his only effective deterrent" (Windrich 1978, p. 58)? The explicit disavowal of the military option is readily explicable by the theory presented here; in essence, the strategy was bad international diplomacy but good domestic politics. The Rhodesian crisis had put the opposition Conservative Party in an awkward position. On the one hand, the policy of making independence conditional on greater African representation had been forged under Conservative rule. On the other hand, the party included a substantial bloc that sympathized with the white minority government (*ibid.*, p. 42). Furthermore, party leaders could read the opinion polls

---

[12] See, e.g., PRO, CAB 148/18, OPD 12 (65) 1 of 5 Mar. 5; CAB 128/39, CC 56 (65) of 2 Nov.

and see that opposing the use of force would have electoral benefits, in addition to mollifying these back-benchers. Hence, the Conservatives staked out the following position: they would back the government in its negotiations with Rhodesia; they would oppose a UDI; but they would not support the use of force to settle the matter.

This stance became evident early on in the crisis. On November 3, 1964, opposition leader Alec Douglas-Home denounced one of the few veiled threats the Labour government made against Smith. Foreign Secretary Arthur Bottomley had said several days earlier that military intervention was not being considered "at the moment." Douglas-Home, noting this qualification, told the Commons: "I hope that this kind of language will cease and that it will be left behind us" (quoted in Young 1969, pp. 168–69). Later, at the Conservative Party conference in October 1965, a strong minority pushed an amendment declaring its opposition to any sanctions, military or economic, in the event of a UDI. Though this amendment was not voted upon, the new party leader, Edward Heath, did put the government on notice that it did not have a "blank cheque from us on Rhodesia." He also deplored the use of terms like "treason" and "traitors" to describe the Rhodesian government, as these labels seemed to invite a forceful response (*ibid.*, p. 250). The party was clearly divided into several shades of opinion on the matter, but opposition to the use of force was one point on which most could agree.

This suggests that Wilson's willingness to threaten force was constrained by the likely response of the opposition party and the resultant impact on his party's electoral fortunes. A threat to use force would have united the Conservatives in vocal opposition. Wilson clearly appreciated this, as he notes in his memoirs: "had we decided to intervene by force of arms [Heath] would have led a united party, and almost certainly won majority support in the country" (Wilson 1971, p. 181). It would not only have been difficult to sustain the government under these circumstances, but it was also unlikely that he could have sustained the bluff. Minutes from cabinet meetings at the time clearly indicate that Wilson thought a threat to use force would be more likely to hasten a UDI than to deter it.[13] Renunciation of the military option, on the other hand, kept the opposition divided and quiescent. Without the prospect of military action against their "kith and kin," the Conservatives had little to oppose and nothing to rally around (Windrich 1978, pp. 65–67). As a result, Wilson could claim bipartisan support for his policies and bolster his image as a

[13] See, e.g., PRO, CAB 128/39, CC 3 (65) 2 of 21 Jan.; CAB 128/39, CC 51 (65) 1 of 14 Oct. 14.

statesman above the political fray (Pimlott 1992, p. 375). The prime minister clearly calculated that the political benefits of forswearing force outweighed any potential benefits that might have come from making a risky threat that he was unprepared to carry out.

For his part, Smith seems to have understood this political calculus. Returning from a trip to London several weeks before the UDI, Smith dismissed his intelligence chief's concerns about a British military response with the observation: "It's not practical politics" (Flower 1987, p. 47). Several months later, Smith elaborated on his reading of the situation facing Wilson:

> I think it [a use of force] would arouse the wrath of the people of Britain and this may be such as to remove him from office, and I believe that there is nothing that Wilson wants more in life than to remain in office. Therefore, he wouldn't take this chance. And in view of the fact that he seems to be entrenching himself without resorting to force – he seems able to run circles round the Conservatives today – why make a dangerous move when he can retain his position without doing so?
>
> (Quoted in Young 1969, p. 328)

Clearly, the British government's political incentives were quite transparent to the Rhodesian leader, who took full advantage of the former's domestic constraints.

Conclusion

Several patterns stand out when these cases are juxtaposed. The first is that, in all four instances, the British government clearly took into account the domestic political reaction which would accompany a threat to use force and the implications this reaction would have for its ability to make such a threat credibly. In the Rhineland and Rhodesia cases, the government understood that political and military conditions were such that a threat to use force would have generated public dissent on which opposition parties would have been happy to capitalize. Since any such threat would have been a bluff, the government abstained from making public commitments from which it would later have to back down. Instead, it took pains to reassure voters that war would be avoided in large part to prevent opposition to war becoming a political issue. In the Boer and Suez cases, the government ultimately decided that the issues at stake and the commitments made required a forceful response; in both instances, however, the knowledge that force would be publicly opposed engendered an element of caution and restraint.

Early in both crises, the government explicitly acknowledged that it was hesitant to threaten force without support from the opposition party. Once Chamberlain and Eden decided that force was needed, they made efforts to counteract the signals that were being sent by their domestic adversaries. This evidence is consistent with hypothesis 8.

There is also evidence of varying quality that foreign decision makers understood the political constraints facing the British government and took advantage of them. Hitler occupied the Rhineland secure in the knowledge that Britain would do nothing to stop him and that the French would not march without the British. Ian Smith was likewise emboldened by his reading of political conditions in Britain, as his own words attest. Less direct evidence exists regarding Nasser's perceptions, and, given the central role of the United States in the Suez crisis, it is important not to overstate how much the image of disunity in Great Britain influenced his decision making. Still, the evidence that does exist suggests that it was a factor. The Boer case is also less conclusive, but suggestive. It is likely that Kruger's early reluctance to make concessions was influenced by the antipathy to war among the British public, which found expression in the Liberal Party's public statements. By late fall of 1899, however, Chamberlain's efforts to stiffen the public's – and the rest of the cabinet's – resolve had borne fruit, and Kruger was aware that the threat of war was now serious. By this point, however, the Boer leader had decided that war was preferable to giving in to Chamberlain's demands, which seemed constantly to grow (Packenham 1979, p. 102). Moreover, the military mobilization which the cabinet set underway created an escalatory pressure that proved hard to escape. If war was approaching, as seemed likely, the Boers needed to strike first, rather than wait to see whether further negotiations could settle the issue. Thus, Britain's efforts to send a strong signal in the face of domestic opposition created an irresistible momentum towards war.

All of these cases illustrate the constraints under which democratic governments operate. Public competition makes it difficult for such a government to conceal factors that make the use of force politically or militarily unattractive. When such factors are present, opposition parties have incentives to reveal them by publicly opposing the use of force. Foreign states observing this signal then have reason to doubt the credibility of the government's threats. As a result, a democratic government that faces the prospect of public dissent is hesitant to make threats and unlikely to engage in bluffing behavior. By preventing the government from monopolizing the signals that foreign decision makers receive, public competition limits the government's ability to use its information opportunistically.

This negative assessment is worth emphasizing given the generally optimistic view of democracy that appears in this book. While the arguments here suggest certain tangible advantages which accompany democratic institutions, these are long-run advantages that do not accrue in every individual instance. In cases like the Rhineland and Rhodesia crises, the loss of control over information, and the resultant inability to bluff, can place democratic states in the undesirable position of having to acquiesce to developments that a threat to use force might have prevented. Moreover, cases like the Boer and Suez wars demonstrate the contingent nature of democracy's benefits. The formal model showed that, *ex ante*, before nature has drawn the state's value for war, the probability that the state will make a threat, the probability that the rival state will resist, and the probability that the interaction will lead to war are all lower if the state is democratic than if it is not. *Ex post*, once the state's type has been drawn, this is not necessarily the case. There are some types for which the probabilities of resistance and war are invariant across political systems. These are precisely the types that experience domestic opposition to the use of force in equilibrium. The fact that competition is associated with a decrease in the probability of resistance on average is cold comfort to any particular government that sees its threats to use force called into question by internal dissent.

8   Conclusions and implications

This book sought to address the following questions: How do domestic political institutions affect the way states behave in international crises? How do the institutions and practices of democracy influence the use of threats to wage war, the way such threats are interpreted, and ultimately whether or not crises can be settled short of war? Answering these questions required that we take a step back to ask a more basic set of questions: Why do states fight wars? What factors determine whether disputes become crises and whether crises escalate into wars? In Chapter 2, I argued that wars occur when states have private information about their expected value for fighting and conflicting preferences over the allocation of international goods. Private information creates uncertainty over the range of negotiated settlements that are mutually acceptable. Conflicting preferences create incentives for states to manipulate their private information strategically, thus complicating efforts to reduce this uncertainty. As a result, much of state behavior in international crises revolves around efforts to reveal and exploit private information through the use of threats and other signals. And the outcomes of crises – who wins, who loses, and whether the dispute is resolved through war or diplomacy – depend crucially on the success or failure of these efforts.

Given this logic, the question of whether democratic institutions affect the likelihood of war could be restated: Do democratic institutions influence the way information is revealed during the course of crisis bargaining? Chapters 3 and 4 answered this question in the affirmative. I argued that institutions designed to facilitate the operation of representative government have unintended consequences for the availability of information internationally. In particular, the public nature of political competition in such systems places constraints on the government's ability to conceal or misrepresent relevant information in a crisis. The political process in democratic countries resembles an open debate in which the government must share the stage with its domestic adversaries. The resulting interaction generates public information about the desirability of different policy choices and the government's domestic political incentives. In nondemocratic systems, by contrast, arguments over public policy – and especially foreign policy – tend to take place in private; their public aspect more closely resembles a monologue than a debate. In such a setting, the government has greater leeway to manipulate its private information for strategic gain.

The core of the theoretical presentation was a comparative-static exercise carried out with the help of a game-theoretic model. Chapter 4 wedded a standard crisis bargaining game with a simple model of two-party electoral choice and asked: holding everything else constant, how do behaviors and outcomes change with the introduction of open political competition in one state? The analysis in this chapter showed that competition at the domestic level helps overcome problems of asymmetric information at the international level. As long as political parties place sufficient weight on the goal of achieving office, the resultant conflict of interests generates informative signals in the crisis game. In particular, the introduction of an opposition party reduces the government's ability to engage in bluffing behavior and creates a mechanism through which governments with high resolve can signal that fact quite credibly. As a result, democratic states were predicted to use threats more selectively, to enjoy greater success with the threats they do make, and fight wars at a lower rate than were states in which political competition is suppressed or takes place in private.

Unlike arguments that have arisen in the democratic peace literature, this finding does not require any assumptions about the relative pacifism of democracies. Democratic states in this theory are not motivated by norms of nonviolent conflict resolution, nor do they necessarily have dovish preferences due to the existence of domestic competition. Instead, the model makes no distinction between democratic and nondemocratic countries when it comes to the distribution of preferences over war and peace. The prediction of fewer wars derives solely from the democratic state's superior ability to signal its true preferences, *whatever those may be*. Indeed, one way democratic states can bring about peace is by convincingly demonstrating unanimous support for war.

The second part of this book, comprising the final three chapters, explored the empirical implications of this theory with an emphasis on differentiating it from other arguments in the literature on democratic distinctiveness. Proving arguments that hinge critically on intangible factors such as information and beliefs presents particular problems due to the difficulties of acquiring reliable and systematic data on what people believe, the probabilities they assign to different events, and the values they place on possible outcomes. In the absence of direct evidence on these matters, the researcher has to rely, not on one decisive test, but on several, mutually reinforcing tests. Hence, although each test in Chapter 5–7 can be judged on its own merits, any evaluation of the theory rests on the picture they present collectively. Two sets of results are worth highlighting.

The first set deals with the decision to turn disputes into crises by issuing threats to use military force. The theoretical presentation suggested that, all other things being equal, democracies should be less likely to make such threats due to constraints on their ability to engage in strategic misrepresentation. Whereas nondemocratic governments have substantial leeway to bluff and probe, democratic governments are less willing to make threats that they do not intend to carry out. Underlying this probabilistic prediction is a specific causal mechanism: democratic governments face domestic competitors who have incentives to oppose the use of force when political and military conditions are unfavorable. As a result, when domestic opposition parties choose to oppose force, foreign observers revise downward their estimate of the government's value for war. Domestic opposition thus casts doubt on the government's willingness and ability to carry through on its threats, and outright bluffing becomes a less attractive strategy. This logic suggests three empirical patterns, all of which found support in the quantitative and historical evidence:

(1) Democracy lowers the probability that a state will initiate a crisis, holding everything else constant.
(2) The prospect of domestic opposition makes a democratic government unwilling to make threats that it is unlikely to carry out.
(3) Foreign decision makers interpret dissent by opposition parties as an indicator that the government has low expected value for war.

The difficulties which democratic states have concealing their constraints or mounting effective bluffs may also make them tempting targets for other states. Though the evidence on this point was mixed, we saw that democracy has at times had dramatic effects on the probability that a state becomes the target of a threat. This was evident not only in the statistical evidence in Chapter 5 but also in the analysis of the Rhineland crisis.

The second set of results deals with how foreign states react when confronted by a threat to use force. Here again, the theory makes both probabilistic predictions and predictions about behavior in individual cases. All other things being equal, threats from democratic governments are less likely to be resisted than threats made by nondemocratic governments. The reason is credibility, which comes from two sources. The first source is the opposition party, which has incentives to support the government's threats when political and military conditions are favorable. As long as the parties are engaged in a competitive relationship, the opposition does not have incentives to collude in a bluff; its support thus serves as independent confirmation that the government has political incentives to carry through on its threat. When faced with a supported threat, decision makers in the rival state revise upward their beliefs about the government's resolve and are consequently more likely to make concessions rather than to escalate the crisis militarily. The second source of credibility comes from the observation, noted above, that democratic governments are less likely to engage in bluffs. If a government is constrained from bluffing, then the threats that it does chose to make are more likely to be genuine. This logic suggests three broad empirical patterns, all of which found support in the evidence presented here:

(4) Militarized actions taken by democratic states are less likely to be reciprocated in kind than are militarized actions taken by nondemocratic states.

(5) Extended deterrent threats made by democratic governments and supported by major opposition parties are more likely to be successful than are threats made by nondemocratic governments.

(6) When domestic opposition parties support a threat to use force, foreign decision makers interpret this support an indicator that the government is willing and able to carry through on the threat.

Together, the combination of selective threats and effective threats led to the prediction that democracy lowers the probability that the state will initiate or become the target of a crisis that escalates to war. The evidence in Chapter 5 supported the first half of this claim, but was mixed in support of the second half.

None of these findings, on its own, serves as conclusive proof of the informational argument developed here, but the overall picture is compelling. Moreover, none of the major alternative arguments about democracy and war anticipates or accounts for all of these findings. Normative theories fall short because all of the results suggest the workings of a purely monadic effect that cannot be attributed to shared liberal norms or values. We saw that democracy leads to a lower probability of crisis initiation, a lower probability of reciprocation, and a higher probability of success in extended deterrence crises regardless of the regime type of the state or states on the other side. The effects of domestic dissent discussed in Chapter 7 were evident even though none of the rival states in the cases considered were democratic. Finally, the case study in Chapter 6, which did examine a conflict between two democracies, found evidence that was inconsistent with this perspective.

The institutional constraints perspective fares better but still does not provide a complete accounting for the results uncovered here. In particular, the finding that threats made by democratic states are more likely to be successful than threats made by nondemocratic states is hard to reconcile with the claim that democratic leaders face systematically higher costs for waging war. Moreover, by implicitly assuming that democratic publics exert a pacifying effect on their leaders, this argument does not adequately anticipate situations, like the Fashoda affair, in which democratic governments can achieve peaceful outcomes by demonstrating in a convincing manner that they have no choice but to wage war unless their demands are met. Such outcomes are best explained by a theory that appreciates the dilemmas associated with bargaining under incomplete information and the role that democratic institutions play in overcoming those dilemmas.

Implications for international relations

What are the implications of this analysis for international relations? Will the spread of democracy, noted at the outset of this book, fundamentally alter the role of force in politics among nations? To a large extent, the answer to this question depends upon whether or not there is a democratic peace – that is, a peace among democracies that can be attributed to their norms and/or institutions. Throughout this book, I have for the most part been silent on this question, and the empirical results I presented do not resolve this debate. Though I could rule out the possibility that democratic peace theories – in either their normative or institutional versions – accounted for my empirical regularities, neither of those theories was truly falsified. As noted in the introduction, my agnosticism on this point is driven by a sense that there are limitations in the available data that make definitive conclusions difficult at this point. Hence, my goal was to articulate a theory that was not inconsistent with the existence of a democratic peace but which explored other avenues.

If there is a real democratic peace, the theory I have presented contributes to but probably does not provide a full explanation. Such an explanation would almost certainly have to include some argument about the nature of preferences, as current theories about the democratic peace generally do. Still, my theory fills a gap in any such arguments – by showing how democratic states might overcome informational asymmetries that can cause bargaining to fail in spite of a shared interest in peace. As we saw in the Fashoda case, democratic states can get into intense crises in which any institutional and normative constraints, if they exist, are overwhelmed by other factors (see also, Layne 1994; Owen 1997). In such cases, the mechanisms of transparency discussed here help explain why war may nevertheless be avoided in these cases. If, on the other hand, there is no democratic peace, then the results here suggest that there are still important consequences of democracy for crisis behavior and the incidence of war.

In thinking about what a world of democratic states would look like, then, the image suggested by this analysis is neither as optimistic as that offered by devotees of the democratic peace, nor is it as pessimistic as that offered by realists. The former operate to one degree or another in the shadow of Immanuel Kant, the title of whose famous treatise on this matter, "Perpetual Peace," states rather succinctly the hopes that underlie these scholars' work. Liberal theory, of which democratic peace arguments are a subset, is fundamentally optimistic about the prospects for progress and holds that, although war has been a recurring feature of international politics, it need not be a permanent feature. To realists, on the other hand, even such modest hopes are unwarranted. Because anarchy is a permanent feature of international politics, so too are conflict and war. And because international factors overwhelm domestic considerations, fundamental change cannot come from within states – only from without. The realist view does not rule out that extended periods of peace are possible. Such periods, however, are only temporary respites brought about by particular configurations of power and interests.

The implications of the argument developed here fall in between the two extremes offered by liberal and realist theories, while at the same time borrowing elements from both of them. The theoretical argument developed in Chapters 3 and 4 and the statistical evidence presented in Chapter 5 both suggest that, all other things being equal, democratic states issue challenges at a lower rate, face resistance at a lower rate, and consequently fight wars at a lower rate than do nondemocratic states. In this sense, it follows that, in a world of democracies, war would be relatively rarer than it has been to date. That said, there are several crucial qualifications to this conclusion.

The theoretical and empirical results in this book are all probabilistic, rather than deterministic, and accompanied by a very strong *ceteris paribus* clause: all other things must be equal. A lower probability of war does not imply an absence of war. Moreover, while institutions have an important influence on crisis outcomes, none of the arguments in this book dispute that interests and power matter too. The informational perspective predicts a lower probability of violence holding constant the frequency and intensity of the underlying conflicts. It is precisely because the level of conflict in states' interests matters that we went to such trouble in Chapter 5 trying to control for unmeasured heterogeneity on this dimension. After all, two autocracies with nothing to dispute can be less likely to engage in militarized conflict than two democracies with a longstanding dispute over highly prized goods. As we have seen, realist accounts that emphasize interests (i.e., Gowa 1999; Farber and Gowa 1995, 1997; Gartzke 1997) are not wrong; they are simply incomplete. This means that efforts to reduce the likelihood of war by addressing underlying conflicts of interest – in Gowa's (1999) words, "building bridges" – are as important as efforts to create change at the domestic level – "building democracies."

At the same time, this logic is consistent with the arguments of Owen (1997), Zakaria (1997), and others, who have argued that democracy coupled with jingoistic, racist, bigoted, or militaristic ideologies does not automatically generate peaceful relations. Democracy, in the argument developed here, does not induce peaceful preferences; rather, it fosters the faithful revelation of voter preferences, whatever those may be. If voters are motivated by ideologies that lead them to place very high value on the acquisition of certain goods – such as historically important territories – and/or to place low value on the human costs of attaining those goods, then those preferences will be carried through into government decision making, certainly leading to a higher rate of challenges and possibly leading to a higher rate of war relative to a state with less belligerent preferences. The comparative static at the core of this book does not imply that a democracy is always more peaceful than a nondemocracy, regardless of the preferences that prevail at the domestic level; rather, it says that, holding such preferences constant, democratic institutions lead to a lower rate of conflict and war. What may seem surprising here is the implication that a democracy suffused with a nationalistic or militaristic ideology is less likely to engage in war than is an autocracy suffused with a similar ideology. The rationale for this goes back to the argument made in the introduction that belligerent preferences, when signaled credibly, can enhance the prospects for a peaceful outcome.

This suggests a related caveat. Throughout this book, I have defined peace rather broadly as the absence of war. It does not mean the absence of conflict, the absence of threats, or the absence of a willingness to wage war. Peace comes about in the crisis bargaining model in three different ways: the potential challenger chooses not to issue a threat; the challenger does make a threat, but the target offers to concede a share of the good; or the challenger makes a threat, the target resists, but the challenger then backs down. Only the first of these outcomes would meet a stricter definition of peace that includes the absence of threats or of other steps that could lead to war. In the argument developed here, democracy increases the likelihood of peace not only by increasing the probability of this "strictly peaceful" outcome, but also by increasing the probability that the target state makes concessions, conditional on a threat having been issued. Thus, democratic institutions do not preclude the use of threats; rather, they imbue those threats with greater meaning, enhancing their usefulness in signaling a state's resolve. Threats and displays of force are a primary means by which states can signal their type under conditions of asymmetric information. As long as such conditions continue to arise, threats should remain an essential component of international politics.

Nor is it the case that democracies need no longer prepare for war by arming themselves and engaging in security alliances. Recall that strategic behavior in the bargaining models is driven by a state's expected value for war. This value determines the minimum a state can expect to get in an international dispute. We have also seen empirically that power bestows benefits. While I emphasized the results showing that democracies enjoy lower rates of reciprocation and higher rates of success in extended deterrence crises, we also saw that relative power produces similar effects. Thus, increases in war-fighting capabilities can lead to increased payoffs from international bargaining – even if no shots are ever fired. Whatever the internal composition of states, the international system is still anarchic, meaning that states must live by a principle of "self-help" (Waltz 1979, p. 111). Unless institutions arise which are capable of distributing international goods based on some other criterion, the ability to prevail in war is a crucial determinant of "who gets what." In sum, then, although democratic institutions help states diminish the likelihood of war, they do not eliminate threats of force, nor do they obviate the need to prepare for conflict.

Implications for national welfare: is transparency in the national interest?

Finally, what does this analysis tell us about the impact of democratic institutions on national welfare? Are democratic states and their citizens better off or worse off as a result of their transparent political institutions? The general question of whether democracy helps or hinders foreign policy is one on which the pendulum of opinion has swung to both extremes in the course of the last century. Influenced by the Western democracies' dismal performance against Hitler in the 1930s, the prevailing viewpoint during that period and the early Cold War was that democracies were at a severe disadvantage in international competition. Democracies were thought to be indecisive, slow to act, weak of purpose, squeamish about using force, and subject to the changing whims of public opinion. By handing foreign policy over to short-sighted politicians and ill-informed voters, democratic politics threatened to divert the state from pursuing its objective national interests (Kennan 1977; Morgenthau 1973, esp. pp. 146–48; Lowi 1967; Lippmann 1955; Friedrich 1938). With the end of the Cold War, however, pessimism has given way to triumphalism. Democracy, it is now argued, encourages better economic growth and more efficient extraction of resources (Lake 1992), promotes soldier morale and battlefield effectiveness (Reiter and Stam 1998), ensures that foreign policy serves the greater good rather than the interests of parochial groups or selfish leaders (e.g., Snyder 1991; Bueno de Mesquita *et al.* 1999) – and, devotees of the democratic peace would add, is the key to "perpetual peace."

On the specific issue of how political competition influences the use of threats in crises, the argument in this book similarly represents a departure from a longstanding conventional wisdom that democratic states are hurt by their openness and transparency. If diplomacy is poker game, who would want to play with all of their cards showing, especially if other players could keep some of theirs concealed? Who would want to play if someone with an interest in seeing them lose could stand behind them and announce their cards? In both popular and scholarly opinion, one sees two related concerns. The first is that democratic institutions inevitably lead to mixed or unclear signals because they make it easy for internal dissent to be openly expressed. As a result, democracies have a harder time convincing their adversaries that they are willing to use force (e.g., Wright 1965; Handlin 1968). In this view, the multitude of signals coming from democracies is confusing rather than informative, and decision makers in other states are more likely to reach the wrong conclusion rather than the right one (Finel and Lord 1999).

A second concern is that, by making it harder for the government to conceal or remain ambiguous about its constraints, democratic institutions deprive the state of its ability to bluff effectively. Henry Kissinger's memoirs contain numerous passages lamenting the way domestic opposition to the Vietnam War undercut his bargaining leverage (Kissinger 1979, pp. 288–303, 512–13, 970–71). Kissinger felt that the only way he could obtain a favorable settlement was if he could make the North Vietnamese believe that there was a chance the United States would stay involved; however, with Congress discussing resolutions calling for an immediate withdrawal, this was a bluff he could not successfully make: "To end the war honorably we needed to present our enemy with the very margin of uncertainty about our intentions that our domestic opponents bent every effort to remove . . . [The North Vietnamese] understood only too well the direction in which we were being pushed" (*ibid.*, p. 979). There is no doubt a self-serving aspect to this interpretation of events, but it is hard to deny that an inability to conceal domestic constraints can put democracies at a disadvantage.

Are these two concerns valid? The first concern, as I hope this book has demonstrated, is misplaced. While democracies may at times send mixed signals, the overall record suggests that they have been very effective at using threats of force. The second concern, on the other hand, is valid. I will argue, however, that these costs are at least partially offset by compensating advantages.

Consider first the argument that democracies cannot use threats effectively. The primary response to this argument is that it is inconsistent with the evidence presented in this book. We saw in Chapter 5 that when democracies wield or threaten force, their adversaries are less likely to respond in kind. We saw in Chapter 6 that democratic defenders have a higher rate of success than do nondemocratic defenders in immediate extended deterrence crises. Given these results, Wright's (1965) conclusion, cited at the outset, is hard to sustain. The evidence in Chapter 6 is particularly useful in refuting the critical view of democracy. Writers in this tradition implicitly assume that democracies are hampered by dissent and that at best they are equal to autocracies when they manage to speak with one voice (Wright 1965, p. 842; Lowi 1967). In fact, this view is wrong. When their threats are supported, democracies do better than their nondemocratic counterparts; it is when democracies face dissent that the success rates of the two types are equal.

While responding at the level of empirical evidence might be sufficient to discard the critical view, the argument presented here can go one step further: by suggesting why it is that conventional wisdom can go astray in this context. Briefly put, the cases that are inconsistent with my general argument tend to be more spectacular – and hence have greater influence on qualitative assessments – than are the cases that are consistent with my argument. Consider the three main patterns predicted by the model:

(1) The government makes a genuine threat, the opposition supports it, increasing the likelihood that the rival state will acquiesce.

(2) The government makes a threat, the opposition dissents, increasing the probability that the rival state will interpret the threat as a bluff and resist.

(3) The government chooses not to make a threat, anticipating that the opposition would dissent if it did.

While the first and third equilibria predict cases in which a democracy speaks with one voice, these are also the cases most likely to end up as nonevents or obscure events. In the first, the rival state is likely to give in, perhaps without taking any escalatory action; in the third, the status quo is maintained. The equilibrium involving mixed messages is the one that is most likely to be associated with resistance, escalation, and war. The same is true of cases that are inconsistent with the first pattern – that is, cases in which the government and opposition both supported force, but the rival state nevertheless did not back down.[1] Indeed, as we saw in Chapter 6, deterrence failures by democracies contributed to some of the most prominent international conflicts of the last century: World War I, World War II, and the Vietnam War. Hence, if one looks back through history at prominent crises and wars – as, for example, Wright (1965) does – there is a danger of overestimating the frequency with which democracies were unable to make their threats credible.[2] It is for this reason that the statistical tests in Chapter 5 tried very hard to get at the frequency of nonevents – that is, the absence of crisis initiation – and obscure events like unreciprocated crises.

What about the concern that democracies are hurt by their diminished ability to bluff effectively? There is no doubt that autocratic governments can take advantage of their superior ability to control information and stifle public dissent. Hitler fully exploited his ability to engage in bluffs and covert rearmament. By concealing the scope of his military preparations early on, he ensured that Western countries would enter the arms race late. By exaggerating the extent of his capabilities from 1935 onward, he reinforced British and French preferences for appeasement and won easy victories in the Rhineland, Austria, and Czechoslovakia (Whaley 1984). As we saw in Chapter 7, the remilitarization of the Rhineland was in all likelihood a bluff from which Hitler would have retreated had the allies chosen to resist. The lack of transparency surrounding German decision making, together with the very public opposition to the use of force in Britain and France, meant that Hitler could exploit his informational advantage, safe in the knowledge that the Western democracies would not oppose him.

Nonetheless, the arguments in this book make it clear that there is in fact a trade-off associated with public competition and the transparency it generates. On the one hand, a government that cannot monopolize information cannot exploit the strategic advantages that private information can bestow. In the context of the crisis bargaining models we have considered, a state successfully exploits its information when it bluffs and gets away with it. The restraining effect implies there are situations in which a democratic government has to accept the status quo when a similarly placed nondemocratic government could bluff and

[1] Though the model presented here predicts that this will never happen, elsewhere (Schultz 1998) I derive the same results using a model that allows a positive probability of resistance against supported threats.

[2] Achen and Snidal (1989) make a similar argument about the difficulties of assessing deterrence theory using case studies.

have some chance of scoring a diplomatic victory. In this sense, transparency is a liability.

On the other hand, a diminished ability to engage in deception goes hand in hand with an enhanced ability to send credible signals. Although domestic competition can undermine a government's threat by revealing political incentives to oppose the use of force, it can also have the opposite effect: strengthening the government's signal by revealing political incentives to support the use of force. The threats that democratic governments choose to make are consequently more effective, on average, than those made by nondemocracies. The evidence shows that democracies are more likely to get their way without having to fight, and they are less likely to end up in unwanted wars – that is, wars that occur when the target of a threat resists because it believes there is some chance the threat is not genuine. In this sense, transparency is beneficial. It is here that the poker analogy mentioned above breaks down. In poker, a person with a very strong hand would like to keep that fact concealed in order to keep other players in the game and betting. If a strong hand were revealed, the player would win nothing. In international crises, a government with a strong hand wants very much to signal that fact in a credible manner. In this case, getting the other side to fold is the best possible outcome.

The result, then, is a trade-off. The model from Chapter 4 cannot tell us in general whether this trade-off yields a net benefit or a net loss in terms of national welfare. Depending upon the actual distribution of the cost terms, the expected value to the voters of playing the game without an opposition party can be either less than or more than the expected value of playing the game with an opposition party. We know that the latter is associated with a lower probability of war, so, to the extent that war imposes costs on the nation, this is a good thing. The wars that are prevented, however, are precisely those for which the state has the highest expected value, or the lowest expected costs. Whether or not the benefit of avoiding these wars outweighs the diminished ability to bluff depends entirely on how often the government could get away with such a move, which in turn depends upon the distribution of costs for the rival state.

What we do know is that the two effects – the inability to exploit private information and the superior ability to send credible signals – are inextricably linked. A state cannot enjoy one without the other. After all, if a state cannot bluff, then the threats it does make must be genuine; conversely, the ability to bluff casts doubt on the credibility of all the state's threats. The liabilities and benefits of transparency inevitably accompany one another.

This linkage is important to emphasize in thinking about the complaints and evasions of democratic leaders who are faced with the downsides of transparency and dissent. Inevitably, efforts to overcome the liabilities – such as by depriving the public and opposition parties of information or creating legal sanctions for dissent – must also deprive the government of the advantages. Laws that prevent opposition parties from opposing the government in a crisis may give the government wider latitude to exploit its private information, but they also undermine the confirmatory signal that opposition parties can send when the government's payoff from war is high. After all, domestic support that is the result of coercion conveys no information whatsoever.

Still, this suggests that, even if there are long-term benefits associated with the trade-off, any given government may face short-term temptations to circumvent or suppress the constraints of democratic competition. There are several reasons, however, why such efforts are unlikely to have the desired consequences. In the first place, the fact that parties tend to alternate in office creates disincentives for a government to impose lasting restrictions on the information available to or the rights to dissent of opposition parties. After all, today's government may be tomorrow's opposition. Not only does the government face the prospect of retaliation in the future, but it knows that any long-term restrictions will affect it should it lose power. An alternative to long-term restrictions would be to impose sanctions on dissent in a particular crisis. This too has shortcomings, though, the most serious of which is that it is likely to be counterproductive. After all, what signal does the government send when it has to pass laws aimed at stifling opposition to its policies? Why would a rival state not interpret this as a sign of domestic weakness? A government that expects support for its policies to be freely given would never have to resort to such actions.

The US experience with the Alien and Sedition Acts illustrates many of these problems. These acts were passed in 1798 during the so-called "quasi-war" with France. The two countries had been allies since the Revolutionary War, but the 1794 Jay Treaty with Great Britain angered the French and led to the seizure of US merchant ships. When American envoys to Paris were asked to pay bribes before negotiations could begin (the so-called XYZ Affair), the resulting outrage in the United States led to repudiation of the US–French alliance, the suspension of trade, and an undeclared naval war in which each side seized the other's ships (DeConde 1966). Although large segments of the public supported President John Adams in these moves, the opposition Republican party was generally sympathetic to France and its revolution and so opposed the government's actions. The Federalists – ostensibly fearing that Republican opposition would give comfort to France, but also seeing an opportunity to wipe out their political rivals – took advantage of their majority in both houses to pass the Sedition Acts. Although the acts were explicitly targeted against "seditious libel" – that is, intentionally and maliciously spreading falsehoods about the government – they could be interpreted quite broadly and were used to intimidate Republican newspapers that engaged in any criticism of the government and its policies (Smith 1956; Miller 1951).

For many of the reasons discussed above, however, these laws ultimately failed to have the desired effects, both domestically and internationally. As predicted, they were designed to be short lived precisely because Federalists feared that they would be used against them should they lose the next election. Most of the sedition laws were designed to expire on March 3, 1801, the last day of the Adams administration. Moreover, while they were politically popular at first, as public ire against France was quite high, they increasingly became a source of internal discord. Prodded by Thomas Jefferson and the Republicans, the state legislatures of Virginia and Kentucky passed resolutions opposing the acts. In one noteworthy episode, a Republican congressman from Vermont who had been prosecuted for sedition campaigned and won reelection from his jail cell (Smith 1956, ch. 11). And, of course, the Federalist party lost the presidency and both houses of Congress in the elections of 1800, in part because of public distaste for the laws and the expansion of federal power they represented (Smith 1956, pp. 431–32; Miller 1951, ch. 13). Ironically, opposition to the acts gave the Republicans a strong plank to run on and allowed them to recover some of the political support they had lost by opposing the conflict with France in the first place. The Federalists would thus have been better off letting the voters punish the Republicans at the polls than trying to silence their dissent through the legal process (Miller 1951, p. 221; DeConde 1966, p. 194).

At the same time, the acts did not eliminate opposition to the government's foreign policy nor mislead the French into believing that Adams had a free hand. The US Constitution explicitly protects members of Congress from prosecution for speeches made from the floor, so the acts could not prevent Republican congressmen from voicing their opposition or voting against the war (Smith 1956, p. 127). French decision makers were consequently well aware of the political divisions in the United States, in spite of the government's efforts. France's main goal in the crisis was to prevent the United States from intervening in its ongoing war with Britain, and French leaders took comfort from Republican opposition to Federalist policies:

> Given the disunity in the United States . . . it was correctly predicted that Adams could not and would not take decisive steps to alienate France further. Instead, the domestic political situation would force him, whatever his personal feelings, to work for a resolution of the problems with France. (Stinchcombe 1980, pp. 39–40)

In February 1799, Talleyrand, the minister of foreign relations, noted that the United States seemed more consumed with internal strife stemming from the sedition laws than it was with its quarrel with France (Lyon 1938, p. 531; DeConde 1966, p. 176). In the final analysis, the effort to silence dissent was certainly a failure and probably counterproductive. It would thus seem that democratic governments must live with the constraints of competition and the possibility of dissent – both for better and for worse.

Whether this trade-off generates a net gain or a net loss depends in part on whether or not there is consensus in the country over what things are worth fighting for. During the 1930s, democracies seemed ill-equipped to use threats in large part because public opinion would not tolerate the risk of war. The inability to conceal these constraints meant that the democratic West was at a disadvantage in confronting Nazi Germany. During much of the Cold War, by contrast, a consensus both at the public and elite levels led to much more effective use of deterrent threats by the United States. The record of the post-Cold War period is mixed, but it is clear that growing divisions over the ends and means of foreign policy have made coercive diplomacy harder to employ successfully. The United States had difficulty speaking with one voice when threatening interventions in Bosnia (1992–95), Kosovo (1999), Haiti (1994), and even the Persian Gulf (1991). In all of these cases, the threat of force alone was not enough (Jakobson 1998).[3] What this suggests is that, if democracies want to enjoy the benefits of their institutions while minimizing the liabilities, the answer lies not in circumventing debate or suppressing dissent but in building true consensus.

---

[3] In the case of Haiti, the military government did not back down until it learned that US planes were *en route*.

Appendices

Appendix A
Solution to the basic crisis bargaining game

This appendix presents the formal solution to the basic bargaining game shown in Figure 2.1. The solution concept employed is perfect Bayesian equilibrium, in which all actors' strategies are sequentially rational given their beliefs and the other actors' strategies, and beliefs are derived from equilibrium strategies with updating according to Bayes' rule. Proposition 1 describes the general form of the equilibrium.

In what follows, it is useful to interpret the cumulative distribution functions F_c and F_t slightly differently from one another. We let F_c denote the cumulative distribution function of the challenger's value for war, w_c, over the range $[p - \bar{c}_c, p]$. We let F_t denote the cumulative distribution function of the target's war costs, c_t, over the range $[0, \bar{c}_t]$.

PROPOSITION 1. The following strategies and beliefs describe a perfect Bayesian equilibrium to this game:

(P1.1) The challenger plays

$$\{\text{Challenge, Stand Firm}\} \quad \text{if } w_c > -a,$$
$$\{\text{Challenge, Back Down}\} \quad \text{if } -a \geq w_c > b, \text{ and}$$
$$\{\text{Status Quo, Back Down}\} \quad \text{if } w_c \leq b,$$

where b is as defined below.

(P1.2) Let q denote the target's posterior belief that $w_c > -a$ given that a challenge has been made. Then,

$$q = \frac{1 - F_c(-a)}{1 - F_c(b)}.$$

(P1.3) The target plays

$$\text{Resist} \quad \text{if } c_t < p \cdot \frac{1 - q}{q} \equiv c^*, \text{ and}$$

$$\text{Concede} \quad \text{otherwise.}$$

PROOF. The expression for q in (P1.2) follows from the challenger's strategies and Bayes' rule. The condition given in (P1.3) is derived in the text as expression (4). We also saw in the text that the challenger stands firm at its final node if and only if $w_c > -a$, as given in (P1.1). What remains is to derive the challenger's equilibrium strategy at its initial node.

Substituting the expression for q into the condition in (P1.3), we find that the target resists whenever

$$c_t < p \cdot \frac{F_c(-a) - F_c(b)}{1 - F_c(-a)}. \tag{1}$$

Based on its prior beliefs, the challenger expects this condition to hold with the following probability:

$$s \equiv \text{Prob}(c_t < c^*) = F_t(c^*). \tag{2}$$

The challenger receives a certain payoff of zero from choosing the status quo. In the event that the challenger makes the challenge and the target resists, the former's payoff is w_c or $-a$, whichever is greater. If the target concedes, then the challenger receives p. Thus, the challenger's expected payoff from making a challenge is

$$\text{EU}_c \text{(Challenge)} = s \cdot \max(w_c, -a) + (1-s)p. \tag{3}$$

It must be the case that a challenger for which $w_c = b$ is indifferent between choosing the status quo and making the challenge. If $b < -a$ (an assumption we will confirm shortly), this implies

$$s = \frac{p}{p + a}. \tag{4}$$

Notice that this probability of resistance makes all types that would incur audience costs at their final node – i.e., all challengers for which $w_c < -a$ – indifferent between making and not making the challenge. Hence, setting b anywhere in this range will satisfy the requirement that the challenger be indifferent at its cutpoint. In equilibrium, though, it must also be the case that the values for s given by (2) and (4) are equivalent. Setting these expressions equal to one another, we find that

$$F_c(b) = F_c(-a) - \frac{[1 - F_c(-a)]}{p} F_t^{-1}\left(\frac{p}{p+a}\right). \tag{5}$$

Because $F_c(x)$ is a cumulative distribution function, it is monotonically increasing for all $x \in [p - \bar{c}_c, p]$. Because the distribution function F_t has only positive values in its support, the second term on the right-hand side is positive. Thus, it must be the case that $b < -a$, as assumed.

Notice that it is possible for the solution to expression (5) to yield a value of b that falls below the lowest possible type of challenger – i.e., $b < p - \bar{c}_c$. This can happen because there is nothing to prevent the right-hand side from being less than zero. In this case, $b = p - \bar{c}_c$, meaning that all types of challenger make the challenge in equilibrium. Substituting this into (P1.2), q simplifies to $1 - F_c(-a)$, and the expression for the probability of resistance is

$$s = F_t \left[p \cdot \frac{F_c(-a)}{1 - F_c(-a)} \right].$$

It is straightforward to confirm that all types of challenger strictly prefer to make the challenge given this expected probability of meeting resistance.

Now consider the modified game in which the challenger's and target's values for war are diminished by d_c and d_t, respectively. The basic form of the solution is identical to that above, except that the cutpoints shift by an amount that depends upon the magnitude of these new terms. Thus, the challenger makes a challenge and stands firm if $w_c > -a + d_c$, and the target resists if $c_t < c^* - d_t$. Making these adjustments, we can derive the new value of b exactly as we did above, which yields

$$F_c(b + d_c) = F_c(-a + d_c) - \frac{[1 - F_c(-a + d_c)]}{p} \left[F_t^{-1}\left(\frac{p}{p + a}\right) + d_t \right]. \quad (6)$$

Depending upon the magnitude of d_c and d_t, some special cases can arise. These are treated in turn.

Case 1: No types of target have incentives to resist, or $d_t > c^*$.
For the target to resist, it must be the case that $c_t < c^* - d_t$. If $d_t > c^*$, then this condition can never be met. Hence, all types of challenger make the challenge, and the target always concedes.

> Prob(Challenge) $= 1$
> Prob(Resistance) $= 0$
> Prob(War) $= 0$

Case 2: All types of challenger have incentives to challenge, or $p - \bar{c}_c - d_c \geq b$.
When the stated condition holds, all challengers fall in the range of types that make challenges in equilibrium, though only those for which

$w_c > -a + d_c$ make genuine challenges. In this case, $q = 1 - F_c(-a + d_c)$, and the target resists whenever the condition given in (P1.3) is met.

Prob (Challenge) $= 1$

$$\text{Prob(Resistance)} = F_t \left[p \cdot \frac{F_c(-a + d_c)}{1 - F_c(-a + d_c)} - d_t \right]$$

Prob(War) $= [1 - F_c(-a + d_c)] \cdot \text{Prob(Resistance)}$

Case 3: General equilibrium described above, which requires $p - \bar{c}_c - d_c < b$.

Prob (Challenge) $= 1 - F_c(b + d_c)$

$$\text{Prob(Resistance)} = \frac{p}{p + a}$$

$$\text{Prob(War)} = [1 - F_c(-a + d_c)] \cdot \frac{p}{p + a}$$

Case 4: No possible type of challenger can make a genuine challenge, or $p - d_c < -a$.
In this case, even a challenger with the highest possible value for war, $p - d_{c'}$ cannot make a genuine challenge in equilibrium. Since bluffing is pointless, all types choose the status quo. Off the equilibrium path, the target always resists.

Prob (Challenge) $= 0$
Prob(Resistance) $= 1$
Prob(War) $= 0$

Appendix B
Solution to the crisis bargaining game with opposition

This appendix presents the formal treatment of the bargaining games in Chapter 4. The solution to the basic game from Figure 4.1 is presented as Proposition 2. I then sketch the proofs for the results underlying Figures 4.2 through 4.5.

PROPOSITION 2. The following strategies and beliefs constitute a perfect Bayesian equilibrium to this game:

(P2.1) The government plays

{Challenge, Stand Firm}	if $w_c > k_{gov}$, where $k_{gov} = -a$,
{Challenge, Back Down}	if $k_{gov} \geq w_c > b$, and
{Status Quo, Back Down}	if $w_c \leq b$,

where $b < -a$ is defined below.

(P2.2) If the government makes a challenge, the opposition plays

Support Force	if $w_c > k_{opp}$, and
Oppose Force	otherwise,

where $k_{opp} \geq -a$ is defined below. If the government chooses the status quo, then the opposition plays

Support Force	if $w_c > 0$, and
Oppose Force	otherwise.

(P2.3) Let q equal the target's posterior probability that $w_c > -a$ after observing the strategies of the government and opposition. Then,

$q = 1$	if the target observes Challenge and Support,

$$q = \frac{F_c(k_{opp}) - F_c(-a)}{F_c(k_{opp}) - F_c(b)} \equiv q^* \qquad \text{if the target observes Challenge and Oppose, and}$$

$$q = 0 \qquad \text{if the government plays Status Quo.}$$

(P2.4) The target plays

Resist $\qquad$ if $c_t < p \cdot \dfrac{1-q}{q} \equiv c^*$, and

Concede $\qquad$ otherwise.

PROOF. Most of the elements of this equilibrium are straightforward to derive. The opposition's strategy after the government chooses the status quo and the government's strategy at its final decision nodes follow readily from the payoffs. The latter does not depend on the opposition's strategy since, in both cases, Stand Firm is preferred to Back Down whenever $w_c > -a$. The target's posterior beliefs, given in (P2.3), are derived logically from the strategies and Bayes' rule. Given these beliefs, the derivation of the target's strategy is exactly as in Chapter 2, expression (4).

What remains is to show that the strategies given in (P2.1) and (P2.2) are sequentially rational and to derive expressions for k_{opp} and b. To do so, we need to derive the two parties' expectations about the target's behavior. If the opposition supports the threat, then, because $k_{opp} > k_{gov}$, the target knows that the government will stand firm in the face of a resistance, or $q = 1$. Given this, the target always concedes, since the condition for resistance in (P2.4) can never be met. If the opposition opposes the threat, then the target updates as shown in (P2.3) above and resists if the condition given in (P2.4) holds. The probability with which this condition holds is

$$s \equiv \text{Prob}(c_t < c^*) = F_t \left[p \cdot \frac{F_c(-a) - F_c(b)}{F_c(k_{opp}) - F_c(-a)} \right]. \qquad (1)$$

For the government's decision rule to hold, it must be the case that a government of type b is indifferent between Challenge and Status Quo. Because $k_{opp} > b$, the opposition would oppose a challenge by this type; because $b < -a$, the government would back down in the face of resistance. Thus, the expected value of a challenge for a government of this type is

$$EU_{gov}(\text{Challenge}) = sr_d(-a) + (1-s)r_d(p). \qquad (2)$$

254

If this type chooses the status quo, the opposition will support the move, so the payoff from this option is $r_a(0)$. Setting these equal to one another, we find that

$$s = \frac{r_d(p) - r_a(0)}{r_d(p) - r_d(-a)} \tag{3}$$

must hold for the government's cutpoint to be rational.

The target's strategy leaves all governments of type $w_c \leq -a$ indifferent between Challenge and Status Quo. Because of this, the cutpoint b separating types which make the challenge from types which choose the status quo can be drawn anywhere in the range $[p - \bar{c}_{c'}, -a]$. In equilibrium, b must be such that (1) and (3) hold simultaneously. Setting these expressions equal to one another, we find that

$$F_c(b) = F_c(-a) - \frac{[F_c(k_{opp}) - F_c(-a)]}{p} F_t^{-1}\left[\frac{r_d(p) - r_a(0)}{r_d(p) - r_d(-a)}\right] \tag{4}$$

As in Appendix A, the fact that the second term is positive implies that $b < -a$, as proposed.

Next consider the opposition's strategy given that the government has made a challenge. For an opposition of type w_c, the expected payoff from supporting the government is

$$EU_{opp}(\text{Support} \mid \text{Challenge}) = 1 - r_a(p), \tag{5}$$

because the target always backs down in this case. The expected payoff from opposing the government is

$$EU_{opp}(\text{Oppose} \mid \text{Challenge}) = s[1 - r_d(w_c)] + (1 - s)[1 - r_d(p)]. \tag{6}$$

Notice that this second expression is decreasing in w_c, so that the opposition's payoff from opposing a threat decreases with the state's value for war. The value of w_c at which (5) and (6) cross determines the value of k_{opp}. Setting these expressions equal to one another, we find that

$$k_{opp} = r_d^{-1}\left[\frac{r_a(p) - (1 - s)r_d(p)}{s}\right]. \tag{7}$$

We can confirm that $k_{opp} > -a$, as proposed, as long as $r_a(p) > r_a(0)$, which is true by the assumption that r_a is increasing in the international outcome. For the opposition's strategy to help separate types, it must also be the case that $k_{opp} < p$, so that there are some types of threats the opposition will support. This condition holds as long as $1 - r_a(p) > 1 - r_d(p)$ – that is, as long as the opposition is better off supporting a threat that leads to concessions than opposing such a threat, which is true by assumption.

The effects of the opposition party

How is the game affected by the introduction of an opposition party? The best way to capture an inactive opposition is to assume that the opposition has no move and that the government's payoff is given by $r_d(x)$. Recall that we interpreted this function as the probability of reelection given that the entire responsibility for the policy rests with the government; hence, this seems like the appropriate utility function for governments without opposition parties. In this case, the equilibrium is similar to that described above, except that there is no opposition cutpoint – or, equivalently, $k_{opp} = p$. Substituting $F_c(k_{opp}) = 1$ into expression (4) yields the expression for b which holds in this case. All other cutpoints remain the same, as does the expression for s in (3).[1] Two changes become apparent when moving from the game without opposition to the game with opposition. First, the cutpoint b increases, meaning that the probability of a challenge goes down. Second, the existence of the opposition creates a new range of types – those that fall in between k_{opp} and p – for which the probability of resistance by the target is zero. In the game without opposition, types in this range are no different from any others that make genuine threats in equilibrium.

The effects of policy preferences

First consider the effects of a dovish opposition, or $\alpha < 0$. Recalculating the opposition's cutpoint as above yields

$$k_{opp} = r_d^{-1} \left[\frac{r_a(p) - (1-s)r_d(p) - \alpha}{s} \right]. \tag{8}$$

Because r_d and hence r_d^{-1} are increasing, this means that k_{opp} is decreasing in α. Thus, a dovish opposition is associated with a higher cutpoint than is a neutral opposition for which $\alpha = 0$. From (4), we know that b is decreasing in k_{opp}. Thus, b decreases when the opposition is dovish. Once α is sufficiently low that k_{opp} exceeds p, then the equilibrium is the same as in the game without opposition.

When the opposition is hawkish, or $\alpha > 0$, the same calculation holds, to a point. As α increases, k_{opp} decreases and b increases. Once k_{opp} falls below $-a$, however, the form of the equilibrium changes, since the

---

[1] Recall that, by assumption, $r_a(0) = r_d(0)$.

hawkish opposition will support some bluffs. The equilibrium depicted in Figure 4.4 holds when

$$\alpha > r_d(-b) - r_d(-a), \tag{9}$$

where b solves[2]

$$F_c(b) + \frac{1 - F_c(-a)}{p} F_t^{-1} \left[\frac{r_a(p) - r_d(-b)}{r_a(p) - r_a(-a)} \right] = F_c(-a). \tag{10}$$

Expression (9) ensures that the opposition will support force when the government bluffs (i.e., when $b < w_c \le -a$) and when the government selects the status quo (i.e., when $w_c < b$). In other words, it ensures that $k_{opp} < b$. Expression (10) was derived as was (4) above, taking into account the opposition's strategy of supporting all bluffs.

The effects of national welfare concerns

National welfare concerns change both the government's strategy in the absence of an opposition party as well as the impact of adding the opposition. Since the purpose of this exercise is to understand how the introduction of an opposition party is affected by national welfare concerns, it is useful to scale the payoffs so that the policy of a government without opposition is insensitive to β. Define

$$g_a(x) = \beta x + (1 - \beta) r_a(x) \text{ and} \tag{11}$$

$$g_d(x) = \beta x + (1 - \beta) r_d(x) \tag{12}$$

as the government's payoffs from outcome x given that the opposition agrees and dissents, respectively. Because both expressions are monotonically increasing in x, the government's decision at its final node – that is, stand firm if and only if $w_c > -a$ – remains unchanged. For a government without opposition – for which g_d describes the appropriate payoffs – the probability of resistance, s, and the cutpoint b are then given by

$$s = \frac{g_d(p) - g_d(0)}{g_d(p) - g_d(-a)} \equiv s_N, \text{ and} \tag{13}$$

$$F_c(b) = F_c(-a) - \frac{1 - F_c(-a)}{p} F_t^{-1}(s_N). \tag{14}$$

---

[2] Because the left-hand side is strictly increasing in b, a solution for which $b < -a$ theoretically exists. Note, however, that this equilibrium can only hold when $r_d(-b) < r_a(p)$, so that the quotient in brackets is positive.

It can be shown that scaling

$$\frac{r_d(p) - r_d(0)}{r_d(p) - r_d(-a)} = \frac{p}{p+a} \tag{15}$$

makes both of these terms insensitive to β. Thus, all changes between panel (a) in Figure 4.5 and those that follow are the result of adding the opposition party, not changes in the government's national welfare concerns.

Define

$$f_a(x) = \beta x + (1 - \beta)[1 - r_a(x)] \text{ and} \tag{16}$$

$$f_d(x) = \beta x + (1 - \beta)[1 - r_d(x)] \tag{17}$$

as the opposition's payoffs. These expressions are either increasing or decreasing in x, depending upon the magnitude of β and the derivatives of the election probabilities. In order to ensure that these utility functions are well behaved, we assume that r_a and r_d are concave functions, or $r''_a(x), r''_d(x) < 0$ for all x. This assumption means that there are diminishing marginal electoral benefits from better international outcomes.

First consider the conditions for which $k_{opp} > -a$, as in panel (b) of Figure 4.5. For the government, the expressions for s in (3) and b in (4) still hold with g_a substituted for r_a and g_d substituted for r_d. We determine the opposition's cutpoint as above, which yields

$$f_d(k_{opp}) = \frac{f_a(p) - (1-s)f_d(p)}{s}. \tag{18}$$

To ensure that $k_{opp} > -a$, it must be the case that $f_d(k_{opp}) < f_d(-a)$, under the assumption that f_d is a decreasing function. This holds when

$$s > \frac{f_a(p) - f_d(p)}{f_d(-a) - f_d(p)}. \tag{19}$$

Solving for β, we find that (19) holds when

$$\beta < \frac{(p+a)[r_a(p) - r_a(0)]}{p[p + a + r_d(p) - r_d(-a)]} \equiv \beta^*. \tag{20}$$

This condition also ensures that f_d decreases from $-a$, as assumed. As long as (20) is true, the basic form of the equilibrium described in Proposition 2 continues to hold.

Now consider the conditions under which $k_{opp} < -a$, which is depicted in panels (d) and (e). In these equilibria, the opposition must be willing to support at least some bluffs. Given that the government is bluffing, the opposition's expected payoffs are

$$EU_{opp}(\text{Support} \mid \text{Challenge}) = sf_a(-a) + (1-s)f_a(p), \text{ and} \quad (21)$$

$$EU_{opp}(\text{Oppose} \mid \text{Challenge}) = f_d(-a). \quad (22)$$

Setting these equal, we find that

$$s < \frac{f_a(p) - f_d(-a)}{f_a(p) - f_a(-a)} \equiv s_{opp} \quad (23)$$

makes the opposition willing to support a bluff. For this to be feasible, it must be the case that $f_a(p) > f_d(-a)$ which requires

$$\beta > \frac{r_a(p) - r_d(-a)}{p + a + r_d(p) - r_d(-a)} \equiv \beta^{**}. \quad (24)$$

Since the opposition's dissent reveals that a challenge is a bluff, no type of government bluffs when the opposition would oppose force, or $b = k_{opp}$. Since the opposition now agrees with whatever the government of type b does, the latter's expected value of making a challenge is

$$EU_{gov}(\text{Challenge}) = sg_a(-a) + (1-s)g_a(p). \quad (25)$$

Setting this equal to the payoff from the status quo, $g_a(0)$, we find that the government is indifferent about making a challenge whenever

$$s = \frac{g_a(p) - g_a(0)}{g_a(p) - g_a(-a)} \equiv s_{gov}. \quad (26)$$

The target state's posterior belief given that it observes a challenge is

$$q = \frac{1 - F_c(-a)}{1 - F_c(k_{opp})}. \quad (27)$$

Substituting (27) into (P2.4) and calculating s as in (1) yields,

$$s = F_t \left[p \cdot \frac{F_c(-a) - F_c(b)}{1 - F_c(-a)} \right]. \quad (28)$$

In equilibrium, the probability of resistance, s, must equal the lower of s_{opp} and s_{gov}. Thus, we can solve for b (which equals k_{opp}) as

$$F_c(b) = F_c(-a) - \frac{1 - F_c(-a)}{p} F_t^{-1}[\min(s_{opp}, s_{gov})]. \quad (29)$$

In the game without opposition, the comparable expression for b is given by (14). Whether b is higher or lower in the game with opposition depends upon whether s_N is higher or lower than $\min(s_{opp}, s_{gov})$, a comparison that is indeterminate without further assumptions. Thus, it is possible under some conditions for the rate of challenges and the probability of resistance to be higher in the game with opposition than in the game without opposition. Notice that, at $\beta = 1$,

$$\min(s_{opp}, s_{gov}) = s_{gov} = \frac{p}{p+a} = s_N, \tag{30}$$

so the two games are identical, as shown in panel (e).

Finally, we consider the conditions for which $k_{opp} = k_{gov} = b$, which corresponds to panel (c). The equilibrium takes this form when $\beta^{**} > \beta > \beta^*$.[3] When this is the case, the opposition wants to support all genuine threats but is unwilling to support bluffs. Under these conditions, the target state should never observe an opposed challenge. In equilibrium, however, it must be the case that the target would resist an opposed challenge with a probability high enough to prevent the government from wanting to bluff and low enough to prevent the opposition from dissenting. Formally, it must be the case that the probability of resistance, s, satisfies

$$\frac{f_a(p) - f_d(p)}{f_d(-a) - f_a(p)} > s > \frac{p}{p+a}. \tag{31}$$

There exists a range of off-the-equilibrium-path beliefs that satisfy this condition.

---

[3] It can be shown that $\beta^{**} > \beta^*$.

Appendix C
Data and methods

This appendix elaborates on the data and methods used in Chapter 5. It discusses considerations that arise in the coding of the dependent variables; it provides the coding rules and sources for the control variables; it justifies and describes the fixed-effect treatment used in the tests on crisis initiation; and it discusses the correction for temporal dependence included in those models. The appendix ends with a list of states coded as having competitive polities according to the method described in the chapter.

Coding of the dependent variables

The probability of initiation: INITIATE

For each event, the MID data set identifies the state or states on the initiating side and the state or states on the target side. The initiating side is defined as the side containing the state which took the first codable action – that is, at least a threat to use force. The data set also distinguishes between revisionist and nonrevisionist states, depending upon whether or not the state sought some revision of the pre-existing status quo. Most states on the initiating side are revisionist, but this is not always the case, and revisionist states can be found on the target side or, in many cases, on both sides of a dispute. From the perspective of the hypotheses considered here, it makes sense to rely on the initiator coding rather than the revisionist coding. Initiation, as defined in the data set, refers to the decision by a state to turn some underlying dispute into a crisis by making at least a threat to use force. Regardless of whether or not that threat is accompanied by a demand to change the status quo, it is the initiator who crossed the relevant threshold. At that point, the choice facing the state on the target side resembles that of the target in the model. Furthermore, while the model has always explicitly assumed that the challenger issues a demand to revise the status quo along with its challenge, none of the theoretical results depend upon this assumption; hence, while revisionism on the part of the challenger is useful for the sake of exposition, it is not a necessary condition for the empirical predictions. Third, the fact that states on both sides of a MID can be coded as revisionist means that, if we were to make revisionism the criterion for a challenge, there would be ambiguity about whom to call the challenger in many cases. Given these considerations, it makes sense to treat as the challenger the state(s) on the initiating side of the MID, regardless of its position relative to the status quo.

A complication arises due to the fact that, unlike in our simple model, not all disputes are one-on-one interactions, involving only a single dyad. In about 20 percent of the cases, there is more than one state on the initiating and/or target sides. Many of the "extra" states on either side joined after the crisis was already underway and, in some cases, after it had already escalated to war. Since the model deals primarily with the initial threat and the response of the target, we have little to say about the diffusion of conflict to other states (see, e.g., Siverson and Starr 1991). The decision whether or not to join an ongoing crisis is made under different strategic conditions than the decision to start a crisis in the first place; indeed, states which join late may do so involuntarily, such as when they are invaded by a state already at war with others (Bennett and Stam 2000). The MID data set codes as "originators" those states that were involved in the crisis from the first day. In coding initiations, it seems appropriate to focus on initiators and targets that were both original members of the dispute.

Thus, INITIATE_{ijt} is coded as one when (a) state i was on the initiating side of a MID against state j in year t, and (b) both i and j were original members of the MID. INITIATE_{ijt} is coded zero otherwise. There are three exceptions to this rule. The first deals with ongoing disputes. Since we are interested only in the probability of a challenge, not the length of the ensuing dispute, INITIATE_{ijt} is coded as one only in the first year of the MID. If the crisis carries over into subsequent years, the variable is coded as missing in those years. The second exception deals with the targets of disputes. In a year in which state i initiates a MID against state j, we do not observe state j initiating against state i; however, we cannot know whether state j would have issued a challenge in that year had state i not done so. Therefore, it would be a mistake to code INITIATE_{jit}

as zero in years when INITIATE$_{ijt}$ is one; such observations are coded as missing. Similarly, since the target cannot challenge the initiator in years during which their MID is ongoing, INITIATE$_{jit}$ is coded as missing in all such years. The third and final exception deals with states that join the MID after the first day. INITIATE is coded as missing whenever both states in the dyad were involved on opposite sides of the same dispute but one or both joined after the first day. For further discussion of these coding rules, see Bennett and Stam (2000).

The probability of reciprocation: RECIP

The coding of RECIP was derived from the MID data set, which provides information on the highest hostility level reached by each dispute participant. This is coded according to a five-point scale as follows: (1) no military action; (2) threat of force; (3) display of force; (4) limited use of force; and (5) full-scale war. For each dispute dyad, RECIP is set equal to one when the hostility level reached by the target state was greater than one and zero otherwise. While dichotomizing the target's response in this way makes intuitive sense, one might imagine alternative ways to operationalize "resistance" which make fuller use of the 5-point scale – for example, was the target's response at a higher level of escalation than the challenger's initial action? Unfortunately, there are two limitations in the data which make such an operationalization impractical. First, the data set only reports the highest level of hostility ultimately reached by each state, making it impossible to say anything about the initial challenge and response of each side. Second, there are legitimate doubts as to whether the hostility levels provide an ordered scale of the underlying concept. For example, putting a country's nuclear forces on alert rates a hostility level of 3 (display), while seizing a fishing vessel merits a 4 (limited use of force). It is quite likely, however, that the former is a riskier, and hence stronger, signal of resolve. On the other hand, the distinction employed here between taking some militarized action and taking no militarized action is clearer.

As before, the sample of MIDs for this test is restricted to original dyads. It would be a mistake to treat as the challenger some state which joined the initiating side long after the original challenge was made and resisted; likewise, it would make little sense to treat as the target some state which joined the target side once the decision to resist had already been made by the original target. There are eighteen MIDs, however, in which the original target(s) chose not to reciprocate, but other states that joined the target side after the first day did take militarized action.

The results are unaffected by the inclusion of dyads involving these states.

The probability of escalation: WAR and FORCE

These variables were coded using the hostility levels recorded in the MID data. WAR equals one when both states in the dyad reached level 5 and zero otherwise. FORCE equals one when both states reached at least level 4 and zero otherwise.

Coding of the independent variables

Power Status

The first method for measuring state power is based on the conventional distinction between major and minor powers provided by the COW project. States were coded as major powers on the basis of consensus among analysts taking into account power, reputation, and involvement in international affairs (Singer and Small 1993). According to this classification, the following states were major powers in the periods designated: the United States (1899–1993), Great Britain (1816–1993), France (1816–1940, 1945–93), Prussia/Germany (1816–1918, 1925–45, 1990–93), Austria-Hungary (1816–1918), Italy (1860–1943), Russia (1816–1917), the Soviet Union (1922–93), China (1950–1993), and Japan (1895–1945, 1990–93). For each directed dyad in each year, dummy variables indicate whether the potential initiator and/or target were major powers according to this classification scheme.

Balance of military capabilities

This indicator is based on the COW's National Material Capability Data (Singer and Small 1993). This data set presents information on demographic, economic, and military characteristics of every state in the international system for the years 1816–1993. Using standard practice, a composite score can be calculated for each state which captures that state's relative performance on six dimensions: population, urban population, iron/steel production, energy consumption, military spending, and military personnel (Singer, Bremer and Stukey 1972). The result is an indicator that reflects, for each state in each year, the share of total capabilities possessed by that state. As designed, a state's capability score in any given year can range from zero to one, and all scores must sum to one each year. The balance of military capabilities in the dyad was calculated by dividing the capability score of the weaker state by that of the stronger state. This variable ranges from zero to one with higher values indicating more equally balanced dyads.

Initiator's share of capabilities

This measure was constructed using the same capability score as above. The score of the initiator was divided by the sum of the capabilities of the two states in the dyad. This variable ranges from zero to one, with higher values indicating a greater advantage for the initiator. Notice that, while this variable is related to the balance variable, the two actually have a correlation of zero in the full population. The reason is that, for each possible balance between zero and one, the initiator's share of capabilities can take on two different values, depending on whether the initiator is the stronger or weaker state. Only when the balance is exactly one is the initiator's share of capabilities constrained to be 0.5.

Contiguity

The data for constructing this variable come from the Correlates of War project. For each directed dyad in each year, a dummy variable was created indicating whether or not the two states shared a land border or were separated by less than 150 miles of water.

Similarity of alliance portfolios

In order to include a control for how similar the two states' strategic interests are, we use a method originated by Bueno de Mesquita (1975, 1981) and refined by Signorino and Ritter (1999). The idea underlying this measure is that states tend to form alliances with partners with whom they have similar interests (e.g., Gowa 1999). Rather than simply determining whether the states in the dyad are directly allied to one another, however, Bueno de Mesquita (1975) proposed a measure which compares alliance portfolios and thus takes into account all of the formal alliances made by each state in the dyad. Signorino and Ritter (1999) proposed an alternative method for measuring alliance similarity which, among other things, weights states' contribution to the portfolio according to their capabilities. This method is adopted here. The measure is generated using the COW's Annual Alliance Membership Data (Singer and Small 1984), which record the membership and years of all formal alliances in the international system from 1816 to 1984. Based on this data, a score is calculated for each directed dyad-year which ranges from -1, if the two states' alliance portfolios were maximally different, to 1, if the two states' alliance portfolios were identical.[1]

Status quo evaluations

The realist literature often distinguishes between "revisionist" and "status quo" powers to capture a state's satisfaction with the international status quo (e.g., Wolfers 1962; Schweller 1996). Kim (1991) suggests that we can get a sense for a state's general attitude toward the status quo by considering how similar its interests are to those of the leading state in the international system. Underlying this contention is the idea that powerful states have a good deal of say in how goods are distributed in the international system. A hegemonic state has undue influence over the allocation of spheres of influence, the distribution of territory, and the design of international institutions (Gilpin 1983). As a result, the argument goes, the most powerful state and its allies are likely to enjoy greater benefits from the international status quo than will those states that are seen as competitors. In the time period studied here, this "power transition" or "hegemonic cycles" school identifies the leading state as Great Britain from 1816 to 1945 and the United States thereafter.

Given that both of these leading states were democratic for all or part of their reigns, one need not buy into the entire vision of this school to recognize the usefulness of including some control for this factor. If we find that these states and their allies initiated crises at a lower rate than other, presumably less satisfied states, we need to be sure that this finding is a result of regime type and not status quo evaluation (Lemke and Reed 1996). Following Kim (1991), a state's evaluation of the status quo is determined by the similarity of its alliance portfolio to that of the leading state in the system at the time, where portfolio similarity is measured as described above. For each state in the dyad, this variable ranges from -1, if the state's strategic interests were diametrically opposed to those of the leading state, to 1, if the state's interests were identical to those of the leading state (or if it was the leading state).

Estimation considerations: the fixed-effects treatment

To understand the rationale behind the fixed-effect treatment, consider the underlying empirical model. Let y^*_{ijt} denote a continuous latent

---

[1] I am grateful to Richard Tucker for making these scores available on his web page (Tucker 1999).

variable that captures the propensity of state i to initiate a crisis against state j in year t. Following standard practice, we assume that the observed dependent variable, INITIATE$_{ijt}$, equals one whenever y^*_{ijt} exceeds a certain threshold, which we can set to zero without loss of generality. In its most general form, the pooled cross-sectional time series model takes the following form:

$$y^*_{ijt} = \alpha_{ij} + \beta X_{ijt} + \mu_{ijt}, \tag{1}$$

where X_{ijt} represents the independent variables, α_{ij} represents the intercept term for the directed dyad ij, and μ_{ijt} is the error term. If we were to assume that all directed dyads have the same base-line probability of experiencing a crisis initiation, then we could re-write (1) as

$$y^*_{ijt} = \alpha + \beta X_{ijt} + \mu_{ijt}, \tag{2}$$

which is the model estimated by most cross-sectional time series analyses in international relations (Green, Kim, and Yoon 2000). By restricting $\alpha_{ij} = \alpha$ for all i and j, this model implies that directed dyads are homogeneous – that is, all of the variation is captured by the independent variables and the (identically distributed) error term. Alternatively, we could assume that directed dyads within the same dyad are homogenous but that dyads differ systematically from one another. This assumption is captured by imposing the restriction that $\alpha_{ij} = \alpha_{ji}$.

Estimating equation (1), which permits a different intercept term for each directed dyad, is clearly the least restrictive specification and the one best suited to capture heterogeneity that is not picked up by the independent variables. Of course, if there are N states in the system, it also requires the estimation of $N(N-1)$ coefficients – one for each directed dyad. Moreover, there are some costs to employing this method, especially when the dependent variable is dichotomous.

The main cost is that we effectively have to drop from the sample all directed dyads in which the first state never challenges the second. The reason is that, if there is no crisis in the directed dyad, then the corresponding dummy variable perfectly predicts the absence of a challenge. So, for example, because there are no crises between the United States and Britain in the Cold War period, we have to drop all observations on that US–Britain and Britain–US directed dyads in this time period. This might seem like a problem for the analysis, but it is necessary because the absence of a crisis between two states is not very informative. Does the absence of a challenge reflect the fact that the potential initiator was constrained by its domestic institutions from making a threat to resolve some underlying dispute, or does it reflect the fact that there was nothing to contest in the first place? Without some variation in crisis behavior over time, the two explanations are observationally equivalent; hence, these observations do not help us test the theory.

The fixed-effects technique also places a premium on units for which there is some variation over time in the independent variables; in particular, the estimates of the coefficients on the regime variables are strongly influenced by those dyads in which a regime transition took place in either state sometime during the period. To see why, consider the case of a dyad in which both states were democratic for the entire period. Since there is no variation across time in the regime variables, these variables obviously do not explain variation across time in the probability of a crisis in that dyad. The only way the outcomes in this dyad would affect the estimates on the regime indicators is through the comparison with other dyads. However, the fixed-effect terms capture all differences among dyads which do not vary with time – including, in this case, any influence from shared democracy. Hence, the regime indicators explain neither variation across time within the dyad nor variation between this dyad and others. Now consider a dyad in which the regime type of the initiator changed at some point in the period. In this case, the regime change permits us to compare the probability of a crisis initiation when the initiator was democratic with the corresponding probability when it was nondemocratic. It is these kinds of observations that drive the estimated coefficients on the regime variables.

Again, this might seem like a shortcoming of the technique, but it makes analytical sense. After all, if one wanted to know whether democracy in state A affects the probability that it will challenge state B, which comparison is better: (a) the probability of a challenge by A against B when A is democratic *versus* the probability of a challenge by A against B when A is nondemocratic, or (b) the probability of a challenge by democratic A against B *versus* the probability of a challenge by non-democratic C against B? Obviously, the first comparison is more informative: assuming that other relevant features of the relationship remain constant, the regime transition by A provides a quasi-experiment. The second comparison is not useless, but it depends on having good control variables to ensure that all other things are equal. The fixed-effect technique makes up for any shortcomings in these variables by picking up all systematic differences between the A–B and C–B dyads, but it also washes out any influence which the difference in regime types between A and C might have had. The advantage is that the results are influenced primarily by comparisons of the first kind. In a sense, then, this technique exploits all of the quasi-experiments inherent in the data.

Because of the costs associated with this method, it is useful to test whether the treatment is really necessary. To determine this, we estimate the model using three different specifications:

(1) Directed dyad fixed effects: each α_{ij} is estimated separately.
(2) Dyad fixed effects: $\alpha_{ij} = \alpha_{ij}$.
(3) Uniform intercept: $\alpha_{ij} = \alpha$ for all i and j.

The first two were estimated using the conditional logit model, while the third was estimated using a standard logit.[2] We test for the correct specification as follows. If the first specification is correct, then the conditional logit will generate consistent estimates, and the standard logit will generate inconsistent estimates. If the third specification is correct, then the standard logit will generate consistent and efficient estimates while the conditional logit will generate estimates that are consistent but inefficient. A Hausman test permits us to assess the null hypothesis that the two sets of estimates are consistent (see, e.g., Greene 1997, pp. 632–33, 900–01). If we can reject the null hypothesis, this means that some form of heterogeneity is present, and a standard logit is inappropriate. We can compare the first and second specifications the same way. In every case, Hausman tests showed that a conditional logit with directed dyad fixed effects was the appropriate specification. Null hypotheses to the contrary were always rejected at below the 1 percent level.

The result of using the fixed-effect treatment is that the tests here differ in important ways from previous ones in the democratic peace literature and have to be interpreted differently. In the first place, because regime characteristics change rarely, if ever, across time, these tests are biased against attributing much influence to them. If a state was democratic for the entire time period, and it initiated no crises in that period,

---

[2] An alternative way to model the intercept terms is through a random effects treatment, which assumes that the α_{ij} are all pulled from a normal distribution. For this treatment to be appropriate, it must be the case that the α_{ij} are uncorrelated with the independent variables. Implementation of random effects in a logit model, which is necessary for comparison with the fixed-effects specification, is somewhat awkward, requiring numerical approximation techniques which may not generate stable results. Nevertheless, the models were estimated in this fashion, but Hausman tests showed that the fixed-effect models were preferred.

this technique assumes that the absence of conflict was due to unmeasured heterogeneity captured in the fixed-effect terms, and not to the state's political institutions. Hence, the tests rely on the conservative assumption that the factors that we cannot measure are highly influential; if a given pattern can be explained either by the regime type or by the unmeasured factors, pride of place should be given to the latter. The second point is that the results in this section do not speak to the frequency of crisis initiation or overall rate of crisis participation, as most tests in this literature do. Rather, they determine how a shift in regime type, holding all other factors constant, changes the probability that a state will initiate a crisis – precisely the comparative-static relationship that the theoretical model addresses.

Correction for temporal dependence

Beck, Katz, and Tucker (1998) warn that data on international conflicts may contain temporal dependence, which means that the probability of a crisis initiation in any given year is a function of how recently the dyad last experienced a crisis. When this is the case, the error terms can have a form of serial correlation, and estimates that fail to control for time effects will be biased. Beck, Katz, and Tucker (1998) recommend dealing with this problem by including variables that capture the number of years that have passed since the last crisis initiation. Unfortunately, this problem becomes more complicated in the presence of cross-sectional heterogeneity, as unmeasured heterogeneity and temporal dependence can be observationally equivalent (e.g., Gowa 1999, p. 58). If at least one of these problems exists, it can be difficult to determine which one is present or if both are. Moreover, using the fixed-effects treatment can induce positive time dependence, since every cross-section that remains in the sample must have had a least one crisis; hence, the longer that unit goes without experiencing a crisis, the higher is the probability that it will do so in the next period.

To deal with this, I estimated the models both with and without the recommended controls for temporal dependence. In particular, I constructed a variable called PEACEYRS which measures, for each directed dyad-year, the number of years that have passed since the last MID in the dyad.[3] The counter was then introduced in linear form and as a cubic

---

[3] When counting the number of years since the last conflict, the counter was reset whenever the two states were on opposite sides of a MID, even if that case did not constitute an initiation, as defined here (e.g., if the states joined an ongoing MID).

spline with knots at 1, 4, and 7 years.[4] In every model, there is evidence of negative time dependence, meaning that the probability of initiation decreases as the time since the last crisis increases. Moreover, the time variables are always collectively significant. In no case, however, does the inclusion or exclusion of these controls affect the substantive results. Results reported here are from regressions that include these controls.

States with competitive polities[5]

Argentina	1937–39, 1973–75, 1983–84
Austria	1920–32, 1946–84
Australia	1901–84
Bangladesh	1972–73
Belgium	1919–39, 1945–84
Bolivia	1982–84
Botswana	1966–84
Brazil	1958–63
Canada	1888–1984
Chile	1935–72
Columbia	1867–85, 1930–47, 1957–84
Costa Rica	1867–1918, 1920–84
Cuba	1902–15, 1918–51
Cyprus	1960–61, 1968–73, 1975–84
Czechoslovakia	1945–46
Denmark	1915–39, 1945–84
Dominican Republic	1978–84
Ecuador	1979–84
El Salvador	1984–84
Estonia	1917–18, 1920–32
Finland	1917–29, 1944–84
France	1848–50, 1898–1939, 1946–84
Gambia	1965–84
German Federal Republic	1949–84
Germany/Prussia	1919–32
Ghana	1979–80
Greece	1880–1914, 1926–35, 1944–48, 1975–84
Guatemala	1944–49, 1966–69
Honduras	1982–84
Iceland	1918–84
India	1950–84
Ireland	1922–84

[4] Though I did not perform a systematic search for optimal knot locations, small perturbations of these numbers did not have any appreciable effect on the results but generally led to lower likelihoods.

[5] This list does not include a handful of states that were never involved in MIDs, either when democratic or nondemocratic, and hence never appear in any estimation sample.

States with competitive polities (cont.)

Israel	1949–84
Italy	1948–84
Jamaica	1959–84
Japan	1952–84
Korea, Republic of	1960
Laos	1958–58
Latvia	1921–28
Lebanon	1971–75
Lesotho	1966–69
Luxembourg	1890–1939, 1945–84
Malaysia	1957–84
Myanmar (Burma)	1948–61
Netherlands	1917–39, 1945–84
New Zealand	1857–75, 1877–1984
Nigeria	1960–63
Norway	1898–1939, 1945–84
Pakistan	1948–57, 1962–76
Papua New Guinea	1976–84
Peru	1980–84
Philippines	1935–40
Poland	1918–25
Portugal	1976–84
Spain	1978–84
Sri Lanka (Ceylon)	1960–76
Sudan	1954–57
Sweden	1917–84
Switzerland	1848–1984
Thailand	1975–75, 1978–84
Turkey	1946–52, 1961–70, 1973–79, 1984
United Kingdom	1880–1984
United States of America	1810–64, 1871–1984
Uruguay	1952–71
Venezuela	1970–84
Yugoslavia/Serbia	1903–15

Appendix D
Coding and sources for opposition stances

1. Penjdeh dispute (1885)
Opposition party: Conservative.
Position: Support.
Evidence: The Conservative Party supported Prime Minister Gladstone's call-up of army reservists as well as his request for war credits. Party leader Salisbury agreed that Britain must draw the line against Russian expansionism (Morgan 1981, p. 196; Jeyes 1898, pp. 100–01).

3. Greece (1886)
Opposition party: Conservative.
Position: Support.
Evidence: The *Annual Register* (1887, pp. 85–86) reports that Prime Minister Rosebery received "applause on all sides" for his firm stance in the crisis.

5. Crete and the Greco-Turkish War (1897)
Opposition party: Liberal.
Position: Oppose.
Evidence: The Liberal Party staunchly favored Greek claims and opposed the efforts of the great powers to coerce Greece from withdrawing from Crete. The party supported the government as long as Prime Minister Salisbury worked to soften the position of the other powers but increasingly distanced itself as Salisbury joined the proposed blockade. Party leader William Harcourt put forward a resolution that force should not be used against Greece or Crete and argued publicly that, despite the government's large majority in parliament, its position on this issue was not reflective of public opinion in the nation (*Annual Register* 1898, pp. 105–07; Gardiner 1923, pp. 438–43).

As noted in the text, this case is supportive of my theory and merits recoding as a deterrence failure. The Liberal Party's opposition to taking strong action against Greece was generally reflective of public opinion in that country and even among some members of the cabinet (Langer 1951, pp. 360–61). Cognizant of these pressures, Salisbury felt constrained against taking a hard line in the crisis. On January 21, he wrote to Queen Victoria that Great Britain "could not now take war-like action against Greece" on behalf of Turkey. On February 17, he noted that the Liberal Unionists within his cabinet were opposed to action (Buckle 1932, pp. 122–23, 133). As a result, Britain was a reluctant member of the great power coalition which, pushed primarily by Germany, sought to institute a blockade against Greece. Salisbury advocated a compromise position, leading the German emperor to despair in late March that a blockade would fail due to British foot-dragging (Germany 1929, p. 457; Langer 1951, pp. 365–66). The Concert powers only managed a blockade of Crete, as British objections stalled and ultimately prevented a more extensive blockade of Greek ports (Langer 1951, pp. 364–65, 368–89). In addition, Langer (1951, p. 366) reports that the Greeks were encouraged by the sympathy for their cause in Great Britain and not particularly troubled by the great powers' threats. Indeed, Greece attacked Turkey shortly after the powers issued a warning to both states on April 6 that, in the event of war between the two, they would hold the aggressor responsible and not permit it to benefit (Langer 1951, p. 369; Perris 1897, p. 231).

In spite of the fact that war broke out between Greece and Turkey over the Cretan issue, the argument for coding this case a deterrence success is that fighting was largely confined to the mainland: Greece attacked Turkey over their European border. Thus, while Turkey failed at direct-immediate deterrence, the actions of Britain and the other great powers successfully prevented a full-scale war on Crete (Huth 1990). This interpretation is based on the assumption that the Greek decision to attack on the mainland was in large part a strategic decision influenced by the fear of British retaliation. It is also likely, however, that this decision reflected military and geographic reality: the Greeks attacked where they could mount the most effective campaign. Greek troops did support the rebels on Crete, who clashed both with Turkish forces and those of the great powers (Langer 1951, p. 365).

Most important, though, the case should be coded as a deterrence failure because Greece did not submit to the Concert powers' demands until after it had been defeated by Turkey. On March 2, the powers demanded that Greece withdraw it troops from Crete and threatened that they were "irrevocably determined not to hesitate at any measures of constraint" (Langer 1951, p. 364). The Greeks rejected this ultimatum, and the ensuing blockade of Crete – as well as the threat of a wider blockade – did nothing to change their attitude. The issue was ultimately resolved only after several lopsided defeats on the battlefield prompted Greece to sue for peace. The Greek government agreed to a total withdrawal on May 8 in return for the powers' support in securing an armistice (Langer 1951, p. 376). Hence, military defeat, not a successful deterrent threat, forced Greece to back down.

I looked at all the cases to determine whether any others should be reconsidered using the same criterion. This is the only case in the data set coded as a deterrence success even though the attacker ended up at war with one of the defenders over the issue in question. Moreover, while a few other successful cases witnessed small-scale uses of force that did not cross the 200 battle-death threshold, in none of these cases was the attacker defeated militarily before backing down.

6. Fashoda (1898)
Opposition party: Liberal.
Position: Support.
Evidence: See text, pp. 188–89.

7. Venezuelan Debt Crisis (1902)
Opposition party: Democratic.
Position: Support.
Evidence: The *New York Herald* of 14 Dec. 1902 reports speeches by members of Congress from both parties supporting President Roosevelt's handling of the crisis. Holbo (1970, p. 436) reports that Secretary of State John Hay used this unity of opinion to impress upon the German chargé d'affaires the firmness of the American position.

8. Panama Canal Crisis (1903–04)
Opposition party: Democratic.
Position: Oppose.
Evidence: This case is somewhat ambiguous, so it was coded to be unsympathetic to my hypotheses. The Democratic Party was divided on the wisdom of Roosevelt's policy of supporting the Panamanian revolution. While many were critical of the level of intervention, the fact that the United States would get the canal under favorable terms made

the policy easier to support. Democratic Senator Arthur Gorman, at the time a prospective presidential nominee, chose to fight Roosevelt on the issue, but his criticism focused more on the US role in the uprising and less on the ongoing effort to deter Colombia from reversing the revolution through force. Still, Colombian General Rafael Reyes took comfort from the Democrats' position and made common cause with them against the treaty and Roosevelt's general policy. In the end, however, the Democrats did not put up a united front, as sixteen of thirty-three Democratic senators voted in favor of the treaty (Collin 1990, ch. 10; Lambert 1947, ch. 13).

11. First Moroccan Crisis (1905–06)
Opposition party: Liberal until December 1905, then Conservative.
Position: Support.
Evidence: There was no difference in party positions in this matter, as evidenced by the continuity in British policy both before and after the Conservative government fell midway through the crisis (Andersen 1930, esp. p. 322).

12. Turkish occupation of Sinai Peninsula (1906)
Opposition party: Conservative.
Position: Support.
Evidence: On May 7, Conservative Party leader Arthur Balfour told parliament that his party would refrain from questioning the government's policy in this dispute (GB, *Parl. Deb.* 4s, 156: 972–93).

16. Agadir Crisis (1911)
Opposition party: Conservative.
Position: Support.
Evidence: Conservative Party leader Arthur Balfour declared support for the government's position in a speech before parliament (GB, *Parl. Deb.* 5s, 28:1828–29).

23 & 24. World War I (1914)
Opposition party: Conservative (also Irish National and Labour).
Position: Support.
Evidence: Early on in the July crisis, Conservative Party leaders pledged to support the government if it went to war, and newspapers aligned with that party were unanimous in calling for Britain to join the coming war. The Irish National Party, which held 84 (of 670) seats pledged its

support, as well. Only the Labour Party, which had yet to become a formidable political force and which held a scant forty-two seats in the Commons, dissented (Steiner 1977, ch. 9).

25. Panama *vs.* Costa Rica (1921)
Opposition party: Democratic.
Position: Support.
Evidence: The US policy of warning off Panama had been initiated by the previous Democratic administration just days before President Warren Harding was inaugurated. A report in the *New York Times* on 6 March 1921 notes that there was close cooperation between the incoming and outgoing administrations. See also approving editorials in the Democratic-leaning *New York Times* on 8 March and 23 August 1921.

26. Chanak (1922)
Opposition party: Labour.
Position: Oppose.
Evidence: The *Annual Register* (1923, p. 107) reports that the Labour Party was "vigorous" in its protests against the possibility of war. In addition, the government's threats were widely criticized in the press (Walder 1969, pp. 228–41, 247–48).

27. Ethiopia Crisis (1935)
Opposition party: Labour.
Position: Support.
Evidence: At the Labour Party's annual conference in October 1935, delegates overwhelmingly approved a resolution calling for "all the necessary measures" consistent with League principles, a position that was widely assumed to include the use of force (Cole 1969, pp. 302–08).

31a. Czechoslovakia (1938, Britain)
Opposition party: Labour.
Position: Support.
Evidence: In September 1938, the Labour Party released a report titled *Labour and the International Situation: On the Brink of War*, which called for collective defense against aggression and urged the government to resist an attack upon Czechoslovakia (Cole 1969, pp. 334–35). In the House of Commons, the Labour Party voted overwhelmingly to reject the Munich agreement.

31b. Czechoslovakia (1938, France)
Opposition: Communist, Socialist, and National Front[1].
Position: Oppose.
Evidence: In general, the parties of the left were more forceful than those of the right, with the Communists calling for a hard line against Germany and the parties of the right generally opposed to any action that might bring the country into war. That said, there was a strong pacifist streak among moderate socialists, and a few on the center and right advocated a firm stance. Still, when the Munich agreement was brought to a vote in the Chamber of Deputies, only the Communists voted against it, suggesting a general consensus against using force to uphold French commitments to Czechoslovakia (Werth 1939, ch. 11; Micaud 1943, ch. 9).

32. Tunisia (1938)
Main opposition parties: Socialist and the National Front.
Position: Support.
Evidence: Though Foreign Minister Bonnet took a firm stand against Italian claims, both Socialists and rightists in parliament criticized his position as overly cautious. Prime Minister Daladier then made a triumphant visit to North Africa, a move that was greeted with unanimous support (Werth 1939, pp. 402–12; Micaud 1943, p. 198).

33. Danzig (1939)
Opposition parties: Labour (Great Britain); Communist, Socialist, and parties of the right (France).
Position: Support.
Evidence: In Britain, the Labour Party supported the commitment to defend Poland and was critical of the government's apparent delay in carrying out that commitment (Cole 1969, pp. 371–33). In France, those on the left and right who had opposed using force to save the Sudetenland generally changed their positions after Hitler invaded Czechoslovakia in March 1939. With only a few exceptions on the extreme right (e.g., the famous "Die for Danzig?" article), there was near unanimity among opposition parties that France should aid Poland

---

[1] The National Front was a collection of center and right parties opposed to the Popular Front of Socialists, Radical Socialists, and Communists. The Popular Front broke down during 1938, especially with the formation of the Radical-led government of Edouard Daladier (April 1938–May 1940). Though the right was nominally in opposition, the cabinet contained a few members from those parties and increasingly relied on their support in the Chamber of Deputies (Werth 1939, p. 133).

(Micaud 1943, ch. 11). Moreover, a poll in March reported that 76 percent of respondents agreed that a German attempt to seize Danzig should be resisted with force (Adamthwaite 1995, p. 179).

35. Turkey (1946)
Opposition party: Republican.
Position: Support.
Evidence: In general, the early Cold War crises were marked by bipartisanship in foreign policy. Republican support for a forceful stance was highlighted by a February 27 speech by Senator Arthur Vandenberg, in which he called for an uncompromising policy toward the Soviet Union. In the speech, Vandenberg explicitly referred to the ongoing crises over the Dardanelles and in Iran (Vandenberg 1952, pp. 247–49). Moreover, Truman's policy was not contested during the November 1946 midterm elections, which took place in the midst of this crisis (Leffler 1992, p. 140).

36. Azerbaijan Crisis (1946)
Opposition party: Republican.
Position: Support.
Evidence: See case no. 35 above and Kuniholm (1980, pp. 311–12, 383).

37. Berlin Blockade (1948)
Opposition party: Republican.
Position: Support.
Evidence: Republican presidential candidate Thomas Dewey supported the government's position, and his foreign policy adviser, Dulles, was included on the negotiating team sent to the United Nations (Shlaim 1983, p. 306). Moreover, Vandenberg made it clear that a GOP victory in the election would not alter the United States position on Berlin (Crabb 1957, pp. 230–31). The only dissent came from Progressive Party candidate Henry Wallace, who was soundly defeated in the 1948 election in the midst of the crisis.

38. Taiwan during the Korean War (1950)
Opposition party: Republican.
Position: Support.
Evidence: Republicans supported the threat of force to defend Taiwan, an issue that united both internationalist and nationalist wings of the party. Some Republicans criticized Truman's decision to position the Seventh Fleet in the Taiwan Straits, but this criticism came from a

hawkish direction. It was felt that this move prevented Taiwan from attacking the mainland (Caridi 1968, pp. 11, 58–63).

40. Taiwan Straits Crisis (1954–55)
Opposition party: Democratic.
Position: Support.
Evidence: Democrats in both houses of Congress voted overwhelmingly in favor of the Formosa resolution, which authorized the president to use armed force to protect Taiwan and, if necessary for this purpose, the off-shore islands of Quemoy and Matsu (George and Smoke 1974, pp. 286–87).

42. Kuwaiti Independence (1961)
Opposition party: Labour.
Position: Support.
Evidence: Party leader Hugh Gaitskell publicly supported the deployment of troops to Kuwait in a speech to parliament (*Keesing's Contemporary Archives* 1961, 18189; Alani 1990, p. 136).

43. Laos (1961)
Opposition party: Republican.
Position: Support.
Evidence: Hall (1971, p. 51) reports that President Kennedy received "strong Republican support throughout the crisis."

45. West Irian (1962)
Opposition party: Labor.
Position: Oppose.
Evidence: On April 5, 1962, the Labor Party put forward a resolution opposing the deployment of reinforcements. The motion was rejected 47:90, with almost all Labor members voting in favor. The motion also drew support from the much smaller pacifist Socialist and Communist parties (*Keesing's Contemporary Archives* 1962, 18848).

46. Malaysian Independence (1964–65)
Opposition party: Labour.
Position: Support.
Evidence: Labour MP P. Williams told the House of Commons that his party welcomed the deployment of British troops to Malaysia (*Parl. Deb.* 5s, 685:1335; Wilson 1971, p. 3).

47. Vietnam (1964–65)
Opposition party: Republican.
Position: Support.
Evidence: The 1964 Republican presidential candidate, Barry Goldwater, was more hawkish than the president. In addition, Republicans voted overwhelmingly in favor of the Gulf of Tonkin Resolution, which authorized the president to take "all necessary measures to repel any armed attacks and to prevent further aggression" in Southeast Asia (Herring 1986, pp. 121–23).

54 & 56. Belize Independence (1974 & 1977)
Opposition party: Conservative.
Position: Support.
Evidence: Conservative MP Reginald Maudling told parliament that his party entirely supported the government in maintaining and carrying out its responsibility to Belize (*Parl. Deb.* 5s, 899: 610–13).

58. Chadian Civil War (1983)
Opposition parties: Gaullist and Union for French Democracy.
Position: Support.
Evidence: Members of the center-right parties supported the deployment of 1000 French paratroopers to Chad, though they criticized the government's move as "too little, too late" (Smith 1983).

References

Achen, Christopher H., and Duncan Snidal 1989, "Rational Deterrence Theory and Comparative Case Studies," *World Politics* 41: 143–69.

Adamthwaite, Anthony 1977, *France and the Coming of the Second World War, 1936–1939*, London: Frank Cass.

1995, *Grandeur and Misery*, London: E. Arnold.

Alani, Mustafa M. 1990, *Operation Vantage*, Surbiton, Surrey: LAAM.

Albrecht-Carrié, René 1970, *Britain and France*, Garden City, NY: Doubleday & Company, Inc.

Aldrich, John H., John L. Sullivan, and Eugene Borgida 1989, "Foreign Affairs and Issue Voting: Do Presidential Candidates 'Waltz before a Blind Audience'?" *American Political Science Review* 83: 123–41.

Alexseev, Mikhail A., and W. Lance Bennett 1995, "For Whom the Gates Open: News Reporting and Government Source Patterns in the United States, Great Britain, and Russia," *Political Communication* 12: 395–412.

Almond, Gabriel A. 1950, *The American People and Foreign Policy*, New York: Harcourt, Brace and Company.

Anderson, Eugene 1930, *The First Moroccan Crisis 1904–1906*, Chicago, IL: University of Chicago Press.

Andrew, Christopher 1968, *Théophile Delcassé and the Making of the Entente Cordiale*, London: Macmillan.

Annual Register, The 1887–1899, London: Longmans, Green.

Aron, Raymond 1973, *Peace and War*. Translated by Richard Howard and Annette Baker Fox. Garden City, NY: Anchor Books.

Bailey, Thomas A. 1974, *A Diplomatic History of the American People*, Englewood Cliffs, NJ: Prentice-Hall.

Barlow, Ima Christina 1940, *The Agadir Crisis*, Chapel Hill, NC: University of North Carolina Press.

Barzilai, Gad 1996, *Wars, Internal Conflicts, and Political Order*, New York: State University of New York Press.

Bates, Darrel 1984, *The Fashoda Incident of 1898*, Oxford: Oxford University Press.

Beck, Nathaniel, Jonathan N. Katz, and Richard Tucker 1998, "Beyond Ordinary

Logit: Taking Time Seriously in Binary Time-Series Cross-Section Models," *American Journal of Political Science* 42: 1260–88.

Bennett, D. Scott, and Allan Stam 2000, "EUGene: A Conceptual Manual" *International Interactions*, 26:179–204. <http://eugenesoftware.org>.

Bennett, W. Lance 1990, "Toward a Theory of Press–State Relations in the United States," *Journal of Communication* 40: 103–25.

Bennett, W. Lance, and David L. Paletz (eds.) 1994, *Taken by Storm: The Media, Public Opinion, and US Foreign Policy in the Gulf War*, Chicago, IL: University of Chicago Press.

Benoit, Kenneth 1996, "Democracies Really are More Pacific (in General)," *Journal of Conflict Resolution* 40: 636–57.

Blainey, Geoffrey 1988, *The Causes of War*, 3rd edition, New York: Free Press.

Bremer, Stuart A. 1980, "The Trials of Nations," in J. D. Singer (ed.), *The Correlates of War II*, New York: Free Press.

1992, "Dangerous Dyads: Conditions Affecting the Likelihood of Interstate War, 1816–1965," *Journal of Conflict Resolution* 36: 309–41.

1993, "Democracy and Militarized Interstate Conflict," *International Interactions* 18: 231–50.

Brody, Richard A. 1991, *Assessing the President*, Stanford, CA: Stanford University Press.

Brody, Richard A., and Catherine R. Shapiro 1989, "A Reconsideration of the Rally Phenomenon in Public Opinion," in S. Long (ed.), *Political Behavior Annual*, Boulder, CO: Westview Press.

Brown, Robert H. 1971, *The Republic in Peril: 1812*, New York: W. W. Norton & Company.

Brown, Roger Glenn 1970, *Fashoda Reconsidered*, Baltimore, MA: The Johns Hopkins University Press.

Buckle, George Earle (ed.) 1932, *The Letters of Queen Victoria*, vol. III, New York: Longmans, Green and Co.

Bueno de Mesquita, Bruce 1975, "Measuring Systemic Polarity," *Journal of Conflict Resolution* 19: 187–216.

1981, *The War Trap*, New Haven, CT: Yale University Press.

Bueno de Mesquita, Bruce, and David Lalman 1990, "Domestic Opposition and Foreign War," *American Political Science Review* 84: 747–65.

1992, *War and Reason: Domestic and International Imperatives*, New Haven, CT: Yale University Press.

Bueno de Mesquita, Bruce, and Randolph Siverson 1995, "War and the Survival of Political Leaders: A Comparative Study of Regime Types and Political Accountability," *American Political Science Review* 89: 841–55.

Bueno de Mesquita, Bruce, Randolph Siverson, and Gary Woller 1992, "War and the Fate of Regimes: A Comparative Analysis," *American Political Science Review* 86: 639–46.

Bueno de Mesquita, Bruce, James D. Morrow, and Ethan R. Zorick 1997, "Capabilities, Perception, and Escalation," *American Political Science Review* 91: 15–27.

References

Bueno de Mesquita, Bruce, James D. Morrow, Randolph M. Siverson, and Alastair Smith 1999, "An Institutional Theory of the Democratic Peace," *American Political Science Review* 93: 791–808.

Butler, Jeffrey 1968, *The Liberal Party and the Jameson Raid*, Oxford: Clarendon Press.

Calvert, Randall C. 1985, "The Value of Biased Information: A Rational Choice Model of Political Advice," *Journal of Politics* 47: 530–55.

Caridi, Ronald J. 1968, *The Korean War and American Politics*, Philadelphia, PA: University of Pennsylvania Press.

Carlton, David 1981, *Anthony Eden: A Biography*, London: Allen Lane.

1988, *Britain and the Suez Crisis*, Oxford: Basil Blackwell.

Carroll, E. Malcolm 1931, *French Public Opinion and Foreign Affairs, 1870–1914*, New York: The Century Co.

Chamberlain, G. 1980, "Analysis of Covariance with Qualitative Data," *Review of Economic Studies* 47: 225–38.

Chan, Steve 1984 "Mirror, Mirror on the Wall . . . Are the Freer Countries More Pacific?" *Journal of Conflict Resolution* 28: 617–48.

1997, "In Search of the Democratic Peace: Problems and Promise," *Mershon International Studies Review* 41: 59–91.

Churchill, Winston S. 1948, *The Second World War*, vol. I, Boston, Houghton Mifflin.

Cohen, Bernard 1963, *The Press and Foreign Policy*, Princeton, NJ: Princeton University Press.

Cole, G. D. H. 1969, *A History of the Labour Party from 1914*, New York: Augustus M. Kelley Publishers.

Collier, Ellen C. (ed.) 1991, *Bipartisanship in the Making of Foreign Policy*, Boulder, CO: Westview Press.

Collin, Richard H. 1990, *Theodore Roosevelt's Caribbean*, Baton Rouge, LA: Louisiana State University Press.

Cook, Timothy 1994, "Domesticating a Crisis: Washington News Beats and International News in the Persian Gulf War," in Bennett and Paletz (eds.).

Coser, L. A. 1956, *The Function of Social Conflict*, New York: Free Press.

Cotton, Timothy C. 1986, "War and American Democracy: Electoral Costs of the Last Five Wars," *Journal of Conflict Resolution* 30: 616–35.

Crabb, Cecil V., Jr. 1957, *Bipartisan Foreign Policy*, Evanston, IL: Row, Peterson and Company.

D'Lugo, David, and Ronald Rogowski 1993, "The Anglo-German Naval Race and Comparative Constitutional 'Fitness,'" in Richard Rosecrance and Arthur A. Stein (eds.), *The Domestic Bases of Grand Strategy*, Ithaca, NY: Cornell University Press.

Dahl, Robert A. 1971, *Polyarchy*, New Haven, CT: Yale University Press.

Dahl, Robert A. (ed.) 1966, *Political Oppositions in Western Democracies*, New Haven, CT: Yale University Press.

Dahl, Robert A. (ed.) 1973, *Regimes and Oppositions*, New Haven, CT: Yale University Press.

Davey, Arthur 1978, *The British Pro-Boers, 1977–1902*, Cape Town, South Africa: Tafelberg Publishers.

DeConde, Alexander 1966, *The Quasi-War*, New York: Charles Scribner's Sons.

Dewar, Helen, and Juliet Eilperin, "Hill GOP Leaders Take Cautious Course on Kosovo," *Washington Post*, 28 April 1999.

Dixon, William J. 1993, "Democracy and the Management of International Conflict," *Journal of Conflict Resolution* 37: 42–68.

1994, "Democracy and the Peaceful Settlement of Conflict," *American Political Science Review* 88: 14–32.

Downs, George W., and David M. Rocke 1995, *Optimal Imperfection?*, Princeton, NJ: Princeton University Press.

Doyle, Michael W. 1983, "Kant, Liberal Legacies, and Foreign Affairs, Parts I–II," *Philosophy and Public Affairs* 12: 205–35, 325–53.

1986, "Liberalism and World Politics," *American Political Science Review* 80: 1151–71.

1997, *Ways of War and Peace*, New York: W.W. Norton and Company.

Drew, Elizabeth 1991, "Letter from Washington," *New Yorker*, February 4, 82–90.

Eden, Anthony 1962, *Facing the Dictators*, Boston, MD: Houghton, Mifflin.

Elman, Miriam Fendius 1997, "The Need for a Qualitative Test of the Democratic Peace Theory," in Miriam Fendius Elman (ed.), *Paths to Peace: Is Democracy the Answer?*, Cambridge, MA: The MIT Press.

Emmerson, James Thomas 1977, *The Rhineland Crisis 7 March 1936*, Ames, IO: Iowa State University Press.

Epstein, Leon D. 1964, *British Politics in the Suez Crisis*, Urbana, IL: University of Illinois Press.

Evans, Peter B., Harold K. Jacobson, and Robert D. Putnam (eds.) 1993, *Double-Edged Diplomacy*, Berkeley, CA: University of California Press.

Eyerman, Joe, and Robert A. Hart, Jr. 1996, "An Empirical Test of the Audience Cost Proposition: Democracy Speaks Louder than Words," *Journal of Conflict Resolution* 40: 597–616.

Farber, Henry S., and Joanne Gowa 1995, "Polities and Peace," *International Security* 20: 123–46.

1997, "Common Interests or Common Polities? Reinterpreting the Democratic Peace," *The Journal of Politics* 59: 393–418.

Fearon, James D. 1992, "Threats to Use Force: The Role of Costly Signals in International Crises," Ph.D. dissertation, University of California, Berkeley, CA.

1994a, "Domestic Political Audiences and the Escalation of International Disputes," *American Political Science Review* 88: 577–92.

1994b, "Signaling versus the Balance of Power and Interests: An Empirical Test of a Crisis Bargaining Model," *Journal of Conflict Resolution*: 236–69.

1995, "Rationalist Explanations for War," *International Organization* 49: 379–414.

1997, "Signaling Foreign Policy Interests: Tying Hands versus Sinking Costs," *Journal of Conflict Resolution*: 68–90.

References

Finel, Bernard I., and Kristin Lord 1999, "The Surprising Logic of Transparency," *International Studies Quarterly* 43: 315–39.

Finer, Herman 1964, *Dulles over Suez*, Chicago, IL: Quadrangle Books.

Fiorina, Morris P. 1981. *Retrospective Voting in American National Elections*. New Haven, CT: Yale University Press.

Fisher, John 1974, *Paul Kruger: His Life and Times*, London: Secker & Warburg.

Fisher, Louis 1995, *Presidential War Power*, Lawrence, KS: University Press of Kansas.

Flower, Ken 1987, *Serving Secretly*, London: John Murray.

Forster, Dirk 1956, "The Rhineland Operation in 1936," *Wiener Library Bulletin* 10 (5–6): 48.

France. Ministry of Foreign Affairs (MFA) 1957, *Documents Diplomatiques Français, 1871–1914*, ser. 1, vol. XIV, Paris: Imprimerie Nationale.

1963, *Documents Diplomatiques Français, 1932–1939 (DDF)*, ser. 2, vol. I, Paris: Imprimerie Nationale.

Freedman, Lawrence, and Efraim Karsh 1993, *The Gulf Conflict, 1990–1991*, Princeton, NJ: Princeton University Press.

Friedrich, Carl Joachim 1938, *Foreign Policy in the Making*, New York: W. W. Norton & Co.

Fudenberg, Drew, and Jean Tirole 1991, *Game Theory*, Cambridge, MA: The MIT Press.

Gamba, Virginia 1987, *The Falklands/Malvinas War*, Boston: Allen & Unwin.

Gardiner, A.G. 1923, *The Life of Sir William Harcourt*, New York: George H. Doran Company.

Gartzke, Erik 1998, "Kant We All Just Get Along? Opportunity, Willingness, and the Origins of the Democratic Peace," *American Journal of Political Science* : 1–26.

Garvin, J. L 1934, *The Life of Joseph Chamberlain*, vol. III, London: Macmillan.

Gaubatz, Kurt Taylor 1998, "None Dare Call it Reason," in R. M. Siverson (ed.), *Strategic Politicians, Institutions, and Foreign Policy*, Ann Arbor, MI: University of Michigan Press.

1999, *Elections and War*, Stanford, CA: Stanford University Press.

George, Alexander L., and Richard Smoke 1974, *Deterrence in American Foreign Policy*, New York: Columbia University Press.

Germany. Auswärtiges Amt. 1929, *German Diplomatic Documents, 1871–1914 (GDD)*, vol. 2, selected and translated E. T. S, Dugdale, London: Methuen.

1962, *Documents on German Foreign Policy, 1918–1945 (DGFP)*, series C, vol. IV, Washington: US GPO.

1966, *Documents on German Foreign Policy, 1918–1945 (DGFP)*, series C, vol. V, Washington: US GPO.

Gilpin, Robert 1975, *US Power and the Multinational Corporation*, New York: Basic Books.

1983, *War and Change in World Politics*, Cambridge: Cambridge University Press.

Gleditsch, Nils Petter, and Håvard Hegre 1997, "Peace and Democracy: Three Levels of Analysis," *Journal of Conflict Resolution* 41: 283–310.

Gochman, Charles S., and Zeev Maoz 1984, "Militarized Interstate Disputes, 1816–1976: Procedures, Patterns, and Insights," *Journal of Conflict Resolution* 28: 585–615.

Goemans, Hein 2000, *War and Punishment*, Princeton, NJ: Princeton University Press.

Goertz, Gary 1993, "Enduring Rivalries: Theoretical Constructs and Empirical Patterns," *International Studies Quarterly* 37: 147–71.

Good, Robert C. 1973, *UDI*, Princeton, NJ: Princeton University Press.

Gorst, Anthony, and Lewis Johnman 1997, *The Suez Crisis*, London: Routledge.

Gow, James 1997, *Triumph of the Lack of Will*, New York: Columbia University Press.

Gowa, Joanne 1995, "Democratic States and International Disputes," *International Organization* 49: 511–22.

1999, *Ballots or Bullets*, Princeton, NJ: Princeton University Press.

Great Britain 1899, *Parliamentary Debates*, 4th ser., vol. 75.

1906, *Parliamentary Debates*, 4th ser., vol. 156.

1911, *Parliamentary Debates*, Commons, 5th ser., vol. 28.

1936, *Parliamentary Debates*, Commons, 5th ser., vol. 310.

1965, *Parliamentary Debates*, Commons, 5th ser., vol. 718.

1974, *Parliamentary Debates*, Commons, 5th ser., vol. 558.

1974, *Parliamentary Debates*, Commons, 5th ser., vol. 899.

Great Britain. Foreign Office 1927, *British Documents on the Origins of the War, 1898–1914*, vol. 1, London: Her Majesty's Stationery Office.

Foreign Office 1976, *Documents on British Foreign Policy, 1919–1939 (DBFP)*, series 2, vol. 15, London: Her Majesty's Stationery Office.

Great Britain. Parliament 1935, *Statement Relating to Defence*. Cmnd. 4827. March.

1936, *Statement Relating to Defence*. Cmnd. 5107. March.

Green, Donald P., Soo Yeon Kim, and David H. Yoon 2000, "Dirty Pool," Yale University, manuscript.

Greene, William H. 1997, *Econometric Analysis*, 3rd edition, Upper Saddle River, NJ: Prentice-Hall.

Grenville, J.A.S. 1964, *Lord Salisbury and Foreign Policy*, London: The Athlone Press.

Grieco, Jospeh 1988, "Anarchy and the Limits of Cooperation: A Realist Critique of the Newest Liberal Institutionalism," *International Organizations* 42: 485–507.

Gurr, Ted Robert, Keith Jaggers, and Will H. Moore 1989, *Polity II: Political Structures and Regime Change, 1800–1986*, Michigan: Inter-University Consortium for Political and Social Science Research.

Hagan, Joe D. 1993, *Political Opposition and Foreign Policy in Comparative Perspective*, Boulder, CO: Lynne Rienner.

Hall, David K. 1971, "The Laos Crisis, 1960–61," in Alexander L. George, David K. Hall, and William R. Simons (eds.), *The Limits of Coercive Diplomacy*, Boston: Little, Brown, and Company.

References

Hamerle, Alfred, and Gerd Ronning 1995, "Panel Analysis for Qualitative Variables," in Gerhard Arminger, Clifford C. Clogg, and Michael E. Sobel (eds.), *Handbook of Statistical Modeling for the Social and Behavioral Sciences*, New York: Plenum Press.

Handlin, Oscar 1968, *Dissent, Democracy, and Foreign Policy*, New York: Foreign Policy Association.

Haraszti, Éva H. 1983, *The Invaders*, Budapest: Akadémiai Kiadó.

Harsanyi, John C. 1967–68. "Games with Incomplete Information Played by Bayesian Players, Parts I-III," *Management Science* 14: 159–82, 320–34, 486–502.

Healey, Denis 1989, *The Time of My Life*, London: Michael Joseph.

Heikal, Mohamed H. 1986, *Cutting the Lion's Tail: Suez through Egyptian Eyes*, London: André Deutch.

Herring, George 1986, *America's Longest War*, 2nd edition, Philadelphia, PA: Temple University Press.

Hickey, Donald R. 1989, *The War of 1812*, Urbana, IL: University of Illinois Press.

Holbo, Paul S. 1970, "Perilous Obscurity: Public Diplomacy and the Press in the Venezuelan Crisis, 1902–1903," *The Historian* 32: 428–48.

Hurwitz, Jon, and Mark Peffley 1987, "The Means and Ends of Foreign Policy as Determinants of Presidential Support," *American Journal of Political Science* 31: 236–58.

Huth, Paul K. 1988, *Extended Deterrence and the Prevention of War*, New Haven, CT: Yale University Press.

1990, "Appendix to *Extended Deterrence and the Prevention of War*," University of Michigan, manuscript.

Huth, Paul, and Bruce Russett 1988, "Deterrence Failure and Crisis Escalation," *International Studies Quarterly* 32: 29–46.

Jaggers, Keith, and Ted Robert Gurr 1996, Polity III: Regime Change and Political Authority, 1800–1994 [computer file] (Study #6695), 2nd ICPSR ed. Boulder, CO: Keith Jaggers/College Park, MD: Ted Robert Gurr (producers), 1995. Ann Arbor, MI: Inter-university Consortium for Political and Social Research (distributor), 1996.

Jakobsen, Peter Viggo 1998, *Western Use of Coercive Diplomacy after the Cold War*, New York: St. Martin's Press.

Jeyes, S. H. 1898, *The Life and Times of the Right Honorable the Marquis of Salisbury, K.G.*, vol. 4, London: J. S. Virtue & Co., Ltd.

Jian, Chen 1994, *China's Road to the Korean War*, New York: Columbia University Press.

Jones, Daniel M., Stuart A. Bremer, and J. David Singer 1996, "Militarized Interstate Disputes, 1816–1992: Rationale, Coding Rules, and Empirical Patterns," *Conflict Management and Peace Science* 15: 163–213.

Kant, Immanuel 1983 [1795], "To Perpetual Peace: A Philosophical Sketch," in *Perpetual Peace and Other Essays on Politics, History, and Morals*, Indianapolis, IN: Hackett Publishing Company.

Karatnycky, Adrian 2000, "Freedom: A Century of Progress," in *Freedom in the*

World: The Annual Survey of Political Rights and Civil Liberties, 1999–2000, New York: Freedom House.

Karsh, Efraim, and Inari Rautsi 1991, *Saddam Hussein,* New York: The Free Press.

Keesing's Contemporary Archives 1961–62, London: Keesing's Limited.

Kennan, George F. 1977, *The Cloud of Danger,* Boston: Little, Brown and Company.

Kennedy, John F. 1940, *Why England Slept,* New York: Wilfred Funk, Inc.

Keohane, Robert O. 1984, *After Hegemony,* Princeton, NJ: Princeton University Press.

Key, V. O., Jr. 1961, *Public Opinion and American Democracy,* New York: Alfred A. Knopf.

Kilgour, D. Marc, and Frank C. Zagare 1991, "Credibility, Uncertainty, and Deterrence," *American Journal of Political Science* 35: 305–34.

Kim, Woosang 1991, "Alliance Transitions and Great Power War," *American Journal of Political Science* 35: 833–50.

Kissinger, Henry 1979, *White House Years,* Boston, MD: Little, Brown, and Company.

Kohut, Andrew 2000, "News Interest Index: A Record of Public Attentiveness to News Stories," The Pew Research Center for the People and the Press, <http://www.people-press.org/database.htm>, accessed 17 July.

Koss, Stephen E. 1981, *The Rise and Fall of the Political Press in Britain,* vol. 1, Chapel Hill, NC: University of North Carolina Press.

Krehbiel, Keith 1991, *Information and Legislative Organization,* Ann Arbor, MI: University of Michigan Press.

Kuniholm, Bruce R. 1980, *The Origins of the Cold War in the Near East,* Princeton, NJ: Princeton University Press.

Kyle, Keith 1991, *Suez,* London: Weidenfeld and Nicolson.

Lake, David A. 1992, "Powerful Pacifists: Democratic States and War," *American Political Science Review* 86: 24–37.

Lambert, John Ralph, Jr. 1947, "Arthur Pue Gorman: Practical Politician," Ph.D. dissertation, Princeton University, NJ.

Langer, William L. 1951, *The Diplomacy of Imperialism, 1890–1902,* 2nd ed., New York: Alfred A. Knopf.

Larson, Eric V. 1996, *Casualties and Consensus,* Santa Monica, CA: RAND.

Layne, Christopher 1994, "Kant or Cant: The Myth of the Democratic Peace," *International Security* 19: 5–49.

Lebow, Richard Ned 1981, *Between Peace and War,* Baltimore, MD: The Johns Hopkins University Press.

Lebow, Richard Ned, and Janice Gross Stein 1990, "Deterrence: The Elusive Dependent Variable," *World Politics* 42: 336–69.

Lees, John D., and Malcolm Shaw 1979, *Committees in Legislatures,* Durham, NC: Duke University Press.

Leffler, Melvyn P. 1992, *A Preponderance of Power,* Stanford, CA: Stanford University Press.

References

Lemke, Douglas, and William Reed 1996, "Regime Types and Status Quo Evaluations: Power Transition Theory and the Democratic Peace," *International Interactions* 22: 143–64.

Levy, Jack S., and William Mabe 1998, "Winning the War but Losing at Home: Politically-Motivated Opposition to War," paper presented at the International Studies Association Annual Meeting.

Lijphart, Arend 1984, *Democracies*, New Haven, CT: Yale University Press.

Lipman, Barton L., and Duane J. Seppi 1995, "Robust Inference in Communication Games with Partial Provability," *Journal of Economic Theory* 66: 370–405.

Lippmann, Walter 1955, *The Public Philosophy*, Boston: Little, Brown and Company.

Lipset, Seymour M. 1959, *Political Man*, Baltimore, MD: The Johns Hopkins Univerity Press.

Livermore, Shaw 1962, *The Twilight of Federalism*, Princeton, NJ: Princeton University Press.

Lowi, Theodore 1967, "Making Democracy Safe for the World: National Politics and Foreign Policy," in James N. Rosenau (ed.), *Domestic Sources of Foreign Policy*, New York: Free Press.

Lucas, Scott (ed.) 1996, *Britain and Suez*, Manchester: Manchester University Press.

Lyon, E. Wilson 1938, "The Directory and the United States," *American Historical Review* 43: 514–32.

Mansfield, Edward D., and Jack Snyder 1995, "Democratization and the Danger of War," *International Security* 20: 5–38.

Maoz, Zeev 1996, *Domestic Sources of Global Change*, Ann Arbor, MI: University of Michigan Press.

Maoz, Zeev, and Nasrin Abdolali 1989, "Regime Types and International Conflict, 1816–1976," *Journal of Conflict Resolution* 33: 3–23.

Maoz, Zeev, and Bruce Russett 1993, "Normative and Structural Causes of the Democratic Peace, 1946–1986," *American Political Science Review* 87: 624–38.

Marder, Arthur J. 1940, *The Anatomy of British Sea Power*, New York: Alfred A. Knopf.

Marks, Frederick 1979, *Velvet on Iron*, Lincoln, NB: University of Nebraska Press.

Martel, Gordon 1986, *Imperial Diplomacy*, Kingston, Canada: McGill-Queen's University Press.

Martinez, Gebe 1999, "GOP's Abiding Distrust Of Clinton Doesn't Stop at the Water's Edge," *Congressional Quarterly Weekly Report*, 1 May: 1038.

Mayhew, David R. 1974, *Congress: The Electoral Connection*, New Haven, CT: Yale University Press.

Micaud, Charles 1943, *The French Right and Nazi Germany 1933–1939: A Study of Public Opinion*, Durham, NC: Duke University Press.

Milgrom, Paul, and John Roberts 1986, "Relying on the Information of Interested Parties," *Rand Journal of Economics* 17: 18–32.

Miller, John C. 1951, *Crisis in Freedom*, Boston: Little, Brown and Company.

Milner, Helen V. 1997, *Interests, Institutions, and Information*, Princeton, NJ: Princeton University Press.

Morgan, Gerald 1981, *Anglo-Russian Rivalry in Central Asia, 1810–1895*, London: Frank Cass.

Morgan, T. Clifton, and Kenneth N. Bickers 1992, "Domestic Discontent and the External Use of Force," *Journal of Conflict Resolution* 36: 25–52.

Morgan, T. Clifton, and Sally H. Campbell 1991, "Domestic Structure, Decisional Constraints and War: So Why Kant Democracies Fight?" *Journal of Conflict Resolution* 35: 187–211.

Morgenthau, Hans J. 1973, *Politics Among Nations*, 5th edn, New York: Alfred A. Knopf.

Morrow, James D. 1985, "A Continuous Outcome Expected Utility Theory of War," *Journal of Conflict Resolution* 29: 473–502.

1986, "A Spatial Model of International Conflict," *American Political Science Review* 80: 1131–50.

1989, "Capabilities, Uncertainty, and Resolve: A Limited Information Model of Crisis Bargaining," *American Journal of Political Science* 33: 941–72.

1994a, "Modeling the Forms of International Cooperation: Distribution versus Information," *International Organization* 48: 387–423.

1994b, *Game Theory for Political Scientists*, Princeton, NJ: Princeton University Press.

Mousseau, Michael 1998, "Democracy and Compromise in Militarized Interstate Conflicts, 1816–1992," *Journal of Conflict Resolution* 42: 210–30.

Mueller, John 1973, *War, Presidents, and Public Opinion*, New York: John Wiley.

1994, *Policy and Opinion in the Gulf War*, Chicago, IL: University of Chicago Press.

Newton, Thomas W. 1929, *Lord Lansdowne*, London: Macmillan.

Nicolson, Nigel (ed.) 1966, *Harold Nicolson: Diaries and Letters, 1930–1939*, London: Collins.

Nincic, Miroslav 1992, *Democracy and Foreign Policy*, New York: Columbia University Press.

Nincic, Miroslav, and Barbara Hinckley 1991, "Foreign Policy and the Evaluation of Presidential Candidates," *Journal of Conflict Resolution* 35: 333–55.

Oren, Ido 1995, "The Subjectivity of the 'Democratic' Peace: Changing US Perceptions of Imperial Germany," *International Security* 20: 147–84.

Organski, A.F.K., and Jacek Kugler 1980, *The War Ledger*, Chicago, IL: Chicago University Press.

Owen, John. M. 1997, *Liberal Peace, Liberal War*, Ithaca, NY: Cornell University Press.

Oye, Kenneth (ed.) 1986, *Cooperation Under Anarchy*, Princeton, NJ: Princeton University Press.

Pace, David 1996, "Nunn Says Opposing Gulf War Ruined Chances at Presidency," *Chicago Sun-Times*, 26 December.

Page, Benjamin I., and Richard A. Brody 1972, "Policy Voting and the Electoral

Process: The Vietnam War Issue," *American Political Science Review* 66: 979–95.

Pahre, Robert, and Paul A. Papayoanou (eds.) 1997, "New Games: Modeling Domestic-International Linkages," a special issue of the *Journal of Conflict Resolution* 41: 1–199.

Pakenham, Thomas 1979, *The Boer War*, New York: Random House.

Penlington, Norman 1972, *The Alaska Boundary Dispute*, Toronto: McGraw-Hill Ryerson.

Penson, Lillian M. 1962, *Foreign Affairs under the Third Marquis of Salisbury*, London: Athlone Press.

Peterson, Susan 1996, *Crisis Bargaining and the State*, Ann Arbor, MI: University of Michigan Press.

Pimlott, Ben 1992, *Harold Wilson*, London: HarperCollins.

Poole, Keith, and Howard Rosenthal 1991, "Patterns of Congressional Voting," *American Journal of Political Science* 35: 228–78.

Popkin, Samuel L. 1994, *The Reasoning Voter*, Chicago, IL: The University of Chicago Press.

Porter, A. N. 1980, *The Origins of the South African War*, New York: St. Martin's Press.

Posen, Barry 1984, *The Sources of Military Doctrine*, Ithaca, NY: Cornell University Press.

Powell, Robert 1990, *Nuclear Deterrence Theory*, Cambridge: Cambridge University Press.

1999, *In The Shadow of Power*, Cambridge: Cambridge University Press.

Putnam, Robert D. 1988, "Diplomacy and Domestic Politics: The Logic of Two-Level Games," *International Organization* 42: 427–60.

Ray, James Lee 1993, "Wars between Democracies: Rare or Non-Existent?" *International Interactions* 18: 251–76.

1995, *Democracy and International Conflict*, Columbia, SC: University of South Carolina Press.

Raymond, Gregory A. 1994, "Democracies, Disputes, and Third-Party Intermediaries," *Journal of Conflict Resolution* 38: 24–42.

Regens, James L., Ronald Keith Gaddie, and Brad Lockerbie 1995, "The Electoral Consequences of Voting to Declare War," *Journal of Conflict Resolution* 39: 168–82.

Reiter, Dan, and Allan C. Stam 1998, "Democracy, War Initiation, and Victory," *American Political Science Review* 92: 377–89.

Riker, T.W. 1929, "A Survey of British Policy in the Fashoda Crisis," *Political Science Quarterly* 44: 54–78.

Risse-Kappen, Thomas 1995, *Cooperation among Democracies*, Princeton, NJ: Princeton University Press.

Roth, Alvin E. (ed.) 1985, *Game-Theoretic Models of Bargaining*, Cambridge: Cambridge University Press.

Rousseau, David L., Christopher Gelpi, Dan Reiter, and Paul K. Huth 1996, "Assessing the Dyadic Nature of the Democratic Peace, 1918–1988," *American Political Science Review* 90: 512–33.

Rummel, R. J. 1983, "Libertarianism and International Violence," *Journal of Conflict Resolution* 27: 27–71.

1995, "Democracies ARE Less Warlike Than Other Regimes," *European Journal of International Relations* 1(4): 457–79.

1979, *War, Power, and Peace,* Beverly Hills, CA: Sage Publications.

Russett, Bruce 1990, *Controlling the Sword,* Cambridge, MA: Harvard University Press.

1993, *Grasping the Democratic Peace,* Princeton, NJ: Princeton University Press.

Sagan, Scott D. 1988, "The Origins of the Pacific War," in Robert I. Rotberg and Theodore K. Rabb (eds.), *The Origin and Prevention of Major Wars,* Cambridge: Cambridge University Press.

Sanderson, G.N. 1965, *England, Europe and the Upper Nile, 1882–1899,* Edinburgh: Edinburgh University Press.

Sartori, Anne 1998, "Deterrence by Diplomacy," Ph.D. dissertation, University of Michigan.

Schelling, Thomas C. 1960, *The Strategy of Conflict,* Cambridge, MA: Harvard University Press.

Schultz, Kenneth A. 1998, "Domestic Opposition and Signaling in International Crises," *American Political Science Review* 92: 829–44.

1999, "Do Democratic Institutions Constrain or Inform?: Contrasting Two Institutional Perspectives on Democracy and War," *International Organization* 53: 233–66.

Schumpeter, Joseph A. 1947, *Capitalism, Socialism, and Democracy,* 2nd edition, New York: Harper.

Schweller, Randall 1996, "Neorealism's Status Quo Bias: What Security Dilemma?" *Security Studies* 5: 90–121.

Senese, Paul D. 1997, "Between Dispute and War: The Effect of Joint Democracy on Interstate Conflict Escalation," *The Journal of Politics* 59: 1–27.

Shay, Robert Paul, Jr. 1977, *British Rearmament in the Thirties,* Princeton, NJ: Princeton University Press.

Sheehan, Neil 1971, *The Pentagon Papers as Published by the New York Times,* New York: Quadrangle Books.

Shin, Hyun Song 1998, "Adversarial and Inquisitorial Procedures in Arbitration," *RAND Journal of Economics* 29: 378–405.

Shlaim, Avi 1983, *The United States and the Berlin Blockade, 1948–1949,* Berkeley, CA: University of California Press.

Sigal, Leon V. 1973, *Reporters and Officials,* Lexington, MA: D. C. Heath.

Signorino, Curtis S., and Jeffrey M. Ritter 1999, "Tau-b or Not Tau-b: Measuring Alliance Portfolio Similarity," *International Studies Quarterly* 43: 115–44.

Singer, J. David, and Melvin Small 1984, Annual Alliance Membership Data, 1815–1965 [computer file] (Study #5602). Ann Arbor, MI: University of Michigan Mental Health Institute, Correlates of War Project [producer], 1966. Ann Arbor, MI: Inter-university Consortium for Political and Social Research [distributor], 1984.

1993, National Material Capabilities Data, 1816–1985 [computer file] (Study

#9903), Ann Arbor, MI: J. David Singer, University of Michigan, and Detroit, MI: Melvin Small, Wayne State University [producers], 1990, Ann Arbor, MI: Inter-university Consortium for Political and Social Research [distributor], 1993.

1994, Correlates of War Project: International and Civil War Data, 1816–1992 [Computer file] (Study #9905), Ann Arbor, MI: J. David Singer and Melvin Small [producers], 1993, Ann Arbor, MI: Inter-university Consortium for Political and Social Research [distributor], 1994.

Singer, J. David, Stuart Bremer, and John Stuckey 1972, "Capability Distribution, Uncertainty, and Major Power War, 1820–1965," in Bruce Russett (ed.), *Peace, War, and Numbers*, New Bury Park, CA: Sage Publications.

Siverson, Randolph M. 1995, "Democracies and War Participation: In Defense of the Institutional Constraints Argument," *European Journal of International Relations* 1: 481–89.

Siverson, Randolph M. (ed.) 1998, *Strategic Politicians, Institutions, and Foreign Policy*, Ann Arbor, MI: University of Michigan Press.

Siverson, Randolph M., and Harvey Starr 1991, *The Diffusion of War*, Ann Arbor, MI: The University of Michigan Press.

Small, Melvin, and J. D. Singer 1976, "The War-Proneness of Democratic Regimes, 1816–1965," *Jerusalem Journal of International Relations* 1: 50–69.

1982, *Resort to Arms*, Beverly Hills, CA: Sage Publications, Inc.

Smith, Alastair 1998a, "The Effect of Foreign Policy Statements on Foreign Nations and Domestic Electorates," in R. M. Siverson (ed.), *Strategic Politicians, Institutions, and Foreign Policy*, Ann Arbor, MI: University of Michigan Press.

1998b, "International Crises and Domestic Politics," *American Political Science Review* 92: 623–38.

Smith, James Morton 1956, *Freedom's Fetters*, Ithaca, NY: Cornell University Press.

Smith, Tom W. 1985, "The Polls: America's Most Important Problems, Part I: National and International," *Public Opinion Quarterly* 49: 264–74.

Smith, William E. 1983, "France Draws the Line; But Mitterrand Creates Controversy in Paris and Washington," *Time*, August 29, 22.

Snyder, George, and Paul Diesing 1977, *Conflict Among Nations*, Princeton, NJ: Princeton University Press.

Snyder, Jack 1991, *Myths of Empire*, Ithaca, NY: Cornell University Press.

Spence, A. Michael 1974, *Market Signaling*, Cambridge, MA: Harvard University Press.

Spender, J. A. 1923, *The Life of the Right Hon. Sir Henry Campbell-Bannerman*, vol. 1, London: Hodder and Stoughton Limited.

Stam, Allan C. 1996, *Win, Lose, or Draw*, Ann Arbor, MI: University of Michigan Press.

StataCorp 1999, *Stata Statistical Software: Release 6.0, User's Guide*, College Station, TX: Stata Corporation.

Steiner, Zara 1977, *Britain and the Origins of the First World War*, London: Macmillan.

Stimson, James A. 1985, "Regression in Space and Time: A Statistical Essay," *American Journal of Political Science* 29: 914–47.

Stinchcombe, William 1980, *The XYZ Affair*, Westport, CT: Greenwood Press.

Stoessinger, James 1974, *Why Nations Go to War*, New York: Random House.

Strom, Kaare 1992, "Democracy as Political Competition," *American Behavioral Scientist* 35: 375–96.

Taylor, A. J. P. 1950, "Prelude to Fashoda: The Question of the Upper Nile," *English Historical Review* 65: 52–80.

Thompson, William R., and Richard Tucker 1997, "A Tale of Two Democratic Peace Critiques," *Journal of Conflict Resolution* 41: 428–54.

Thorold, Algar Labouchere 1913, *The Life of Henry Labouchere*, London: Constable.

Tint, Herbert 1980, *France Since 1918*, 2nd edition, New York: St. Martin's Press.

Tucker, Richard 1999, "The Similarity of Alliance Portfolios, 1816–1984," <http://www.vanderbilt.edu/~rtucker/data/affinity/alliance/similar/>, accessed 24 September.

Tullock, Gordon 1987, *Autocracy*, Dordrecht: Martinus Nijhoff.

Turner, Lynn W. 1971, "Elections of 1816 and 1820," in Arthur M. Schlesinger, Jr. (ed.), *American Presidential Elections, 1789–1968*, New York: Chelsea House.

United Nations. General Assembly 1956, *First Emergency Special Session, 561st Meeting*, Official Records.

United States. Congress 1989, "Instances of Use of United States Armed Forces Abroad, 1798–1989," Congressional Research Service Report, 4 December.

United States. Department of State 1976, *Foreign Relations of the United States, 1950*, vol. 5, Washington: US GPO.

1990, *Foreign Relations of the United States*, vol. 16, Washington: US GPO.

United States. Senate 1999, Armed Services Committee, *Hearing on Kosovo*, 106th Congress, 1st sess., 15 April.

Van Belle, Douglas A. 1997, "Press Freedom and the Democratic Peace," *Journal of Peace Research* 34: 405–14.

Van Belle, Douglas A., and John R. Oneal 1998, "Press Freedom as a Source of the Democratic Peace," paper presented at the 1998 Annual Meeting of the American Political Science Association.

Vandenberg, Arthur H., Jr. (ed.) 1952, *The Private Papers of Senator Vandenberg*, Cambridge, MA: The Riverside Press.

Vasquez, John A. 1993, *The War Puzzle*, Cambridge: Cambridge University Press.

Verrier, Anthony 1986, *The Road to Zimbabwe, 1890–1980*, London: Jonathan Cape.

Wagner, R. Harrison 2000, "Bargaining and War," *American Journal of Political Science* 44: 469–84.

Walder, David 1969, *The Chanak Affair*, London: Hutchinson.

Waltz, Kenneth N. 1959, *Man, the State, and War*, New York: Columbia University Press.

1967, *Foreign Policy and Democratic Politics*, Boston: Little, Brown, and Company.

1979, *Theory of International Politics*, New York: McGraw-Hill.

Ward, Michael D., and Kristian Gleditsch 1997, "Democratizing for Peace," *American Political Science Review* 92: 51–62.

Weede, Erich 1984, "Democracy and War Involvement," *Journal of Conflict Resolution* 28: 649–64.

Werth, Alexander 1939, *France and Munich Before and After the Surrender*, New York: Harper and Brothers Publishers.

Whaley, Barton 1984, *Covert German Rearmament, 1919–1939*, Frederick, MD: University Publication of America, Inc.

Wheeler-Bennett, John W. (ed.) 1937, *Documents on International Affairs, 1936*, London: Royal Institute of International Affairs.

White, Stephen 1979, *Britain and the Bolshevik Revolution*, London: Macmillan.

Williams, Philip M. (ed.) 1983, *The Diary of Hugh Gaitskell, 1945–1956*, London: Jonathan Cape.

Williamson, Oliver E. 1985, *The Economic Institutions of Capitalism*, New York: The Free Press.

Wilson, Harold 1971, *The Labour Government, 1964–70*, London: Weidenfeld and Nicolson.

Windrich, Elaine 1978, *Britain and the Politics of Rhodesian Independence*, New York: Africana Publishing Company.

Windrich, Elaine (ed.) 1975, *The Rhodesian Problem*, London: Routledge & Kegan Paul.

Wintrobe, Ronald 1998, *The Political Economy of Dictatorship*, Cambridge: Cambridge University Press.

Wolfers, Arnold 1962, *Discord and Collaboration*, Baltimore, MD: The Johns Hopkins University Press.

Woodward, Bob 1991, *The Commanders*, New York: Pocket Star Books.

Wright, Alan H. 1951, "The Fashoda Affair: A Study in the Age of Imperialism," A.B. thesis, Princeton University, Dept. of History.

Wright, Quincy 1965, *A Study of War*, 2nd edition, Chicago, IL: University of Chicago Press.

Young, Kenneth 1969, *Rhodesia and Independence*, London: J. M. Dent & Sons.

Zakaria, Fareed 1997, "The Rise of Illiberal Democracy," *Foreign Affairs* 76: 22–43.

Zaller, John 1992, *The Nature and Origins of Mass Opinion*, Cambridge: Cambridge University Press.

1994a, "Strategic Politicians, Public Opinion, and the Gulf Crisis," in Bennett and Paletz (eds.).

1994b, "Elite Leadership of Mass Opinion," in Bennett and Paletz (eds.).

Zaller, John, and Dennis Chiu 1996, "Government's Little Helper: US Press Coverage of Foreign Policy Crises, 1945–1991," *Political Communication* 13: 385–405.